THE THEFT OF THE COUNTRYSIDE

'This other Eden, demi-paradise . . . '
William Shakespeare

The Theft of the Countryside

by

Marion Shoard

with a foreword by
Henry Moore

Temple Smith : London

First published in Great Britain in 1980
by Maurice Temple Smith Ltd
37 Great Russell Street, London WC1

© Marion Shoard 1980

Third impression 1981

ISBN 0 85117 200 8 Cased
     0 85117 201 6 Paper

Photoset in Garamond by
Robcroft Limited, London WC1

Printed and bound in Great Britain
at The Pitman Press, Bath

The photographs originate as follows:
Heather Angel: Plate 21
Mike Abrahams: Plates 3, 6, 7, 15, 18
Bob Bray: Plate 1
Power Farming: Plates 4, 5, 13, 14
Kenneth Scowen: Plates 2, 17, 19
Marion Shoard: Plates 8, 9, 10, 11, 20
Peter Wakely: Plate 12
Bertram Unne: Plate 16

Contents

Foreword by Henry Moore   7
Introduction: Paradise Threatened   9

Part One – An Agricultural Revolution

  1 Technological Transformation   15
  2 Subsidies for Destruction   21

Part Two – The Impact on the Countryside

  3 Hedgerows   34
  4 Hedgerow Trees   43
  5 Woods   47
  6 Roughlands   58
  7 Downs   65
  8 Moors   76
  9 Wetlands   83
Conclusion to Part Two   98

Part Three – Toothless Watchdogs

10 Farming and Forestry – Above the Law   100
11 The Education Experiment   119
12 Graffham Down: Victim of the System   129
13 The National Parks   136
Conclusion to Part Three   154

Part Four – Economics

14 The Farmers' Case   155
15 The Tourism Bonanza   165
Conclusion to Part Four   169

Part Five – Future Landscapes and Future Lives

16 A Threatened Record   173
17 Disappearing Wildlife   183
18 Impoverished Lives   191
Conclusion to Part Five   200

Part Six – Stop, Thief!

19 The Planning Weapon   204
20 Regions to the Rescue   218
21 Opening up the Countryside   226
22 National Parks for the Nation   239

Regaining Paradise: What You Can Do   255

References   261
Index   270

Foreword

by Henry Moore

Our surroundings are part of what we are. And the special quality of the English countryside has helped shape the English character. Certainly it has shaped much of England's art. From the Beowulf poet to Shakespeare, Chaucer to the Brontes, our literature has sprung at our writers from the natural environment. Our painters and our musicians too are inseparable from the landscape which inspired them. Try and imagine Constable, Gainsborough, Turner or Elgar having been born and brought up in a foreign country. Sculptors have proved no less dependent on the English countryside. My own work would have been different had not the shapes of the Yorkshire landscape existed first. This may seem a puzzling statement since the subject of most of my work has been the human figure, but it is forms that I have come across in the natural world – from pebbles or tree trunks to a whole valley – which have often shown me how to interpret the human body. My work is a marriage of man and landscape, which is why I prefer to have it displayed out of doors with the sky, clouds and trees. And I believe that something of the same synthesis of man and nature makes up the character of us all, whether or not we are artists.

Such a view necessarily commits me to a deep concern for the English countryside. It is a concern I have found to be among the most widely shared of all the concerns of my fellow countrymen. And yet, the countryside which is so much a part of our nation now stands in real danger of destruction. I am in no doubt that the loss of our countryside would be universally perceived as the unprecedented catastrophe it would undoubtedly be. Yet there is almost universal ignorance of the imminence of this catastrophe. If people knew what was happening, they would rise up and stop it. I have not the slightest doubt about that. This book explains what is happening and how it could be stopped. Please read it, for your sake, for the sake of your children, and for the sake of your country.

For Catherine, born three weeks before Chapter One
and
in memory of Harold Shoard

Acknowledgements

I wish to thank the Sidney Perry Foundation for providing most of the funds which enabled me to scour England for eighteen months to prepare this book. I am also grateful to the Joseph Rowntree Charitable Trust, which contributed additional funds, and the Centre for Environmental Studies, which provided me with an office.

The following people kindly looked at particular sections of the book and I am grateful for their helpful comments: Carolyn Adams, Richard Bacon, Dr Peter Fowler, Michael Hudson, Professor David Lowenthal, Roy Millward, Nick Morris, Christopher Robbins, Dr Judith Rossiter and Professor Gerald Wibberley. I should like to thank Vivien Bowler for drawing the maps and Sandra Sutton and Betty Franolic for typing the manuscript.

My most grateful thanks go to David Cox for his help throughout.

INTRODUCTION

Paradise Threatened

England's countryside is not only one of the great treasures of the earth; it is also a vital part of our national identity. All of us – even those who rarely step outside our towns – cherish somewhere in our souls the same vision of our real homeland: a rural vision, nowadays conjured up as faithfully by margarine commercials as it was once by Shakespeare's plays. Virtually all of us know and value the world's most celebrated landscape and cherish rural England's patchwork quilt of fields, downs and woods, separated by thick hedgerows, mossy banks, sunken lanes and sparkling streams. For hundreds of years, our English countryside has given us such ideas as we have had of what paradise might be like. Peopled by badgers, skylarks and nightingales, scattered with bluebells, poppies and cornflowers and studded with oak, elm and hawthorn, our countryside has knitted itself into our idea of ourselves as a nation as thoroughly as it has delighted and amazed strangers who have travelled from the far corners of the earth with no other purpose than to feast their eyes on it. Our empire may have passed away; our industrial strength may be tottering; but the matchless charm of our countryside – that was ours before imperial power or economic hegemony, and it survived them. Until now.

Although few people realise it, the English landscape is under sentence of death. Indeed, the sentence is already being carried out. The executioner is not the industrialist or the property speculator, whose activities have touched only the fringes of our countryside. Instead it is the figure traditionally viewed as the custodian of the rural scene – the farmer.

A new agricultural revolution is under way. If allowed to proceed unhindered, it will transform the face of England. Already a quarter of our hedgerows, 24 million hedgerow trees, thousands of acres of down and heathland, a third of our woods and hundred upon hundred of ponds, streams, marshes and flower-rich meadows have disappeared. They have been systematically eliminated by farmers seeking to profit from a complex web of economic and technological change. Speedily, but almost imperceptibly, the English countryside is being turned into a vast, featureless expanse of prairie. Its surface is given over either to cereal growing or to a grass monoculture fuelling intensive stock-rearing. This new English landscape can offer little delight to the human eye or ear. It cannot sustain our traditional wild flowers, birds and animals. But each year it takes over hundreds more square miles of England. Already, much of the east of the country looks disappointingly familiar to tourists from the American Mid-West. And unless something is done to curb agricultural intensification, virtually the whole of the countryside will be no more than a food factory by the early part of the next century.

If we do allow our children to be cheated of their birthright in this way, they may find it hard to forgive us. As opportunities for work diminish in post-industrial Britain, the need for leisure outlets will grow steadily more insistent. And quite apart from its other claims on us, the countryside is a vast treasury of so far largely untapped recreation opportunities. We can ill afford to stand by and see it destroyed now – and destroyed quite unnecessarily.

We do not have to eliminate the character of our landscape to produce food efficiently. If we take certain steps, we can safeguard our rural heritage *and* enable farmers to profit from new methods. At present there is no machinery whatever to require farmers to reconcile their plans with the needs of all the rest of us who value the English scene. That is why agricultural change is proceeding in such a destructive way. It need not be so. The deep regard for the countryside that lies entrenched in so many English breasts has yet to make itself felt. But it still can. The theft of England's countryside is under way, but not yet completed. We can save our countryside, if we choose to.

PART ONE
An Agricultural Revolution

Writing just after World War II, George Orwell was still able
to describe the kind of English rural scene that had enthralled
English writers for hundreds of years before his day: 'the
railway cuttings smothered in flowers, the deep meadows
where the great shining horses browse and meditate, the slow-
moving streams bordered by willows, the green bosoms of the
elms, all sleeping the deep, deep sleep of England'. When
Orwell was writing, the peace of the English countryside had
survived a history of energetic economic exploitation and
periods of intense and far-reaching change. The Industrial
Revolution had devastated certain areas and twentieth century
development sprawl had pushed its fingers all through
England. But the countryside had proved it could live with all
these intrusions, just as it has since shown it can live with the
other intrusions of advanced industrial society – from pylons
to motorways, quarries to hypermarkets. Today the pace of
this kind of development has slowed and the threat it poses
has been contained. Now, as for most of our history, agriculture remains in control of the landscape – over 70 per cent
of the land surface of England is farmed. It is farming more
than any other single force which created the glories of the
English countryside. But in the years since Orwell wrote, the
nature of our great rural industry has changed. Today, far
from enriching and conserving the landscape, farming has
started to destroy it. The 'deep, deep sleep of England', which
survived the factory, the car, the bungalow and the electricity
power-line, is at last being shattered – by, of all things, farming.
An Agricultural Revolution, which is now in full swing, will
destroy the character of our landscape completely if allowed
to proceed unhindered.

England's landscape has been evolving through what has
been described as the 'centuries-long conversation between
man and nature' since Neolithic Man first made clearings in
the great forest that once clothed virtually all of England in
order to grow crops and graze livestock. The landscape we see

today – land tilled and land left uncultivated, paths and roads, hamlets and villages – is for the most part the product of gradual social and economic change over a period of six thousand years. At three points in this long history there have however been periods in which a change in agricultural methods has produced dramatic effects on our landscape over large areas. The changes which occurred in the first two such 'Agricultural Revolutions' enriched our countryside immeasurably. They established many of the features which have given our traditional landscape its distinction. We are now living through the third major transformation. But unlike its two predecessors, this present Agricultural Revolution is devastating rather than enriching the environment in which it is occurring.

The first Agricultural Revolution was the discovery in Neolithic times, probably about 3,800 BC, that the same piece of land could grow crops more than once if it was left fallow between periods of cultivation. This breakthrough, combined with the availability of strains of grass suitable for cultivation as crops and animals that could be domesticated, enabled nomadic tribes to settle in one spot. The first Neolithic and Bronze Age villages sprang up as the centres of settled agricultural communities, laying the foundations of the medieval manorial system with its open fields and rotational farming. Under this system, the land around a village was owned by the lord of the manor, but the peasants had a right to cultivate a strip or strips of the common fields (to iron out differences in soil fertility across the fields, strips were allocated in rotation). In addition, peasants could graze their animals on the common pastures of the village. Although the strip cropping system survives today in England at only one or two places, most famous of which is Laxton in Nottinghamshire, England's one million acres of common land, situated mainly on the Pennine moors and Dartmoor, but also including stretches of uncultivated lowland country from Dunstable Downs and the Malvern Hills to Port Meadow at Oxford and the Strays of York, are the relics of the common grazing pastures.

The second Agricultural Revolution, which occurred mainly between 1750 and 1850, partially dismantled this system. The population of England was increasing sharply, and rising demand made new methods of producing more food highly lucrative. Developments in stock rearing held out new hope of enhanced profit. But these could not be exploited as long as landowners' animals were able to mate freely in common pastures shared with peasants' animals, in accordance with traditional practice. So the landowners decided to enclose fields hitherto farmed in common by villagers. They imposed a network of hedges, stone walls and roads on the countryside to divide up the land into units suitable for scientific stock-rearing and other new forms of arable farming that were more productive than those they replaced.

The roots of the third (and current) Agricultural Revolution lie in World War II. The war stimulated demand for home-produced food, just as population increase had done in the eighteenth century. For most of the hundred years leading up to 1939, agriculture had been in decline. Britain had relied on cheap food from abroad to feed her population. Around 70 per cent of the nation's food was imported from overseas, in particular from the wheat farmers of Canada and the United States, the beef farmers of Argentina and the sugar cane farmers of the Caribbean, who produced food far more cheaply than their British counterparts because they were operating on a larger scale, climatic conditions were more suitable or wages were lower.

It was the U-boat campaign in the Western Approaches in the 1940s which revived interest in domestic agriculture by demonstrating the risks of reliance on imported food. After the war, the belief that a healthy agriculture was a strategic necessity led to a wide-ranging programme of government support for farmers. Since 1945 demand for home-grown food has been artificially stimulated through tariffs on imports and direct subsidies of many different kinds to British farmers from the taxpayer and consumer. Against the background of a guaranteed income, farmers have become businessmen anxious to make the most of new opportunities for financial gain. And, as it has happened, this change in attitude has coincided with a breakthrough in technology on a par with those of the two earlier agricultural revolutions. New tech-niques have made it possible to turn food production into a large-scale industry run quite differently from pre-war agri-culture. And the combination of technological change and highly favourable financial conditions has made farming far more profitable than anyone would have imagined possible in 1945. As a result, big business is turning the countryside into a huge production line. Of course, everyone has forgotten that the original reason for boosting home production – fear of a blockade of imports – is no longer very real. And it makes no difference that much of what is produced in Britain joins the EEC's mountains of surplus food.

The traditional English landscape is an inconvenient obstruction to the activities of the agri-businessmen. They could adapt the new methods to fit the environment they have inherited. But instead they are dismantling it. Profit dictates this course, and there are no real counter-pressures. Few of the people involved are unthinking vandals. Many of them are attached to the countryside and some are active in certain forms of conservation. But they have been taken over by a new professional orthodoxy which is propped up not only by the agricultural establishment but by the Government too, which is speeding the transformation with financial incentives and technical advice. In practising what is now understood to be their trade to the limits of their ability, farmers, mesmerised by the combination of technological change and excessive subsidies, have become the often unwitting agents of destruction. The two main forms of technological development are outlined in Chapter One, though others will be referred to elsewhere in this book. The subsidies are described in Chapter Two.

1

Technological Transformation

Mechanisation

The central process in the current agricultural revolution is the replacement of men and animals with machines. Machines enable farmers to reduce their labour costs, and to cram more crops into a rotation: harrowing, harvesting and so on can be done much more quickly by tractors than by horses. Machines also enable farmers to produce a better crop, as mechanical operations can be timed more accurately than those dependent on human activity. In 1920 there were only 10,000 farm tractors in Great Britain compared to more than 500,000 today. Meanwhile, the 300,000 horses that were still working on our farms in 1950 have now virtually all disappeared.[1]

There are two main reasons why the acquisition of machinery leads farmers to remove hedgerows, woods, clumps of trees and any other landscape feature on uncultivated land. First, the machines need large sweeps in which to turn: a lot of the equipment in which farmers have been investing heavily in recent years has a width of 20 or 30 feet, and it is clearly easier to operate if hedges and copses – 'obstructions' in the agricultural machinery trade's vocabulary – are removed, so that the spaces in which the machines work are larger and more regular. The other reason is that since the point of mechanisation is to enable farmers to shed workers and cut labour costs, they want the operation of their new machines to consume as few man-hours as possible. So they want to see their machines driven as quickly as possible round unencumbered fields.

The bigger a machine, the greater the incentive to clear away any areas that are not intensively cropped on the farm where it is to be used. The trend is towards the development and acquisition of more and bigger machines, so the outlook for such landscape features as have escaped the agricultural bulldozer so far looks bleak. 'Farmers want more tractor power and the figures prove it', declared an article in *Farmers'*

Weekly (2 November 1978), reporting a Ministry of Agriculture machinery census which showed a big jump in the number of tractors in use of over 82 horsepower. The weight of these powerful machines has to be spread or the soil would compact too much: the spreading of the weight on dual tyres attached to each wheel increases the width of the track. This is often extended further by giant attachments put on behind, like the twelve-furrow plough.

To clear the path for these new machines, other machines, mainly bulldozers and hydraulic lifters, have been developed. These make operations ranging from the clearance of a wood to the creation of a moorland road much easier than they used to be. By attaching special blades and a lifter to his tractor, a farmer can rid himself of a mile-long hedge in an afternoon; thirty years ago the task would have taken him several days. Another range of machines has been developed to make possible the 'reclamation' of rough uncultivated land on steep slopes. Many of these, like crawler tractors, are tracked vehicles whose design is based on the tank principle.

It is easy, then, to see how mechanisation leads directly to the destruction of landscape features on farmland. But it has also had indirect effects on features not directly involved in rationalisation plans. As a result of the mechanisation process, agricultural workers too have been leaving the land. The impact of continuing mechanisation and other labour-saving techniques has come at a time when other industries are still able to provide the prospect of higher wages and better working conditions, so there has been little resistance from the farm-workers to the de-manning that has taken place. Since the war, the farm workforce has been shrinking by about 7,000 a year. In 1948 there were nearly 563,000 regular full-time farmworkers in England and Wales; by 1979 the number had fallen to 133,000, a reduction of 66 per cent. So the new machines have not only stripped many parts of rural England of landscape features; they have also provoked change in the countryside's social structure.[2] As in other declining communities, it is the able, younger people who leave. And once the population of an area of countryside falls below a certain level or reaches a certain degree of imbalance, it ceases to work as a real community. A spiral of decline sets in, involving further depopulation, the loss of more and more local services and therefore more and more people. The only counterbalancing force has been the mixed blessing in some parts of the countryside of an influx of retired people and second-home owners. The arrival of such people can only do a limited amount towards the creation of healthier communities.

The decline of rural communities has a further impact on the landscape. Since fewer people are available to work on farms, the maintenance of landscape features on marginal land has become more difficult to arrange. If hedgerows, for instance, are to be really effective as stock-proof barriers, they need to be 'laid' by hand every five years; that is, the bushy top of the hedge has to be cut off, and the stems that remain have to be interwoven. In her country diary for 1906, Edith Holden notes that 'hedging-and-ditching are going on everywhere' in January. In her day, there were about five times as many farmworkers as there are today, and they were set to maintain hedges, woods and so on in the slack months of the farming year. The reduction in numbers of permanent farmworkers coupled with new-found reliance on contract labour to help out at harvest time has meant that there are now fewer spare man-hours to be filled with secondary work. And the disappearance of labour needed to maintain items like hedges has made their removal all the more urgent for many farmers. Where hedges are kept, they are nowadays often cut as quickly as possible by a man driving a flail cutter alongside them and chopping them off almost to the stumps – a method which destroys most of their landscape value.

The new machines' steady march into the countryside is heavily subsidised by the taxpayer. One of farmers' many tax concessions is the entitlement to write off the entire cost of new machinery (and buildings) against tax in the year of purchase. So it becomes worthwhile for farmers to buy machines they would otherwise not bother with. But the extra machinery will still only pay its way if it is exploited fully. So more land is reclaimed to keep the new equipment busy. This taxpayers' subsidy to farmers obviously benefits wealthy farmers much more than the little man. And it probably costs the British taxpayer something like £200 million per year in lost tax revenue.[3]

Fertilisers and pesticides

Until the present agricultural revolution, farming operations were closely conditioned by the natural biological processes

of the earth. The idea was still: 'We plough the fields and
scatter The good seed on the land But it is fed and watered By
God's Almighty Hand.' Now, however, farming is a capital-
and energy-intensive process in which industrial products are
turned into other industrial products that happen to be edible.

Before 1945, nearly all extra nutrients for crops and grass
pastures came either from manure applied to the ground or
from alluvium deposited by rivers in flood. But now huge
amounts of artificial inorganic fertilisers are used almost everywhere. Nitrogen-based fertilisers are the most important.
About one million tons of them, manufactured mainly from
natural gas, are applied to farmland in the UK every year: the
amount increased eight-fold between 1953 and 1976. Phos-
phate fertilisers are manufactured from ores imported from
Morocco and Florida: their use has increased by a half over
the post-war period. The use of potassium-based fertilisers,
imported from Russia, Israel, France, Germany and Spain,
has more than doubled.

The large-scale use of chemical pesticides, too, is a post-war
development. Between 1944 and 1975 the number of approved
pesticides in use on British farmland increased twelve-fold.
To keep down crop diseases and competition between crops
and weeds farmers no longer rely on the use of clean seed,
hoeing, and the restriction of cultivation to the times of the
year that favour the crop rather than the weed. Instead, they
spray herbicide on the land to kill weeds, as well as fungicides,
insecticides, molluscicides, rodenticides and avicides.

The increase in the use of fertilisers and pesticides has gone
hand in hand with mechanisation. Farmers can hitch special
devices to the backs of their tractors to spray chemicals on to
their land; without such mechanical aids, chemicals would
not have acquired their present grip.

Chemical fertilisers and pesticides have undoubtedly increased yields dramatically. And they enable farmers to abandon
crop rotations. The soil is no longer allowed to rest under a
root crop or fallow field every three or four years in order to
recover naturally the fertility it lost under intensive cultivation: fertility is maintained at as high a level as possible
almost indefinitely through the application of huge quantities
of fertiliser and pesticide. What this means is that farmers can
now grow crops like barley in the same field for up to thirteen
consecutive years instead of just one in four. This is, of course,

much more profitable than turning the land over to a less lucrative crop every few years. The abandonment of rotation has provided farmers with another reason for hedge removal. When crops are rotated, land is left fallow some of the time and animals graze it. So each field needs to be stock-proof. But when crop rotation has been abandoned, farmers can specialise completely in arable farming and get rid of all their animals. When they have done this, hedges are no longer needed and they can be bulldozed away. But this is far from being the only ill effect of the chemical takeover of farming.

Arable land occupies nearly 30 per cent of the land surface of Great Britain. And the most obvious direct impact of chemical pesticides and fertilisers here has been the elimination of wildlife. Thirty years ago wildlife in our countryside was not, as it is today, effectively confined to uncultivated, marginal land – hedgerows, woods, marshes and so on. Even productive arable land growing barley, wheat, cabbages, peas and potatoes also supported abundant wildlife, though it was less rich than that of uncultivated land. English cornfields were splashed with red poppies. Cornflowers grew among the ears of wheat, and here and there the delicate, rose-coloured blossoms of the bind-weed on their green, string-like stems twined themselves in and out of the wheat stalks. A walk after harvest revealed little plants which had been hidden by the tall crop, like the tiny heartsease or wild pansy with its single creamy flower, dabbed with a spot of deepest yellow streaked with purple at its centre. Hares and partridges were thick on the ground. Now, however, farmers have the means to grow 'clean crops', so all 'weeds' are banished by pesticides. Animals are affected in turn by the elimination of weeds. The survival of the partridge, for instance, depends on an adequate supply of insects to feed its newly-hatched chicks. The Game Conservancy estimates that the partridge chick survival rate is now running one-third lower than the level of the 1930s, and it attributes this to starvation of chicks through the elimination of insect 'pests' by pesticides.[4] Stubble-burning, which accompanies chemical control, accentuates the impact on wildlife. When wheat or barley is harvested, farmers burn the stubble to destroy it as quickly as possible so they can sow another crop at the first possible moment after the last one was harvested. Stubble-burning burns or chars not only the remains of the crop, however, but also the microfauna and flora of the soil surface. In one study, stubble-burning reduced the number of insects living above ground by 85 per cent, the number of insects emerging in the following year by 71 per cent and the number of species present by 61 per cent.[5] One of the more visible effects of this process is the absence of flocks of birds feeding on the stubble. Thirty years ago most fields were visited after harvest by large numbers of lapwings, finches, buntings, larks, pipits and wagtails. But now that their food has turned to ashes, few turn up.

Like mechanisation, the switch to chemical fertilisers and pesticides was a product of the era of cheap oil. The manufacture of fertilisers for UK agriculture alone requires the energy equivalent of two million tons of oil every year – about one-fifth of the total annual energy input to UK agriculture.[6] And the efficiency of our agriculture in terms of output per man, which is undoubtedly high, exacts a high price in energy use. Between 1952 and 1972, the energy input per man employed in UK agriculture tripled. Through heavy use of fertilisers, pesticides, processed animal feedstuffs and machinery, UK farmworkers now consume as much energy per man as workers in heavy engineering industry. Gerald Leach of the International Institute for Environment and Development wrote in 1975 of a comparative study he had made of energy inputs and outputs of different UK industries: 'It is one of the most striking results of this study that the worker normally associated with the power-hungry machinery of the factory and production line should be backed by no more energy than the man who tills the field and tends the cows.'[7] Now that the real cost of energy has increased, the benefits to the nation of such energy-intensive agriculture are even less obvious than they were.

2

Subsidies for Destruction

Technological change would not in itself give rise to the wholesale destruction of the countryside we are now experiencing. Some landscape features would doubtless be destroyed to facilitate new forms of operation. But many of these features lie on patches of ground which would not be worth cultivating, even with the new methods, were it not for the incentives to production provided artificially by the state. The most important of these incentives is the artificial support of agricultural food prices to guarantee farmers' incomes through what is in effect a tax on food. Guaranteed minimum price levels have been pegged so high that it is profitable for farmers to plough up almost any kind of uncultivated land – woodland, marsh and down, for example – to increase their output, even if much of it is destined for the Common Market's stockpiles of surplus produce. The next most important incentive is the provision by the British taxpayer of direct cash grants to encourage farmers to make landscape changes to increase output. But there are others too, like reliefs from rates and taxes.

Price support

Price support was an essential ingredient of Clement Attlee's 1947 Agriculture Act (the cornerstone for British agricultural policy through most of the post-war era), though the form of price support changed when Britain entered the EEC in 1973. It arose naturally enough from the thinking behind the Act, which was designed to stabilise prices for farm produce, to lift agriculture out of its pre-war depression, to raise farmers' incomes and to increase the output of home-grown food to a level which would ensure strategic security. 'For the first time in history', announced Tom Williams, the Minister for Agriculture, as he introduced the Bill, 'the farmers will be able to plan ahead with certain knowledge of market and price . . . I fully believe that this machinery for providing stability represents the most far-reaching step that has ever been taken in the history of agriculture.'

The means of price support chosen in 1947 was the system known as deficiency payment. The Government guaranteed farmers minimum prices for the main farm products and these were set at levels that would ensure that farming was profitable. As long as the market price was higher than the guaranteed price, then the market price was what the farmer received; but when it fell below the guaranteed price, the farmer received a 'deficiency payment' from the taxpayer to make up the difference. At the same time, food imports were subjected to tariffs and quotas.

Since Britain has been a member of the EEC, more of the burden of supporting agriculture has been switched from the taxpayer to the consumer. During the transitional period, from 1973 to 1977, the price of food in Britain moved up ahead of the retail price index as the changeover to the new price level was completed.[1]

Prices are supported in the EEC in two main ways. First, a trade barrier has been erected right round the collective borders of the member countries to prevent cheap food from overseas from competing with the produce of EEC farmers. This would be a real threat, as those areas from which Britain used to import so much food are still producing it at prices far below those at which it is produced in Europe. At present potential competition from such countries is controlled by the imposition of levies on food imported into the EEC from outside. Before New Zealand butter, for example, can get onto our supermarket shelves, a levy is imposed at the port of entry, so its price to the consumer is increased. EEC housewives pay the levies in higher food prices and this money is then channelled to Brussels to help finance the Common Market as a whole. What this means is that for certain commodities our housewives are forced to pay prices way above those they would have to pay if they were allowed access to the world market. For instance, the average retail price of butter in Common Market countries is more than double the price in Hong Kong, according to calculations by the Institute of Fiscal Studies.[2] Similarly, the retail price of sugar in the EEC is nearly three times the world price, that of barley is two and a half times the world price, and cheese and beef are nearly twice as expensive.

But even more important than the EEC levies on food from

overseas is the system of price guarantees for farmers inside the EEC. This requires a subsidy not only from the consumer but also from the taxpayer. The guaranteed prices offered to EEC farmers are based on a principle quite different from the deficiency payment system which operated in Britain before we joined the EEC. There are no deficiency payments, as prices to the consumer are never allowed to fall below the guaranteed minimum level. Up till now, the guaranteed prices have nearly always been set too high for production and consumption to be kept in balance. High prices have encouraged farmers to produce more than EEC consumers either want or can afford to buy. The result has been surpluses far larger than those that would result simply from variations in output from harvest to harvest. To fulfil the guarantee to farmers that all their produce will sell at a fixed minimum price, the EEC's Intervention Boards have to buy up any produce farmers cannot sell on the open market at the minimum price or above. As a result, the EEC Commission has accumulated massive stockpiles of butter, skimmed milk, cheese, beef, veal, wine, wheat, barley, rye, olive oil and pigmeat. These foodstuffs are sold off at knock-down prices outside Europe or destroyed. Much surplus skimmed milk is even fed to farm animals, which then produce further surpluses. In 1980, the Community was planning to spend 60 per cent of its whole budget – nearly £6 billion – on dealing with surpluses.[3] Through levies on non-EEC food and through price guarantees to EEC farmers, the Common Agricultural Policy (CAP) increases the retail price of food in the UK by 12 per cent, according to calculations by economists at the University of Cambridge.[4] But by no means all the surpluses are generated in the rest of Europe, as the National Farmers' Union and the Milk Marketing Board sometimes seem to be implying is the case. The most recently published annual report of the Intervention Board for Agricultural Produce in the UK (and most surplus foods dealt with by this board originate in the UK) shows that our own Exchequer paid out £90 million in 1978 on buying and storing surplus food.[5] At the end of 1978 Britain's surplus stocks of skimmed milk powder, for example, amounted to 59,000 tons and were worth nearly £30 million – this only after 56,000 tons had been disposed of. These 56,000 tons were unloaded only with the help of a special subsidy on the purchase of skimmed milk powder which is to be used as feed for animals.

The price support system makes farmers the only group of producers who are guaranteed that whatever they produce will be sold at an acceptable price regardless of the level of demand and regardless of the overall level of production. And the existence of an infinite market obviously tempts farmers to expand indefinitely. That means 'reclaiming' any uncultivated land they can. In a world where any amount of production is saleable at an attractive price, every unfelled wood or undrained wetland represents forfeited profit.

Since price support is a benefit for British farmers, if not for British consumers and taxpayers, the cost of price support to Britain only emerges when the total gain to our farmers is subtracted from the total cost to UK consumers and taxpayers. The Institute of Fiscal Studies has calculated that in 1980 the total gain to UK farmers from the CAP works out at £1,558 million. The total loss of UK consumers from the CAP is £2,813 million. To this net loss of £1,255 million must be added the sum of £1,050 million paid by the UK taxpayer to support the CAP in 1980,[6] minus the rebate of £710 million Mrs Thatcher secured in June 1980. Of course, Britain is particularly badly placed to benefit from the CAP: farmers form a tiny proportion of our population compared to consumers. But in the Community as a whole something like £4 billion a year disappears on the journey from consumers and taxpayers to farmers. The Institute has worked out the consequences of the CAP for the Community as a whole to be as follows: 'The policy raises the income derived from European agriculture by about £14.4 billion, or approximately £1,700 per person employed in agriculture. It does so at a total cost (exclusive of central administrative expenses) of £18.4 billion, or £70 per head of population.' The missing billions seep away mainly through loss of consumer demand and increases in feedstock costs, both caused by artificially high prices, storage costs and administration costs. So the CAP does not just transfer money to farmers from the rest of us: it also destroys a lot of money in the process.

This bizarre system seems most unlikely to change significantly. Farmers in both France and Germany are a powerful political force and their governments are anxious to avoid alienating them through steps like the freeze on the intervention prices of products that are in continual surplus, which

Britain has advocated. If such a freeze were achieved, it would stem the build-up of surpluses and probably also slow down the conversion of uncultivated land supporting hedges, woods, wetlands, downs and so on to intensive agricultural land. But when Peter Walker became Minister of Agriculture in 1979, he made it clear that he wanted to improve the position of farmers in the UK and to increase output even of products in long-term surplus. So although he has pressed for a freeze on the EEC guaranteed minimum prices of products in long-term or 'structural' surplus (*not*, of course, freezes on the retail prices of these products), he has also at the same time taken several major steps to encourage UK farmers to produce more. Thus during Mr Walker's first eight months of office as Minister of Agriculture (up till the end of 1979), he introduced the biggest-ever subsidies to hill farmers. These will encourage the spread of intensive agriculture on our moorlands, even in national parks. He announced two major increases in the price of milk, and secured three devaluations of the green pound, the device by which EEC agricultural prices are related to sterling. Each one per cent devaluation of the green pound transfers £37 million from UK consumers to UK farmers, according to the Institute of Fiscal Studies.[7] The total of four devaluations of the green pound between March 1979 and March 1980 benefited UK farmers to the tune of £340 million, and put up the food price index by 4 per cent, according to Roy Mason, the Opposition Spokesman on Agriculture.[8]

Capital grants

The second way in which the taxpayer has funded the current Agricultural Revolution has been through the provision of a series of capital grants to farmers. There are now two main grant schemes: the farm capital grant scheme, financed solely by the British Government, and the EEC Farm and Horticulture Development scheme of which the British taxpayer meets one quarter of the cost direct. In 1979-80 an estimated £171 million was paid to farmers in the two forms of capital grants; the direct cost to the British taxpayer was £108 million.[9] The British system of grants was introduced soon after the war to encourage farmers to expand production. Under both schemes grants are available to cover up to three-quarters of the cost of putting up buildings and carrying out 'improvements' which very often mean the removal of hedges, trees, woods, rough grasslands, streams and ponds.[10] Eighty-eight thousand pounds, for example, were paid to farmers in England in 1979 under the farm capital grant scheme to uproot bushes and small trees to uncover extra farmland, £680,000 to make farm roads, £584,000 to put up new fences (frequently as we shall see to replace hedges) and £659,000 to kill natural grass pastures – moors, downland turf, hay meadows and so on – and to replace them usually with a ryegrass monoculture which is converted to milk more quickly than our natural grasslands. Unfortunately the grants, which are available on demand, have been administered by the Ministry of Agriculture with almost total disregard for the implications of the activities that it is funding for other interests in the countryside.

The capital grants, together with price guarantees and tax concessions on new farm machinery, feed a spiral of rising food production and accelerating landscape destruction. There is no limit to the number of steps a farmer can take to increase (perhaps only fractionally) the output of his farm largely at the taxpayer's expense. A farm is like a sponge: it has the ability to soak up limitless sums of money. Even if all opportunities could be exhausted, a farmer could happily go back to replace worn-out drainage systems, buildings, fences and so on. As farmers increase their profits through improvement, they have more money to plough into new machinery, buildings, fertilisers and the exploitation of uncultivated land. And if the taxpayer is ready to put his own cash into almost any scheme a farmer dreams up, the farmer who fails to invest in improvement loses twice over.

But although the taxpayer helps finance the installation of new drainage schemes, the erection of buildings, the under-grounding of watercourses and so on, the Ministry administering the grants applies no test whatever of the project's value. In 1970 James Prior, the then Minister of Agriculture, abolished the test that had existed up till then on the grounds that if a farmer thinks it is worth spending his own money on a particular scheme, the Government should put in its share too without asking questions. The Ministry of Agriculture sees its role as merely to react to proposals farmers put forward. Although the £108 million given to farmers in 1979–80 is justified in terms of the need for Britain to produce extra quantities of certain foodstuffs, applications for grant are judged solely on technical viability (whether a drainage scheme proposed will actually work) and on whether or not the proposal will provide the maximum possible profit for the individual farmer who has submitted the application.

What this means is that if a farmer puts in an application for grant for say £60,000 to install drains to turn a marsh into an arable field in order to produce extra quantities of a product that is in surplus, the Ministry would not make the grant conditional on the growing of a product that was in short supply. If 'improvement' increases surpluses, then the Ministry argues that that is a problem for the EEC. In any case, the Ministry contends that it could not possibly ensure that a particular crop was grown after a capital improvement scheme had been installed. In fact, it is not easy to see why this would not be possible.

Farmers' means are not examined before they receive a grant – as are those of citizens seeking legal aid or rent rebates, for instance. A visiting delegation from West Germany, where capital grants are only given to farmers who could not otherwise afford to make improvements, asked officials at our Ministry of Agriculture whether they would have given a grant to Paul Getty if he had applied for a grant to increase the profitability of his land. Our officials replied, yes, they would. The Ministry administers the capital grants scheme on the assumption that all farmers in Britain – whether they are full-time or part-time, owner-occupiers with a small area and relatively low income or financial institutions with annual profits running into millions – are entitled to a taxpayers' grant to do whatever they like to increase the profitability of their land.

Neither does the Ministry discriminate against farmers who have run into objections to what they propose, for instance from people who consider the scheme will impair landscape beauty, destroy wildlife or archaeological remains or rob a local community of recreation land. It would be unfair, it argues, to deny grants to certain farmers just because they happen to have land over which there is a conservation interest. The Ministry does not keep records of any grants it refuses but it is clear that at most a handful and perhaps only one farm capital grant application (that for Lockton Moor, see pp111-12) has ever been turned down on conservation grounds. This despite the duty Parliament laid on the Ministry to 'have regard to the desirability of conserving the natural beauty and amenity of the countryside' (Section 11, Countryside Act 1968).

In February 1980, amidst much publicity, Mr Peter Walker, the Minister of Agriculture, announced cuts in the numbers of staff administering the capital grants system. The purpose of these cuts was twofold: first, to release technical staff for other purposes,[11] and, second, to meet the 3 per cent target for cuts in manpower required as the Ministry's main contribution to the general round of public expenditure cuts.[12] But these moves certainly will not help the countryside. Quite the reverse. The manpower cuts are leading to reductions in the system of controls surrounding the grants. Before Mr Walker's change, farmers needed the Ministry's approval before beginning the work for which they intended to claim a grant. Once the application had been received, a Ministry of Agriculture local official usually visited the farm to see what was planned and to advise the farmer about cost and other considerations. This visit also provided an opportunity for some discussion of the impact of what was proposed on wildlife, archaeology, recreation and other non-agricultural interests. Under the new proposals, however, farmers will simply carry out the work and then send the Ministry a bill. So this move will almost certainly mean that the grants will inflict even more damage on the countryside than they have done already.

The one move that would have helped curb the destruction of the countryside which the grants help to cause – and would have fitted in with the Thatcher government's philosophy – is not being made. This would have been the imposition of a ceiling on the total amount of money available for grants in any one year. Apart from the proposed abolition of prior approval, Mr Walker made two other changes in the grants system designed to cut costs: in January 1980 he introduced a limit of £136,000 on the total investment that can now be approved for grant, together with a slight reduction in the rates of some grants. But essentially, despite the savage cuts and ceilings being imposed in other areas of public expenditure, the agricultural grants budget will remain a bottomless pit, the amount of money being paid out depending on the number of applications received. And even after changes in the rates, the grants remain mouth-watering. Field drainage is funded at 37 per cent under the farm capital grant scheme, 50 per cent under the farm and horticulture development scheme, and 70 per cent under the FHDS in hill areas; the ploughing of open moorland is backed to the tune of 22 per cent, 32 per cent, or 50 per cent in hill areas.

Total net cost of agricultural support

The feather-bedding of British farmers does not end with price support, capital grants and protection from overseas competition. There are other measures designed to increase the general profitability of farming as part of our system of farm support. Unfortunately, most of these other measures stimulate the destruction of the beauty of the countryside, though less directly than grants and price support.

The English countryside can be regarded as a vast tax haven. And not only do farmers and foresters enjoy very substantial tax concessions from central government: they also enjoy complete relief from local taxes – that is, rates. It was in 1929, when the agricultural industry was in a particularly depressed state, that Parliament decided to grant all agricultural land and buildings total exemption from payment of rates. Although agriculture is now at least as well able to pay rates as any other industry, this anomalous arrangement still stands. It probably costs the people of England and Wales about £150 million every year. (The Layfield Committee on Local Government finance, which reported in 1976, estimated the cost to the nation of the de-rating of agriculture at £120 million a year.[13] Rateable values are tied to rental values: between 1975, when the Committee carried out its calculation, and 1979, rental values on farmland in England and Wales rose by more than 60 per cent. Farmers would, however, be able to write off payment of rates against income tax as a business expense, so the net benefit to the Exchequer if rating of agricultural land and buildings were introduced now would be something in the region of £150 million a year.) At the moment, this particular subsidy to agriculture is made largely by the taxpayer in the form of rate support grant, for the exemption of farming and forestry from rates makes predominantly rural counties, like Lincolnshire and Northumberland, much less able than they would otherwise be to support public services for country people.

In income tax law, farming is treated just like any other industry. This means two main concessions are available. The first is the ability to write off against tax the cost of the purchase of new machinery or buildings. If we assume that farmers would have had to pay income tax at the rate of 40 per cent on the estimated £1,075 million they spent in 1979 on the purchase of new machinery and buildings[14], this represents a gift from the taxpayer to the farmer of £430 million in that year. In addition there is the allowance for depreciation. Depreciation allowances for farmers in 1978 amounted to £616 million[15]; if income tax had been payable on this sum at the rate of 40 per cent, this relief would have represented an additional £246 million in terms of tax revenue foregone. Farmers are also allowed to average out their profits for tax purposes so that they are not unduly penalised by fluctuations in profit brought about by good or bad harvests: this concession was worth £10 million in income foregone in 1978–79.[16]

In capital transfer tax, farmers enjoy special exemptions. The combined effect of agricultural relief and business relief is to allow a 50 per cent relief from CTT on all working farmers' assets, that is machinery as well as land and buildings, without upper limit.[17] If farmers seek to reduce their CTT bill further through tax planning – and the Northfield Committee of Inquiry into the Acquisition and Occupancy of Agricultural Land, which reported in 1979, considered it essential to assume that farmers would inevitably do this – then the tax they pay is of course reduced still further. Alistair Sutherland, a lecturer in economics at Cambridge University, who worked for a time as special advisor to the Northfield Committee, wrote in an unpublished report for the Committee: 'A widow paying standard CTT and leaving a house plus financial assets worth £50,000 to her children has a CTT tax rate of ten per cent. To pay at that rate a farmer's widow, with no tax planning, has to leave a farm business worth about £170,000. If there is effective tax planning via a suitable family partnership, a farm worth £510,000 will pay ten per cent.'[18] The cost of agricultural relief in 1978–79 was £20 million; the amount of business relief claimed by farmers is not recorded.[19]

The £94 million which the taxpayer paid in 1979–80[20] for the administration of the Ministry of Agriculture is the last significant capital sum diverted to agriculture. If it were not for the policy of heavy state support to agriculture, we probably would not need a separate ministry for agriculture. After all, we do not have a ministry for the retail trade, or for steel or motor-car manufacture. Most of this £94 million goes to pay the Ministry's 13,600 employees. In addition, the Ministry spent an extra £44 million in 1979–80 on sponsoring research,[21] much of this into techniques for land 'improvement'. All told, then, taking into account price support, grants, subsidies, tax and rate reliefs and the financing of a separate and large ministry, agricultural support now costs the British taxpayer and consumer in the region of £5 billion every year.

What all this means is that far more than any other comparable group of producers – including those in the much-maligned heavy manufacturing industrial sector – our farmers are 'pensioners of the state', in Sir Keith Joseph's phrase. Each year the British taxpayer and consumer subsidises each farmer in England to the tune of something like £8,500[22] – nearly five times the £1,800 per year which, as the Conservative Government was reminding us in January 1980, was the average annual subsidy to each employee of the British Steel Corporation at that time. It might be supposed that in return for the support farmers receive from the community at large they could be expected to pursue their activities in ways which would harmonise with the needs of the rest of the community. Nothing could be further from the truth. For on top of the privileges conferred on farmers which I have listed, they have also been granted almost total exemption from the operation of the town and country planning system which was set up in 1947 to give the community a voice in the shaping of the environment. This exemption gives farmers *carte blanche* to do whatever they want to our countryside.

PART TWO

The Impact on the Countryside

The English landscape is a symphony whose unique sound depends on the harmonious orchestration of a wide range of instruments. It is the overall balance of features in our countryside that matters. But the best way of appreciating how agricultural change is turning harmony into discord is to anatomise its impact on each of the instruments which contribute to our rural symphony.

The following seven chapters describe the impact of agricultural intensification on the seven landscape features that are affected most acutely.

3

Hedgerows

Hedgerows provide the framework of the English country-side. In the form in which we know them in Britain, hedge-rows exist in only a handful of other spots around the world, principally central Tasmania, Normandy, Ireland and New England. Hedgerows have defined field and territorial boundaries in our countryside from Saxon times. And the pattern they have imposed on our fields, built up gradually over thousands of years, does more to distinguish our landscape than any other feature. By providing abundant cover, hedgerows have made England's wildlife richer by far than that of other lands: the primrose and the violet, the hedgehog and the dormouse owe their abundance to the hedgerow; and it is our network of bushy hedges which has made England *par excellence* the country of small songbirds. Most important of all, however, it is the hedgerow that has given our landscape the peculiar intimacy that distinguishes it from all others. As Richard Jefferies wrote in 1884, 'without hedges, England would not be England'.

Today, however, our hedgerows are disappearing fast. Farmers removed a quarter of the hedgerows in England and Wales between 1946 and 1974, about 120,000 miles in all, or 4,500 miles a year.[1] The loss is continuing, as the hedgerow gets in the way of a wide range of new agricultural techniques. In 1978, 74 miles of hedgerow in England and Wales were grubbed out in the course of preparation for new drainage schemes alone to stop their roots fouling new drains.

The regional variations that provide much of the subtlety of our countryside are intimately bound up with differences in the composition, shape and layout of hedgerows. The low, square, beech hedges of Exmoor are quite distinct from the tall hedgebanks of Devon and Cornwall, as the oak studded hedges of the Weald are quite unlike the straight hawthorn and ash hedges of the Midlands, and these distinctions are vital to the differences in the character of these areas. Geology, geography and biology all play a part in distinguishing these hedge types from each other, but the most important distinguishing feature is age. It is a popular misconception that the basic structure of the lowland landscape is only two hundred years old, a creation of eighteenth-century enclosure. Our different kinds of hedgerow illustrate perhaps better than any other landscape feature the basic law of landscape history that everything in the landscape is much older than it seems. The 18th century enclosures, which divided up the old open-field parishes, had a widespread effect only on that part of England where the open-field system was well-established – the Midlands[2]. Outside the heart of England, in such counties as Northumberland, Durham, Suffolk, Essex, Kent, Sussex, Devon, Cornwall, Cheshire and Lancashire, the open-field system had never had the hold it achieved in the Midlands and by the beginning of the 18th century most of the hedgerows that survive today were already in existence, created from the times when the first settlers enclosed fields from the forest. Even in Midland counties like Oxfordshire, Leicestershire and Warwickshire many hedgerows date back much further than the eighteenth century. Half of Oxfordshire's hedges pre-date the Georgian and Victorian periods, according to landscape historian Frank Emery. He calculates that 15 per cent of Oxfordshire's hedge-miles marked out fields carved straight out of the great forest that once clothed almost all of Britain. Some of these hedges are more than one thousand years old; early enclosure of common fields and more forest between 1450 and 1750 account for the other 35 per cent.[3] By the 18th century most of the hedgerows that survive today were already in existence.

Most of our hedges, then, have quite a history. To see how variations in this history condition landscape, we could do worse than look at the countryside of Shropshire.

In north-eastern Shropshire, parliamentary enclosure in the eighteenth century created a landscape of fields bounded by a geometrically regular pattern of hawthorn hedges and wide, straight roads. This area has none of the intimacy of central and southern Shropshire. We find here a mosaic of smaller, irregular fields, bounded by sunken lanes and thick hedges, dating largely from the medieval enclosure of individual fields direct from the untamed forest wilderness. The rocky Stiperstone Hills in the west of the county are characterised by circular, roughly built stone walls: sixteenth-century sqatters, who were often miners working part-time as farmers, enclosed islands of the rough grass heathland with walls of stones gathered from the land.

Shropshire has done well to hold on to as varied a landscape as this. In other areas, where, of course, stone walls have suffered the same fate as hedges, monotony has taken over.

Hedges in west Cornwall are constructed on quite a different pattern from those in the rest of England. In the Land's End peninsula in particular they are typically very old (their bases are estimated to date in some cases from the Bronze Age). Here hedges consist of stone-faced walls filled with earth, with a drainage ditch on either side, and on top a carpet of thick turf and wild flowers (brightly-coloured cranesbills, stitchworts, campions and harebells) crowned by gorse and hawthorn bushes. Here in the westernmost tip of England, conditions were too exposed for hawthorn hedges and hedge-row trees. But stone-based hedges could be put up simply from boulders cleared off the small, irregular fields they bordered. These hedges are themselves of great historical interest, but even more ancient remains lie underneath many of them – the remains of Iron Age villages, burial chambers and subterranean refuges. When the hedges are removed, as more and more of them are being, these archaeological treasures go too. At the moment there is almost nothing to prevent a Cornish farmer from bulldozing away all the ancient hedges on his land if he wishes to. Uprooting a Cornish hedge is deceptively easy: without tree or hawthorn roots to anchor it to the earth, all that is needed is a powerful bulldozer and somewhere to dump the stones. Twenty-three miles of hedge were taken out in an eight-square-mile area of West Penwith near St Buryan between 1888 and 1976, according to Nicholas Johnson of the Cornwall Committee for Rescue Archaeology, who estimates that more hedges were removed in West Penwith during the thirteen years between 1963 and 1976 than were grubbed out during the seventy-five year period up to 1963.[4]

The impact on the landscape of hedge removal can be seen clearly at Trevorian Farm just outside Sennen Cove. In the early 1970s, two farmers from Kent bought six farms near the Cove covering a total of about 900 acres, the largest of which was Trevorian. In order to clear a path for the machines which were an essential feature of their plans to grow cereals, carrots, potatoes and bulbs, they cleared away eleven miles of hedge-bank, thus increasing field sizes eightfold. Of course, it would be unreasonable to demand the preservation of all existing hedges. But too many operations like that at Trevorian will rob Cornwall of part of its identity. Trevorian is already indistinguishable from many farms in the east of England.

Cornwall is only one area whose regional character is disappearing with its hedgerows. The Vale of York, central and southern Devon, the Northumberland plain, central Herefordshire, the Lake District's Eden Valley, the Weald of Kent and Sussex, Nottinghamshire and Lincolnshire are just some of the areas suffering in this way. In Norfolk, Cambridgeshire and even the Cotswolds you can now drive for miles and not see a single substantial hedgerow; this is one reason why these areas now seem almost identical.

The impact of hedge removal on a landscape does of course vary widely. If there are plenty of hedges to start with, it is easier to bear the loss of a few. But the bulldozer is not respecting such niceties. The Worcestershire countryside has been turned into much more of a prairie than neighbouring Herefordshire has. But this is not because hedgerow removal has been taking place faster in Worcestershire. It is because Worcestershire started with fewer hedgerows. The county lost an estimated 1,087 miles of hedgerow between 1900 and 1976 whereas farmers in Herefordshire managed to clear away an estimated 3,730 miles during the same period.[5] Worcestershire may have lost a third as many hedges, but it misses them much more.

In the 1950s and 1960s, it was on the arable lands of East Anglia and, to a lesser extent, on the mixed farming lands of southern England that most hedge removal was taking place. Hedges were removed to create more cropland and to make way for the big new machines in which arable farmers were investing heavily. The doubling of England's barley acreage in the 1950s was just one sign of an aggressive drive to squeeze more out of the English soil which spelt doom for hedges. Hedgerows are of no real use to the arable farmer: in the past they may have helped stop soil erosion by acting as wind-breaks, but now this can be achieved more efficiently by the application of mulches and oils to the soil surface. The arable farmer has no call for stock-proof barriers and little need for the proprietary boundary that many hedgerows originally provided. Hedgerows need maintaining and they harbour 'pests'. So our arable farming lands (especially those in Norfolk, Suffolk, Cambridgeshire, Hertfordshire, Lincolnshire, Nottinghamshire and Humberside) have been stripped of a large proportion of their hedges: 45 per cent of Norfolk's hedgerows (a length of 8,000 miles) were removed by farmers between 1946 and 1970, for example.[6] Many of those that remain have been cut right down to a level about two feet off the ground, at which they cease to fulfil any real landscape or wildlife function.

Until the 1970s, on the other hand, dairying remained a form of farming that really helped conserve the landscape against unwelcome change. For the last few years, however, the dairy farming areas of England have been subjected to even more dramatic change than arable areas. For now a revolution in dairy farming has touched off a new wave of hedge removal that is beginning to wipe out the distinctive character of parts of our non-arable areas. In these places, hedgerows are as redundant in cattle country as they are on arable farms. Dairy farming is particularly widespread in England: a majority of British farmers depend on it while more than half of the land in England and Wales is occupied by farms on which milk production is the major interest. Counties in which dairying is the dominant type of farming include Cumbria, Cheshire, Shropshire, Staffordshire, Warwickshire, Avon, Somerset and Dorset.

Two new practices are taking grip. The first is paddock grazing. Farmers are replacing the old natural pastures with specially developed strains of grass, sown as a virtual monoculture, which are converted to milk more quickly than the original grasses. But these new pastures do not protect the underlying soil from trampling in the way that natural grass pastures do, since they lack the thick matt of interwoven roots of our natural pastures: they consist simply of bare earth and blades of grass. For this and other reasons, farmers are anxious to minimise the amount of trampling the new pastures receive. So they try to direct grazing by confining the animals to small paddocks, moving them on to another paddock every day or two, or even twice in the same day. For this system, they require movable field boundaries. Post and wire fences can meet this need, hedges cannot; so hedges are being replaced. In winter the animals subjected to paddock grazing are kept indoors and fed on silage (fermented grass) which was cut from the fields in summer and stored until needed. The second new method in dairying involves carrying this idea to its logical conclusion. To control the feeding of cattle even more precisely, farmers in some areas no longer risk allowing their cattle to stray out of doors at all. Instead, the cows are housed together in sheds and fed on grass harvested from the fields where the cattle once grazed, supplemented by concentrates brought in from outside. Under this system, hedgerows just get in the way of the big machines harvesting and fertilising the grass.

Somerset is one county where paddock grazing is likely to gain a stronger and stronger grip. A study in 1972 revealed that on one 265-acre dairy farm near Crewkerne, two and a half miles of hedgerow had been removed so that grazing could be reorganised: the old nine-acre fields bounded by hedgerows made way for fields nearly five times as large divided up into much smaller areas by movable wire fences.[7]

The advantages of paddock grazing for farmers are only marginal, however, if they exist at all. Observation by the Ministry of Agriculture showed very little difference in either total milk yields or cow weight changes during the grazing period when cows in paddock grazing were compared with others in extensive grazing systems.[8] Nor are wire fences any cheaper to maintain than hedgerows: maintenance costs for wire fences are actually higher: 75p per chain for fences compared with 73p per chain for hedges since fences need replacing every twenty years.[9] Nonetheless, more and more farmers are switching to controlled grazing systems, with encouragement from the Ministry of Agriculture in the form of advice and grant. (The cows, by the way, much prefer traditional extensive grazing, and therefore produce more milk, according to one Ministry of Agriculture study.[10] But we can hardly expect their views to carry much weight if even the human community fails to make its voice heard in these matters.)

The Weald of Kent and Sussex is one area that looks particularly vulnerable to a switch to 'battery dairying'. Secrecy is the key to the charm of the Weald. And it is the wide, thickly timbered hedgerows of the Weald, locally known as 'shaws', that shelter the Weald's secret delights. For thousands of years the heavy clay soils and the marshy character of much of the land made it difficult to clear through the efforts of men and animals alone. Early settlers were forced to leave wide belts of wood around the tiny fields they managed to carve out of the primeval forest, called in Saxon times 'Andredsweald', or the land where nobody dwells. Many 'shaws' are relics of this ancient forest. At the moment only the walker who takes to the Weald's dense web of public footpaths can really penetrate the secrets of this area, for only walking uncovers the wealth of surprises that lie hidden behind the shaws and close-spread coppices: hundreds of ponds, little rivers, rushy fields thick with orchids, yellow flags and ragged robin, churches, stately parklands, timber-framed manorhouses with encircling moats and, most beautiful of all, the long, narrow hammer ponds. If the hedgerows and shaws are cleared away – as they are being cleared over larger and larger areas of the Weald – the discreet charm of these features will evaporate. Sometimes these features are rooted out along with the hedges. Hedgerow removal rarely occurs alone. In the Weald it is usually accompanied by drainage as part of a general tidying up operation. As a Ministry of Agriculture official put it to me: when farmers are installing drains they usually 'take the opportunity' of removing hedgerows.

Dr Peter Brandon, who has studied the evolution of the Wealden landscape in detail, has estimated that shaws (characteristically full of bluebells, wood anemones, celandines and campions), other hedgerows and copses will almost certainly disappear from all but the marshiest parts of the Weald by 1990 unless action is taken to control their destruction. 'The loss of shaws is particularly disturbing since ... these are amongst the oldest regional characteristics of the Wealden landscape', he wrote in 1974.[11] 'The landscape of the Sussex Weald is a priceless national heritage which will be visually degraded and its record of historical development on the ground largely destroyed unless some inducement is offered to farmers for retaining something of its present character.' As woodland is cleared, ponds and marshes drained, streams canalised or piped underground, grass reseeded, wire fences and lines of gleaming silos added, the land loses its Wealden feel and becomes just like any other stretch of the England of the 1980s.

Hedgerows, especially the thicker specimens – Wordsworth called them 'little lines of sportive wood run wild' – are a microcosm of the natural world. Deep down among their tough, ancient roots and in the recesses of their thorny, intertwined boughs, our common mammals have their home and refuge – the hedgehog, vole and mole, the field-mouse, harvest mouse and dormouse, the stoat and the weasel, the common shrew and Britain's smallest mammal, the long-nosed pygmy shrew which weighs less than a fifth of an ounce. These animals are just one part of the web of life for which our hedges provide a haven. Preyed on by owls and kestrels, they themselves find food among the multitudes of slugs, snails, spiders and insects which in their turn feed on the disorderly tangle of shrubs, trees and creepers that crowd along our hedgerows. Rupert Brooke in 'The Old Vicarage, Grantchester', written in 1912, captures the unique character of our English hedgerows when comparing their vitality with the dreary monotony of the German landscape:

> Unkempt about those hedges blows
> An English unofficial rose.

In his day, Cambridgeshire hedges would have teemed with holly, hawthorn and honeysuckle, wayfaring tree and woody nightshade, whitebeam and the spindle tree; in the autumn they would have been aflame with the bright, glossy reds, yellows, blacks, browns and russets of the fruits and seeds of these wayside plants, the whole array clothed in the feathery white seeds of old man's beard looking like long strands of sheep's wool caught on the rose briars. Today, hedgerows in Cambridgeshire are few and far between. A survey of an area in the north-east of the county in 1972 found that 40 per cent of the area's hedgerows were taken out between 1945 and 1972, or thirty-five miles in an eight-square-mile area.[12] Most of those that remain have been cut back severely.

If England continues to be denuded of hedgerows at anything like the rate of the last thirty years, the populations of 250 of our plant species will be severely diminished, according to Dr Max Hooper of the Nature Conservancy Council.[13] Continued hedgerow removal could well lead also to the extinction in parts of the English countryside of 30 plant species, says Dr Hooper, including such attractive plants as the tiny green moschatel appropriately known in some areas as fairy's clock, the sweet violet, the vivid blue greater and lesser periwinkles, golden rod, hedge bedstraw and lady's bedstraw, scented agrimony, and shrubs including crab apple, the wayfaring tree, dogwood and the spindle tree.

Hedge removal is as yet threatening no animal species and only three plant species with extinction in England, for hedgerows are not an exclusive habitat for most of our wild creatures: they also live in woodland or shrubland or on rough grassland. But these alternative habitats are disappearing too. And in view of this, hedgerow removal is in the end likely to be accompanied by the disappearance from many parts of our countryside even of common species, from wild roses to celandines and badgers to dormice.

4

Hedgerow Trees

The depredations of Dutch Elm Disease during the 1970s became a national talking point. The disease claimed the lives of over 11 million elms in England. However, agricultural change since the war has probably stripped the countryside of over twice as many of the deciduous trees that stand in our fields and hedges outside woods.[1] Few people talk about the disappearance of these trees. For, unlike Dutch Elm Disease, which has left the fields and hedges peppered with the spectral corpses of its victims, the farmers have killed by stealth and disposed of the evidence. In the process they have committed the perfect crime, stripping the landscape of its sinews.

Deciduous trees have been grown in England's countryside throughout our history. They were planted to provide shelter and shade for stock; or for timber that could be used for a wide variety of purposes, from making fencing, weatherboarding and field-gates to water-pumps, staircases and cow-stalls. Sometimes they were planted as cover for game; or, particularly in the case of country parklands, to make the landscape beautiful. Often they did all four things. Kipling's 'huge oaks and old, the which we hold / No more than Sussex weed', for instance, were sown for centuries along the hedgerows of the Weald to provide timber for ships, beams for churches and farmhouses, bark for tanning and acorn mast for pigs; and those that remain still give parts of Sussex the open park-like landscape which has been such an attractive feature of the county. The irregular and generous distribution of deciduous trees in our countryside in the form of small woods, copses and spinneys, along roads and hedgerows, and singly or in clumps in parks and on farms has come to be accepted as a vital component of our countryside. In southern England and the Midlands it is mainly oak, beech and horse chestnut that enhance the rural scene; meanwhile, the wych elm, ash and sycamore soften the aspect of the bleaker districts of the north: without the stately mountain ashes spaced along their drystone walls, the Yorkshire Dales, for instance, would be a different, emptier place.

Increasingly, however, hedgerow trees, along with other trees scattered individually round the countryside, in fields for instance, are being cut down. In the past, trees used to be very useful to farmers. Now they are usually seen as a hindrance. So they are cut down, either because they slow down farm machines, or because they shade crops, slightly reducing yields, or to create a little more ploughland, or for all three reasons. Unfortunately for the trees, their main agricultural function, keeping the midday sun or the winter wind and rain off the backs of cattle, is disappearing. Grazing is becoming more and more controlled: animals are increasingly being kept indoors and fed on grass harvested from fields by machines which find hedgerows and hedgerow trees as much of a nuisance as the combines on arable fields. Between 1947 and 1972, 2,300 hedgerow trees were cleared away in an eight-square-mile sample area of Huntingdonshire, according to a Countryside Commission study.[2] This figure amounted to 80 per cent of the hedgerow trees in the sample area. One-third of the hedgerow trees were cleared in a four-square-mile sample area in the North Riding, and in a Commission sample area in Somerset, where agriculture is based almost entirely on dairy farming, two-thirds of the hedgerow trees disappeared during the same twenty-five-year period. Norfolk is currently losing 8,000 hedgerow trees a year.[3] As the trees go, so does the wildlife.

The oak supports more species of insect than any other tree – 284. It is also a food plant for 114 species of moth, which in turn provide food for animals and birds. Where trees have gone, the numbers of all these creatures have dwindled. But it is the impact of this destruction on the landscape that is most noticeable. In a poem entitled 'Going' (1951), Philip Larkin encapsulated the tree's importance in the landscape: 'Where has the tree gone, that locked / earth to the sky?' Our deciduous trees do hold the landscape together in a way that buildings, for example, do not. Trees also enable a landscape to accommodate even the most unsightly buildings without being destroyed by them. Remove the trees and hedgerows in most parts of England and you expose not just bare earth but sewage works, broiler houses, ramshackle sheds and lines of pylons, their angular edges nakedly dominating the landscape in a way their builders never imagined.

Trees that are cut down are not usually replaced, as their importance in agriculture is now much less than it was in the past. There are those who argue that our present generation of farmers is making a big mistake in failing to appreciate the value of trees. For although trees may shade crops and there-fore prevent even ripening, they also check soil erosion, help reduce extremes of wind and climate in their immediate vicinity, and increase the movement of water in the soil. But even if those people who believe in trees could persuade farmers of their value, there would still be problems in accom-modating trees in modern agriculture. New methods of hedge maintenance are not geared to the fostering of sapling trees. When hedge maintenance was carried out by hand, the saplings could be looked after quite easily. Now hedges are cut by big flail cutters: the machine is driven alongside the hedge, chopping off its head. It would require extra work (although not that much) to ensure that any sapling trees in the hedge were exempted from decapitation. At present, farmers can see no reason for going out of their way to save England's trees. Their business is agriculture, not landscape conservation. And at present there is almost nothing the rest of the community can do to save our trees.

The scale of the problem is masked by the afforestation that is taking place. The figures do not suggest that England is losing her trees. Anything but. As fast as deciduous trees disappear from our hedgerows, country parklands and woods, large areas of conifers are planted over our upland moors, and on the sites of felled deciduous woods. What is happening is a complete shift-round of trees. In 1951, one third of the total volume of hardwood (deciduous) timber growing in England was in trees growing along hedgerows and in parklands.[4] If a similar survey were carried out today, the proportion would be quite different, perhaps less than 10 per cent. Certainly the volume of all kinds of timber, softwood as well as hardwood, that is now found along our hedgerows is tiny. Our traditional species of trees are being removed from much of our farmed lowland countryside while plantations of alien conifers occupy a larger and larger proportion of the land surface. Effectively, timber factories are appearing to match the food factories which the farms have become. The separation of trees into forestry reservations is just one aspect of change

which is sweeping across our countryside as different uses –
farming, recreation and forestry in particular – are being
separated. Rural England is becoming less of a place where
the different activities of different groups of people go on side
by side. Instead, particular uses are being relegated to
separate plots.

Nonetheless, stopping the eradication of trees through
deliberate action (such as drainage schemes) would not mean
that England's trees would be safe. Stand on the Malvern Hills
and look westwards, and you can still see everyone's dream
picture of rural England: a colourful chequerboard of fields of
innumerable shapes and sizes, separated by thick hedges and
studded with thousands of bushy-topped trees – ash, elm,
oak, and chestnut, here standing singly, there in a coppice and
all, at a distance, looking like thousands of green bubbles
massed together. But the bubbles are popping one by one.
Here in southern and western Herefordshire, hedges and
trees are being ripped out much less frequently than elsewhere in England. But here, as in nearly all the rest of the
country, new trees are not being planted to replace those that
die. To ensure eventual replacement, allowing for sapling
mortality, the number of saplings in a hedge at any one time
needs to be equal to the number of live trees of all other ages
added together. But the ratio of saplings to other live trees in
the Countryside Commission's study area in Herefordshire
was not 50:50 but 27:71.[5] The situation was even more serious
in their study area in Somerset where saplings made up only
one-ninth of the total live tree population. So, on current
trends, even if no more trees were deliberately felled for
agricultural purposes, hedgerow trees would still gradually
die out.

5

Woods

Mossy, silent but for the song of birds and strewn with primroses and bluebells underfoot, the woods are the very centrepiece of the English pastoral dream. But the stretches of
deciduous woodland dotted haphazardly throughout the lowlands are now being transformed by two great changes. First
of all, many of them are being bulldozed away wholesale by
the agricultural revolution. But those that escape the bulldozer do not necessarily survive unscathed. Instead, many of
them are being surreptitiously transformed into a dark and
dismal travesty of their former selves. Leaving only a thin
outer screen of deciduous trees to deceive the passer-by,
landowners are scooping out the guts of our native woodlands. And our native broadleaved species, such as oak, ash,
beech and lime, are being replaced with serried ranks of
conifers, whose permanent canopy stifles undergrowth and
changes woodlands once alive with flowers and birds into
gloomy timber factories.

The combination of coniferisation and clearance for agriculture is gradually eliminating the traditional English woods.
Go down to the woods today and you will not find them; if
you do, you may wish you hadn't.

Two spot findings from survey data: 16 per cent of the
broadleaved woods in a sample area in west Cambridgeshire
were cut down to make way for arable cropland between 1946
and 1973; and nearly 30 per cent of the broadleaved woodland in a sample area of central Lincolnshire was felled and
replaced with conifers during the same period.[1] Both figures
reflect the beginnings of processes that are now snowballing.
The clearance of woods for agriculture and the coniferisation
of many of those that remain have already had a visible impact
on the appearance of eastern England. In other parts of the
country, woodland has been suffering in the same way, but
the effects have up till now tended to be masked by the
hedgerows and spinneys which still survive west of the
Greenwich meridian. Even in Devon, the small woods that

are among the most vital elements in the county's landscape tapestry are rapidly being grubbed out or coniferised: a survey by women's institutes in Devon in 1972 found that in the preceding twenty years, 20 per cent of the county's broad-leaved woods had been cleared away for agriculture, reduced in size or converted to conifer plantations.[2] So concerned is the Nature Conservancy Council about the erosion of deciduous woodland that it wrote in 1979: 'The active con-version of broadleaf woodlands [to conifers], combined with their clearance for agriculture and other uses, has now reached the stage where the continued existence of semi-natural broadleaf woodland outside nature reserves is seriously threatened in many parts of Britain.'[3]

Ancient woods

Deciduous woodland is the natural vegetation of England. After the last ice sheets retreated and a hospitable climate returned to Britain around 8000 BC, it was deciduous forest – oak in the highlands and lime, oak, hazel and ash in the lowlands – which came to dress the wounds the ice had made as it etched out England's valleys and rounded the once rug-ged hills. By 3000 BC Britain was covered in a mixture of forest types that were just beginning to be affected by human activities. For virtually the whole period in which man has occupied England, deciduous woodland has remained the characteristic vegetation: remnants of the post-Ice-Age forest cover have been taken into management for timber produc-tion; deciduous rather than coniferous trees have been planted for timber elsewhere; and cleared land has naturally reverted to deciduous woodland when grazing or cultivation has ceased.

The solidly deciduous pattern of our traditional woodland has not entailed any lack of variety. We have maple woods, alder woods, hazel woods, lime woods, and several sorts of elm wood as well as the more common woods of beech, oak or ash. In eastern England alone, any one of at least fourteen native trees can predominate locally, each particular blend of species resulting from the interaction of geology, geography, biology and management by man. Nearly every deciduous wood has its individual peculiarities. Particularly in surviving remnants of the post-Ice-Age forest cover – the ancient wood-land, or 'Wildwood' as it is called – the tree mixture varies even from one part of the wood to another.

In such counties as Devon, Essex, Suffolk and Lincolnshire, a high proportion of the woods we see today are ancient woodlands: in other words, the land has never been cleared for agriculture. From medieval times until recently, these woods were usually managed without much replanting; foresters exploited one intriguing characteristic of trees: they do not have a fixed life-span. Trees and shrubs were coppiced so that the cut-down stumps would yield long, straight boughs suitable for poles; or they were pollarded – that is, cut down to a height of about ten feet, leaving a permanent trunk which sprouted in the same way as a coppice stool, but at a height at which grazing animals could not reach the shoots. Both these techniques yielded an indefinite succession of crops of poles. Management of this kind enabled the woodland, and in particular its ground vegetation, to retain ecological links with earlier times, which is why ancient woods contain irreplaceable communities of plants and animals, reflecting the thousands of years of evolution they have undergone.

These woods also reveal much about rural life during historical times, as they have played a vital role either in timber production or grazing for animals. Both woodmanship (the art of cropping timber without destroying the existing vegetation) and wood-pasture (the art of growing trees in the presence of grazing animals without too many young shoots being bitten off in the process) involved skills which were not described in books and can be reconstructed only from field and archaeological evidence. In the past, a large proportion of our population depended on woods for their livelihood. Timber was used for a wide variety of agricultural, domestic and industrial purposes, and whole communities based their existence on woods, as Hardy's novel *The Woodlanders* demonstrates. Even one tree in an ancient woodland can embody a wealth of information about what has gone on around it: its very existence, its shape and branching, the scars of old injuries, embody information about land-use and woodland management.

During the last thirty years, coniferisation and clearance for agriculture have destroyed nearly a third of the ancient woods that had survived in Britain until 1945, according to Dr Oliver Rackham of Cambridge University. Despite the particular scientific and historical importance of our ancient woods, the evidence suggests that they are being cleared for farming or coniferised just as rapidly as more recent woods. So far, Britain's town and country planning machinery has completely failed to protect them. 'In recent local studies,' writes Dr Rackham, 'between a third and a half of the ancient woodland remaining in 1945 has been found since to have lost its characteristics. The most common cause has been 'coniferisation', followed by grubbing-out for agriculture. Quarrying comes well behind, while the inroads of housing, roads, and industry are generally insignificant.'[4] Elsewhere Dr Rackham writes:

> Casual observation suggests that a similar story could be told of nearly every sheet of the Ordnance Survey: of Dorset, the steep oak woods of mid-Wales, the Wye gorge, the Forest of Wyre, the hilltop woods of the Welsh Border, and the romantic lichen-hung corkscrew oaks of the deep valleys of Dartmoor and Bodmin Moor. The long arm of destruction has reached from the Lizard Peninsula to remote Argyll.[5]

Clearance of woodlands

Of course, not all our woods are remnants of the Wildwood. One of the distinctive features of the Leicestershire landscape to this day is the spattering of small woods planted by the great landlords in the 1790s as coverts for foxes to breed in. Elsewhere, woods large and small were planted for a myriad of purposes – to provide cover for pheasants and partridges, to provide timber for all sorts of uses on country estates as well as for house, factory and public-building construction. In their struggle against clearance for agriculture, all our woods face the same forces as hedges and hedgerow trees. Like these features, woods, copses and spinneys obstruct the new generation of farm machines, and they occupy potentially profitable farmland. So they have been swept away. Thirty per cent of woods of less than two and a half acres in size (about the area of Trafalgar Square) were cleared away between 1947 and 1972.[6] Clearance is encouraged by the Ministry of Agriculture which provides twenty and thirty per cent grants to clear away tree stumps when land use is being changed to agriculture. On the whole, the Common Agricultural Policy's price guarantees ensure that farming is more profitable than forestry, as did price support through deficiency payments before Britain entered the EEC.

In many parts of our countryside the clearance of deciduous woodland can be expected to accelerate as patterns of ownership change. Estates are passing from the hands of gentleman farmers into those of financial institutions –insurance companies, pension funds and property unit trusts. Such institutions seem bound to pursue profit more single-mindedly than traditional landowners. The objective of an estate manager employed by a trust is to maximise the return on the shareholders' investment. In contrast, the maximisation of income is often only one of a number of the objectives of the private owners of our large landed estates. Such landowners may also want to make their own environments as pleasing as possible, and not to antagonise the local people among whom their families may have lived for generations. Another of their attitudes which may also benefit landscape conservation is a desire to hand on their estates to future generations in as unchanged a form as possible. But the most significant of these attitudes by far is a desire to indulge personal whims like blood sports and in particular a fondness for pheasant shooting.

The consequences for the countryside of a transfer of ownership from large private landed estates to financial institutions can already be seen in North Hampshire. A few miles south of Newbury, between Basingstoke and Hungerford, stretches a ridge of chalk hills embracing some of the loveliest scenery in England. Many of the individual hills along the ridge are still covered in rough downland turf; hedgerows and small woods too are much more common than in other areas of similar geology and agricultural potential, like the East Sussex Downs. Here, as in many of the other corners of our countryside that retain a thick clothing of deciduous trees, the woods have been maintained not for the timber they provide but as cover for pheasants. The 6,500-acre Highclere Estate south of Newbury shows clearly the role pheasants play in defending landscape features on marginal land. Seven thousand pheasants are reared at Highclere every year to provide sport for the owner and his guests, and to guarantee the availability of this sport, much of the uncultivated land throughout the estate has been left unreclaimed. Pheasants flourish in countryside rich in woods with undergrowth providing plenty of cover, interspersed with parkland, fields and, ideally, streams, rivers and lakes. And largely for the benefit of pheasants, the whole of the northern third of Highclere has been maintained as woodland – a good mix of broad-leaved trees, mainly beech, interspersed with conifers and two lakes, used for fishing. Much of the central third of the estate is parkland; rolling green pasture studded with fine, spreading trees and supporting a few cows. Two magnificent chalk hills occupy much of the southern third of the estate. They are still carpeted in rough chalk downland with its characteristic galaxy of wild flowers or clad in beech woods. These beeches have been deliberately left to grow naturally on the hillsides since their presence ensures better sport. Shooting is most satisfactory when game is high in the air, but the pheasants are by nature reluctant to take to the wing. To solve the problem at Highclere, beaters drive the game over the tall, stately beeches. If profit were the only consideration in the management of Highclere, the downland, woods and parkland would have been replaced with fields of wheat. As it is, only a relatively small proportion of the area is devoted to intensive agriculture, and even this arable land is broken up by thick hedgerows to provide extra cover for the birds and beats for their pursuers.

Up till now, conservation by private landowners with a penchant for shooting has been of little benefit to the public, as the landowners involved have been among the most reluctant to create public access to their land. Nonetheless, the makings exist of an alliance between landscape conservationists and private landowners who are interested in pheasants. In contrast, investment trusts are unlikely to be so easily diverted from the single-minded pursuit of the profits available from intensive agriculture.

Just outside the walls of Highclere lies a smaller though equally attractive estate, the Ashmansworth Estate. In 1978, Ashmansworth was bought by a financial institution, the Abbotstone Agricultural Property Unit Trust. Soon afterwards the Trust put forward plans to clear away much of two woodlands containing 2,500 trees and several hedgerows containing another 90 trees, the whole area involved covering 33 acres. The main woodland concerned is hundreds of years old. It consists of oak trees and hornbeam coppice covering a series of large flint-based banks up to five feet high. These are thought to be the boundaries of prehistoric fields and at the time of writing the woodland is preserving a complete-archaeological landscape. Bluebells, red campion, primroses, yellow archangel and ferns flourish on the woodland floor The intention at Ashmansworth is to turn over the land cleared to agriculture. This step can be expected to increase the value of the land concerned fivefold. It is difficult to tell just yet how great the impact of the arrival of the institutions will be. But in the 250 square miles of rolling chalk country-side, including Highclere and Ashmansworth for which Basingstoke District Council is responsible, financial institutions accounted for only 17 per cent of felling licence applications for the conversion of woodland to agricultural land between March 1978 and March 1979. The following year they accounted for 67 per cent – involving proposals to clear 7,000 trees covering a total of 100 acres. Too much should not be made of such a limited sample, but a trend in this direction seems inevitable.

In 1977, financial institutions bought more than 10 per cent of all land sold in England and Wales.[7] Financial institutions tend to buy large estates, often from private landowners. In 1977 they bought nearly 37,000 acres, or 20 per cent of all land which changed hands in parcels of over 300 acres.

The rate of acquisition of farmland by financial institutions shows no sign of diminishing. It was the sudden rise in the value of farmland between 1972 and 1973, when the price of an acre rose from £300 to £800, that first attracted the institutions into farmland on a large scale. Since then the price of farmland has more than doubled (in the first four months of 1980 farmland in England with vacant possession fetched on average £1,600 per acre). Agricultural land thus provides an inflation-proof investment. What's more, financial institutions have their own ready source of capital to pay for schemes to intensify production. So we can expect them to continue to move into farmland, and in particular into land like that in north Hampshire or western Hereford-shire where there are big profits to be made from turning old shooting estates into barley prairies.

Coniferisation

The coniferisation of deciduous woods is not something

practised only by financial institutions. Traditional landowners are planting many of the conifers springing up in
hitherto deciduous woodlands. The reason for coniferisation
is this: conifers grow more quickly than deciduous trees, so a
conifer wood yields a profit more quickly and more often
than a deciduous wood. Beech trees planted in 1980 would
take about 120 years to reach maturity, whereas sitka spruce
or douglas fir would be fully grown after about 60 years. And
the conifers would yield their first income from thinning
about ten years earlier than the deciduous trees. The harvested
beech could be expected to sell for about twice as much as the
softwood timber, but because income would come much
later and since profits from forestry like most other investment activities are calculated in such a way that the later a
return is made the less it is worth, the profits from the beech
would be worth less than those from the spruce or fir.

The taxation system provides the wealthiest members of
our society with an incentive to make as much money as they
can from forestry. The taxpayer does not do much to subsidise
the conversion of hardwoods to softwoods directly, in the way
he directly subsidises the drainage of wetlands, or the
ploughing of the downs. What he does is to pay out millions
of pounds each year to make forestry a specially attractive
form of economic activity for people with large taxable
incomes. Because it is hard for such people to make large
after-tax profits elsewhere, they try to do this through forestry.
And to make the most of their chances, they plant conifers.

The income tax privileges for private foresters work like
this. When the plantation is being established – the ground
cleared of natural vegetation and the trees planted and
managed – the owner of the trees can write off the costs
incurred against income tax that would be payable for other
reasons – for instance, from an agricultural business or profits
made in the City. When the trees are ready to be felled, a
simple tax avoidance measure (switching from Schedule D to
Schedule B) enables the timber to be sold entirely free of tax.
There are other reasons, too, why the wealthy owners of large
estates find it worth their while to devote a substantial proportion of their estates to timber. They are allowed to write
off the costs of establishing and managing the plantation
against tax incurred in other ways. When the trees are growing,
they provide an effective hedge against inflation which the

burdens of capital transfer tax and capital gains tax bear relatively lightly. They also provide the ideal means of storing up money to meet future capital transfer tax bills. And in almost all cases, softwood trees will meet landowners' requirements better than hardwoods.

The taxpayer, then, subsidises coniferisation negatively, through tax reliefs rather than positively through grants. For his pains, any fears he may have about timber shortages are partially allayed. In fact, however, the amount of timber that can be produced in our lowland countryside, even in woods of 1,000 acres, is insignificant compared to what can be produced in the vast Forestry Commission plantations on the moors of northern England, Wales and southern and central Scotland. Sales of timber from private estates bring in millions of pounds a year, considerable proportions of which must be subject to tax relief. But the community is not rewarded with a say in the way foresters behave, in the way the community controls the environmental activities of far less favoured industries. Coniferisation does not require planning permission.

Dorset is a county in which the influence of land ownership on the character of woodland is particularly striking. In 1811, 95 per cent of Dorset's total woodland area consisted of deciduous trees; only 3 per cent was coniferous (the rest was coppice or mixed wood). By 1972, pure deciduous woodland formed only 23 per cent of the total woodland area of Dorset. Fifty per cent of Dorset woodland area is now coniferous, and much of the remainder consists of conifers mixed with deciduous trees.[8] This dramatic change in woodland character occurred in two main waves. First, the Forestry Commission acquired and planted with conifers large tracts of Dorset's heaths (Hardy's 'Egdon Heath') just before and immediately after World War II. This has now stopped, but the coniferisation of deciduous woods by private landowners has gathered pace and shows no sign of slowing down. Eastern Dorset, in particular the old hunting forest area of Cranborne Chase, is a land of estates large enough to attract substantial capital transfer tax bills; small wonder then that the landowners in this area are busily planting conifers. In western Dorset, in contrast, the land holdings are smaller, landowners pay less income tax and capital transfer tax and, consequently, they are less anxious to switch to conifers. So the little Vale of

Marshwood, west of Bridport, for example, is still rich in deciduous woods and copses, partly because the heavy clay soil makes clearance of woods difficult but also because ownership is in the hands of people for whom coniferisation offers only limited financial gain.

Wildlife suffers heavily from coniferisation. English deciduous woods harbour peculiarly rich communities of plants and animals. Primroses, bluebells, early purple orchids and red campion may survive for a short while on the site of a felled wood if wide grassy rides are left and if the land is not bulldozed (which compacts the soil and crushes ground vegetation) and if trees are not uprooted (which also disturbs the soil). But once conifer replanting is under way, they and other typical deciduous woodland species are likely to disappear. The dense all-year-round canopy of conifer plantations makes them much darker than deciduous woods, and the exclusion of sunlight from the forest floor combines with the accumulation of needles, which make the ground acidic, to alter completely the ground vegetation. Badgers and bluebells, wood anemones and wild garlic, the silver-washed fritillary butterfly and the green woodpecker are a few of the characteristic species of England's deciduous woods that are virtually unknown in conifer plantations. These missing plants and animals are not replaced by other, equally interesting species. The coniferous world is silent and dead. Fungi, which live on dead matter and do not need sunlight to manufacture their own food like flowering plants, take over as the most conspicuous vegetation. A few tits are soon virtually all that remains of the bird population. To demonstrate how much poorer are the trees of conifer plantations than those of our native hardwoods we need only compare the following figures. Fir is the food plant for only 16 different species of insect, compared with the 284 that live off oak. This more limited supply of insect food in turn cuts down the number of bird, mammal and reptile species.

Woodland clearance and coniferisation work together to destroy our countryside's specifically English character. Deciduous trees are our natural vegetation and the environment of many of our most characteristic birds, flowers and mammals, while the rounded forms of bushy-topped trees provide a necessary visual complement to the soft curves and hollows of England's topography. The spiky tops and regular form of conifers may fit mountainous landscapes, but they strike a chill into lowland English landscapes as well as stripping them of the seasonal variety provided by the ever-changing colour and form of our traditional deciduous foliage. In areas like Hertfordshire where many woods have been cleared, autumn is now marked by the harsh blackness of burnt stubble rather than by the rich reds, yellows, browns and russets that used to clothe England. When conifers are present – as in so many parts of Dorset, for instance – the English seasons are similarly obscured. Such areas know no delicate tracery of bare branches against the pinks and blues of a winter sky, nor the burst of bright green life of an English spring. Only after clearance or coniferisation does it really become apparent how much the subtle variety of the English countryside depends on the variety of form, colour, texture and age of our deciduous trees.

6

Roughlands

Variety is at the heart of the attraction of the English countryside. Unlike his counterpart in America, Scandinavia or even France, the traveller through England is never surrounded by any one type of scenery for long. The underlying reason for this lies in our surface geology, which is peculiarly diverse. Belts, crescents and loops of chalk, sandstone, limestone and clay span our little country; in the South-West and the uplands, great bosses of ancient granites, gneisses, schists and shales obtrude through the younger sediments; and glacial drift deposits of sand and gravel compound variety still further.

Traditionally, this rich geological diversity has been reflected above ground and it is England's grazing pastures more than any comparable landscape feature which have ensured that this has happened. The range of grasslands in England is as varied as England's dialects. The springy turfs that clothe the sand dunes of Northumberland, spangled with blood-red cranesbills and the tall blue viper's bugloss, are quite different from the gorse-strewn cliff roughlands of Cornwall or the watery summer pastures of the Somerset Levels, with their drifts of marsh marigolds and ragged robin. The daffodil meadows of the Lake District, the buttercup and green-winged orchid pastures of the old ridge-and-furrow fields of the Midlands, the heather moors of Dartmoor, Exmoor and Bodmin Moor and the rough chalk downlands of the south and east are different again. But post-war agricultural change is wiping out this variety. At the same time, it is wiping out roughland altogether and with it opportunities for walking, picnicking and so on which this kind of country has traditionally provided.

Seven of our best-known and most distinctive types of grassland are:

1. *Hay meadows:* areas of permanent grassland on neutral soils that have been cut for hay for centuries and may also be grazed in summer by cattle. They are fertilised by farmyard manure or alluvium but not chemically manufactured

products. There are two specially beautiful sub-types: hay meadows on carboniferous limestone at altitudes between 700 and 1,000 feet in the north of England, like the Yorkshire Dales, and the flood meadows of Suffolk, Herefordshire and Oxfordshire customarily strewn with the fritillary, cowslip, green-winged orchid and meadowsweet.

2. *Water meadows:* wet, alluvial grassland used as grazing for cattle in summer but frequently flooded in winter. These meadows harbour a wide range of grass and herb species and often provide important feeding grounds for migrating birds. Most of such water meadows that survived until the war have since been drained and converted to intensive farmland, but some unimproved water meadows still survive. The larger areas are in the Somerset Levels, the Yare Marshes that encircle the Norfolk Broads and the Pevensey Levels in Sussex.

3. *Chalk downland turf:* rough downland turf on the alkaline soils of our chalklands once covered most of England's chalk belt from Dorset to the Yorkshire Wolds. Fragments of downland still survive in parts of the Yorkshire and Lincolnshire Wolds, Cambridgeshire, the Chilterns, the North and South Downs of Kent, Surrey, Sussex and Hampshire, and the Downs of Dorset and Wiltshire.

4. *Lowland heaths:* heather or rough grass areas, usually on sandy acidic soils, like those of Breckland, eastern Dorset, Bagshot, the Suffolk coast, Charnwood Forest, and the Lizard peninsula in Cornwall. These lowland heaths provide a home for all six of Britain's reptiles, many varieties of dragonfly and butterfly and the Dartford warbler.

5. *Moors:* our most common remaining roughland. These are treeless lands, dominated by heather, sedges and grasses which occupy the uplands of west and north-west Britain from Bodmin Moor, Exmoor and Dartmoor in the South-West to the Welsh Mountains, the Lake District, the Pennines, the Yorkshire Dales, the North York Moors and the Cheviots of Northumberland.

6. *Cliff roughland:* the rough turf that edges some cliff-tops like those of Cornwall, here carpeted in sea-pink, sea-campion, the little blue hyacinth-like squill, and gorse. This type of roughland is one of our most 'natural' vegetation types, as is the next type:

7. *Coastal marshland:* rough grassland on salt marsh and mudflats off our coast, once a common habitat type but now

restricted mainly through agricultural reclamation to the Wash and the coasts of north Norfolk, north Kent and Lancashire.

The processes that are transforming our roughlands are of three main types: the replacement of rough grassland with arable crops, chiefly barley (which is mainly taking place on our chalk and limestone hills, coastal marshlands and water meadows); afforestation with conifers (which is mainly taking place on our moors and lowland heaths); and the conversion of rough pasture to chemical ryegrass monoculture designed to produce milk more quickly (which is changing all types of roughland, save, so far, sand dunes). Of the three agricultural processes that are transforming our roughlands, the ryegrass revolution is the most damaging, partly because it affects a higher acreage than ploughing or coniferisation, but also because of its particularly sinister side: this change robs our countryside of its wildlife and recreation value just as much as the other two, but the casual observer may not notice anything has changed: the grass still looks green, even if it is a different shade.

Chalk downland turf in Dorset alone harbours more than 20 different kinds of grass, and nearly 120 different species of flowering plant including 7 kinds of orchid.[1] The plants of the downs interweave above the soil to support a springy turf in which literally millions of creatures live. On one small stretch of limestone grassland in Berkshire an observer in 1962 found 141 different species of spider alone.[2] Coastal saltings, hay meadows and water meadows are three other types of roughland that embody in their natural state a particularly rich variety of herbage. For thousands of years our roughlands, fertilised only by animal droppings, farmyard manure and alluvium deposited by rivers in flood, provided rich pasture for sheep, cattle and horses. But now, farmers no longer feel that the output of natural pastureland is enough. More and more of them are changing to new methods of stock rearing, particularly dairy farming. Those that have become fashionable since the 1950s require the elimination of the old pastures and their replacement with perennial ryegrass which happens to be converted to milk more quickly than any other grass species. So specially bred strains of this grass (with names like S23, S24 or S32), mixed with small quantities of New Zealand or Danish white clover and timothy, are replacing the natural species of England's roughlands from Land's End to Berwick-on-Tweed. Thousand-year-old rough chalk downlands, open heather moors, peaceful marshland saltings, old hay meadows from the Yorkshire Dales to Suffolk and cliff roughlands are being sliced up by the plough so that huge quantities of lime, fertiliser and pesticide can be sprayed on to the soil. Treated fields are then sown with Italian ryegrass – the pioneer crop for perennial ryegrass which replaces it after about a year. Steep slopes present few problems for the ploughing machines. Four-wheel-drive or crawler vehicles can now make short work of slopes that would have been beyond the reach of earlier machines. If slopes are too steep even for vehicles like these, the old sward is killed by herbicides rained down from fixed-wing aircraft or helicopters. Paraquat, which rapidly scorches plant tissues, is one such herbicide. Dalapon is another: it is absorbed by the natural grasses and causes a slow but profound disturbance of the normal processes of growth and eventual death. After the herbicides have done their work, huge doses of fertiliser are sprayed onto the dead or dying herbage, and this is followed by new seed. So now there are virtually no roughlands from Dorset to the Yorkshire Wolds or the heather moorlands on our steep upland hills which can't be 'brought into the twentieth century', as an official at the Ministry of Agriculture's Grassland Research Institute put it to me.

The effect of these operations is to make all grassland exactly the same. Regional variations in the topography of England are being ironed out as more and more of our open, natural grasslands are squared off, fenced in and replaced with exactly the same variety of artificially fertilised grass. Of the total acreage of permanent grassland (that is, land on which grass is not cropped on a one-year rotation but remains year after year) less than 2 per cent was ryegrass pasture in the 1930s. But by the early 1970s, at least 40 per cent of permanent grassland was ryegrass, according to a study by the Grassland Research Institute, carried out between 1970 and 1972.[3]

The ryegrass revolution is not only eliminating the rich variety of our grassland plants and what W. H. Hudson called the 'fairy fauna' of tiny creatures scrabbling through the grass stems. Butterfly populations are also being decimated. Twenty-four of our butterfly species can live in natural permanent pastures: indeed such grassland is the main habitat for the majority of British butterflies; but not a single species can live in reseeded ryegrass. The Nature Conservancy Council has estimated that if present trends in farmland 'improvement' continue, 95 per cent of the butterfly species of England's farmed landscape will be lost.[4] Many will become extinct in England. The apparent extinction in Britain of the Large Blue Butterfly in 1979 followed the destruction of twenty-nine of its thirty known colonies through the ploughing of turf or its colonisation by bushes and trees after grazing had ceased.[5] Many other butterfly species now seem fated to go the same way as the Large Blue.

The transformation of natural pastures into intensive food factories, whether for monoculture grassland or arable crops, destroys a valuable recreation amenity, as well as wildlife. The greater part of our rough grasslands, moors, heaths and downs, have traditionally been open to everybody, in practice if not in law: landowners have allowed people to wander across them as they have had nothing to lose by doing so. The areas involved – Dartmoor, Exmoor, and the Sussex Downs, for example – have given visitors from towns a sense of wilderness, as they have rambled across them unimpeded by fences, ploughland or evidence of modern civilisation. But when rough pasture is converted to intensive production, it is almost invariably fenced against walkers. Italian ryegrass needs to be carefully sheltered to protect it against the cold (to which it is much more sensitive than our hardier natural grasses) and against fungal diseases, to which it is particularly vulnerable. Ryegrass monocultures are also easily bruised by trampling. Barbed wire fences are therefore strung round most of the fields that are reseeded. Nearly sixty square miles of rough moorland, most of it with *de facto* access, were fenced off and 'improved' for intensive farming or planted with conifers in the North York Moors National Park between 1950 and 1975.[6] The National Park Officer estimated in 1975 that most of the moorland of the park would have disappeared within the next hundred years if these trends continued. The only stretches of open moorland which would survive in this national park would be the few areas which have been specially purchased for conservation and odd areas like a stretch around the Fylingdales Early Warning Station where open moorland is maintained for security reasons. At the other end of the country, virtually half the wild, flower-spangled chalk downland turf on the Wiltshire Downs was ploughed up between 1937 and 1971; 64,000 acres in all, according to Wiltshire County Council calculations. And the wild, furzy heaths of the Suffolk coast, to take another typical example, have all but disappeared: 73 per cent of the heathland behind the coast stretching from Lowestoft to Ipswich was ploughed up or afforested between 1920 and 1968.[7] Access may still occasionally exist after roughland areas have been 'improved' but few people enjoy walking over fields of grass which never vary throughout their length any more than they wish to walk through prairie-style barley fields. Those who try may be risking their health. These fields are normally sprayed with at least one of the thirty or so types of pesticide commonly used on intensive farmland known to cause serious illness. Picnickers in fields recently treated with these chemicals risk anything from blurring of vision to cancer.[8]

There is a danger to our food supplies as well as to picnickers in the newly fashionable approach to grassland cultivation. The fragile 'hothouse' product of chemicals and biological engineering could easily be wiped out overnight. It is a basic law of ecology that the less the genetic variation in any one species, the less well placed that species is to resist natural disasters from disease to cold. The reason is that among a wide range of genotypic structures, some individuals will be likely to possess the requirements to resist whatever threat the species faces. The ryegrass revolution is cutting down not only the range of grass and herb species but also on genetic variation, since plant breeders have deliberately eliminated strains other than those few that perform most productively. All this leaves Britain's grasslands much more vulnerable to disease, other natural disasters or even man-made catastrophes like nuclear radiation leaks than they used to be. John Christopher's *The Death of Grass*, the science fiction story in which an incurable disease befalls the world's grasslands, including wheat, barley and grass pasture, threatening starvation, is much more likely to come true if we try to eliminate one of the main ways in which Nature has always tried to ensure that at least some individuals, and therefore the species as a whole, survive disasters.

The agricultural lobby like to point out to those seeking to preserve roughlands that they are 'not natural'. Chalk downland turf, for instance, would not exist if Man did not graze his animals on it. And farmers like to argue that if agriculture shaped the traditional English landscape, agriculture is entitled to create a new English landscape. If they feel sufficiently bold, they may go on to argue that their endless monoculture fields and tower silos are quite as attractive in their way as the 'fussy' patchwork quilt of the traditional English landscape.

It is true that England's roughlands are man-made. Only a few kinds – coastal marshlands, cliff-edge roughlands, grassy sand dunes and moorlands above the 2,000 foot contour – are entirely 'natural' in that their existence has no connection with any activity of Man. Most of our chalk downs, moors, meadows and lowland heathlands were once covered with the mixed deciduous woodland that colonised England after the last Ice Age. As our forefathers carved space out of the forest to grow crops, or to provide grazing pasture or timber, chalk downland turf, heather moorland and other forms of roughland spread where geological conditions allowed and where the continued grazing of animals prevented the regeneration of tree seedlings. This means that our roughlands are threatened not only by twentieth-century agriculture but by the deciduous woodland that would, in the end, replace them, if Man ceased his activities in the English countryside.

None of this has much to do with the case for conserving our roughlands. This rests not on their origin, but on their present value to the people of England. Ultimately, of course, a subjective value judgment is involved. But while there may be those who prefer the uninterrupted sweep of the pale green monoculture expanse to the landscape Constable painted, the evidence is that most people do not. On the contrary, the loss of roughland countryside seems to be profoundly upsetting to almost all those people who comment on the change.

Of our almost endless range of roughlands in England I have singled out two for special attention in the next two chapters. These two, chalk downland and heather moorland, make the most distinctive contribution to the landscape of England. But it should not be forgotten that the vast range of nondescript bits and pieces of countryside about which I could not possibly generalise are at least as valuable.

7

Downs

Our chalkland hills, clothed in rough turf for hundreds, in some cases thousands, of years, are as peculiarly English as our hedgerows. Rudyard Kipling encapsulated their charms in the poem 'Sussex' in 1902:

> No tender-hearted garden crowns,
> No bosomed woods adorn
> Our blunt, bow-headed, whale-backed Downs,
> But gnarled and writhen thorn –
> Bare slopes where chasing shadows skim,
> And through the gaps revealed,
> Belt upon belt, the wooded, dim,
> Blue goodness of the Weald.

In Kipling's time, downland turf could be found in abundance from Dorset through Salisbury Plain, the North and South Downs and the Chilterns, through Cambridgeshire, Norfolk and the Lincolnshire and Yorkshire Wolds. Now, however, it is largely confined to small stretches on steep slopes.[1] The springy turf is made up of the fibres of countless grasses, interlaced in a thick layer with clovers and other herbs. Its appeal to walkers rests not only on its well-sprung feel – you can walk all day on the downs without feeling tired – but also on its fresh herb smell, which derives from the presence of many tiny aromatic plants like wild thyme, marjoram and round-leaved mint. Downland turf is the home of most of our native orchids and many of the most beautiful of our other plants. It also supports large populations of butterflies, like the chalkhill blue and the marbled white; and in those areas where it has lain untilled for hundreds, sometimes thousands of years, the thick turf is freckled with the remains of long-dead peoples that lived on the downs in prehistory. Barrow humps and thickly turfed ramparts winding serpent-like around the hilltops used to be found all over the downs.

Of all the charms of our chalk downlands the wild flowers are perhaps the most widely appreciated. It is a curious fact that although all plants require certain minimum amounts of nutrients and trace elements to live and grow, some of our tallest and some of our most spectacular plants – like the lizard orchid, pyramidal orchid, man orchid, lesser butterfly orchid, monkey orchid, bee orchid, fly orchid, spider orchid, musk orchid, lady's tresses, giant mullein and viper's bugloss – do best on soils that can offer only the barest minimum of nutrients. The reason why there are so few nutrients is that chalk is so permeable that rainwater drains away before it can deposit minerals. And in a way that ecologists do not yet understand, this shortage of nutrients, combined with the low acidity of the chalky soils, allows extremely diverse assemblies of plants to grow cheek by jowl without any one species coming to dominate the rest. Our chalk downs support nine species of wild orchid, as well as a great variety of tiny plants – harebells and autumn gentian, wild mignonette and lady's bedstraw, rock-rose and squinancywort, milkwort and bird's-foot trefoil, musky storksbill and hairy violet, to name but a few. Of this galaxy of wild flowers W. H. Hudson wrote:

> Looking round upon the living garment of many colours, especially where the glowing orange-yellow patches of ragwort are most conspicuous, one can fancy that the strayed pack-horses of a silk merchant of olden time have passed this way, and that the sharp claws of the brambles have caught and pulled the package to pieces, scattering far and wide the shining fabrics of all the hues of the rainbow.[2]

In contrast to the austere diet of the wild 'fairy flora', as Hudson called it, the specially bred strains of ryegrass which farmers are now using as pasture depend on huge quantities of inorganic nitrates and phosphates, which have to be applied artificially. So even if downland turf is not ploughed up, it may still be destroyed: the application of a few tons of nitrogen fertiliser soon decimates the plant species living on rough downland. The ryegrasses crowd out the other plants: they are at a competitive advantage because they alone can thrive on the rich diet now provided. The process is usually accelerated by the application of herbicides to kill the existing plants. Then even on slopes too steep for the tractor, the ryegrass seed can be sprayed onto the dying vegetation.

Two hundred years ago, rough chalk downland was one of Britain's main landscape types. Great stretches of the chalk lands of lowland England were carpeted in springy turf supporting flocks of sheep and a galaxy of wild flowers and butterflies, on the same scale that grass and heather moorland covers much of the north and west of England. The economy of these areas was based on sheep and corn: sheep were run on the open downs by day; overnight they were folded on arable land in the valleys. But towards the closing decades of the eighteenth century, technical innovation (in particular the introduction of new fodder crops) made it possible to incorporate sheep husbandry into the management of the new enclosed arable farms which arose through the increasing numbers of Enclosure Acts. Thus the vast tracts of open downland began to go under the plough. The trend accelerated during the Napoleonic Wars, when extra food was needed for the troops.

Nonetheless, throughout the first half of our own century large areas of unploughed, unfenced turf still survived in Dorset, Wiltshire, Berkshire and Sussex. They served not only as sheep ranches but as open spaces on which city-dwellers could ramble and picnic, and botanists, lepidopterists and archaeologists could hunt their prey. The naturalist W. H. Hudson was just one of many who spent weeks holidaying in the Sussex Downs delighting in 'wild nature and a wide prospect in unenclosed country, an elastic turf under foot, and full liberty to roam whithersoever we will'.

So important were the Downs of Sussex and Hampshire as playgrounds for the people that a government committee in 1947 recommended that they should become a national park. The committee wanted these areas of downland specially protected against building development so that the opportunities for open-air recreation they offered could be conserved and enhanced. 'There is no other area within easy reach of London which provides such opportunities for the enjoyment of lovely scenery and peaceful walks and, it should be added, such perfect terrain for riding', wrote the committee.

Here the town dweller can enjoy, often in surprising solitude, the sweeping views of the chalk uplands, the springy turf under his feet, lark song and the crooning of turtle doves, and the scent of wild thyme and hawthorn; or he may wander in the silence of beech woods or explore the many charming villages which are hidden in the folds of the downs or strung out along the foot of the escarpment.[3]

However, when the National Parks Commission (the government agency set up in 1949 to select national parks) came to consider this area in the 1950s, it decided against making it a national park: so much of the open access land in it had been ploughed by then that it was no longer worth protecting with national park status. Today, rough downland in Sussex east of the River Arun covers barely a sixth of the area it occupied immediately after the war. The downs of East Sussex that had rolled in a smooth grassy swell from Eastbourne past Lewes, Brighton, Hove, Shoreham and Worthing to Arundel, with every fold and coombe in between strewn with constellations of flowers, have been stripped naked. Ploughing machines have scraped the surface from their majestic flanks, destroying the ancient earthworks that lay in their path. Barbed wire fences split the sprawling masses of the hills into geometrically shaped barley fields, in the process eliminating freedom to roam. In place of the buzzards, wheatears and stone curlews who used to live here, in place of the vivid chalkhill blue and adonis blue butterflies that used to hover among the harebells and scabiouses, farm labourers, high up in tractor cabins, their ears muffled like those of factory workers, are the only creatures visible in the enormous enclosures of barley and ryegrass that have taken the place of the turf.

The novels of Thomas Hardy have made the downs of Dorset familiar even to people who have never visited them. This is particularly true of the rolling coastal downs (where Gabriel Oak of *Far from the Madding Crowd* worked as a shepherd). One of our most recently established long-distance paths, the Dorset Coastal Path, runs along these cliff-tops amidst downland flowers whose vivid colours seem that much more intense alongside the glittering sea below. Kestrels hover overhead, riding on the salt-laden winds. Yet even here, along the cliff-top, as in the rest of Dorset, rough downland turf is going under the plough. The only substantial stretch of coastal downland still untouched is the Army ranges at Lulworth. But although these whaleback downs are magnificent to look at, walkers are not allowed on them because of the presence of unexploded shells. Elsewhere on the Dorset coast no substantial stretches of uninterrupted turf survive.

During the eleven years between 1956 and 1967, the following areas were among the victims of the plough: the soaring crest of Ballard Down, north of Swanage, 100 acres of downland near Lulworth Cove that had been designated by the Nature Conservancy Council as a Site of Special Scientific Interest, the crown of downland at St Alban's Head, and a 2½ mile stretch of rough turf at Kimmeridge in the Isle of Purbeck. A leading conservationist of the 1930s, Vaughan Cornish, proposed that a belt of country 100 yards wide should be conserved against all change along the then undeveloped coastline of England. Planning controls have prevented the post-war ribbon growth of the seaside bungalows and chalets which Cornish feared. But nothing has been able to save many of the last strips of downland reaching up to the cliff-edge.

In Dorset as a whole, 11,000 acres, or one quarter of the county's downland turf, went under the plough between 1957 and 1972.[4] But what remains has not survived unscathed. Much of the remaining downland is confined to steep slopes which can be ploughed only at considerable risk to the worker, so these areas are obvious targets for 'improvement' from the air. Newly developed methods of spraying pesticide, fertiliser and ryegrass from aeroplanes have turned an additional area of unknown but clearly substantial extent into a different kind of pale parody of its former self.

Undisturbed chalk downland turf is usually extremely rich in archaeological remains. Clusters of upstanding remains, from circles of standing stones. henge monuments, causewayed camps and hillforts to less dramatic but equally tantalising burial chambers, field systems, trackways and crossdykes, can add magic to any landscape they happen to grace. Now, however, such relics have been banished from most lowland landscapes. Since most of our lowland countryside has been cultivated more or less continuously for hundreds, often thousands, of years, any evidence of prehistoric life it may have harboured has either been destroyed completely, or shows up only as 'crop marks' – circles and lines visible from low-flying aircraft. These occur because crops grow more vigorously in soil covering silted-up ditches and pits dug into the ground in earlier times. For any more complete reflection of times past, we have to rely on the small proportion of the land surface that was ploughed or settled in prehistory but afterwards withdrawn from intensive use and left untouched.

Only certain parts of our chalk downlands, heather moorland and woodlands meet this requirement, and of these types of country, the chalk downlands were the richest storehouse. Since World War II, however, downland ploughing has swept away entire visible archaeological landscapes, embodying not only a unique treasury of information about our nation's past but also features that distinguished England's chalk downs for centuries. An account by Sir Richard Colt Hoare of a journey over the Wiltshire chalklands in 1812 provides a tantalising glimpse of the way things used to be: 'On traversing the extensive downs of Wiltshire our attention is continually arrested by the works of the Ancient Britons: strong fortresses, circles, barrows and other inequalities in the ground which are evidently contrary to nature.'

The present agricultural revolution has turned the Wiltshire Downs into a vast barley prairie, whose monotony is relieved only by barbed wire fences and oil stores and, in autumn, by the charred stubble. Less than 3 per cent of the chalk downland of Wessex now remains intact as old, undisturbed grassland. The upstanding earthworks that attracted Colt Hoare's attention have been levelled, and with them volumes of irreplaceable information about our history as well as much of Wiltshire's landscape character. In just ten years, between 1954 and 1964, 250 out of a total of 640 scheduled ancient monuments in Wiltshire were destroyed or badly damaged, according to a survey by the Council for British Archaeology.[5]

Now the great expanses of downland apart from Salisbury Plain and the Lulworth Ranges have all disappeared, it is the remaining pockets that are being mopped up, like those on the Isle of Wight. A Jutish cemetery, the remains of four Roman villas, the remains of three Iron Age/Romano-British field systems, the earthworks of a medieval manorial settlement, and three medieval field systems, as well as 42 per cent of Bronze Age round barrows on the island were being destroyed by ploughing in 1978, according to a survey by Mrs. H. V. Basford, the county archaeologist.[6] The disappearance of these features and of the other charms of chalk downland will not help the island's holiday industry, which attracts 1.3 million visitors every year, thus providing much local income and employment. These visitors include foreigners who find within this little corner of England types of scenery unknown in their great continents – like the American journalist who, after a stroll across the open downlands of the island in 1975, declared turf on chalk 'the best walking country in the world'.[7]

Our chalk downlands no longer offer city-dwellers the opportunity to wander at will for hours on end. But the small stretches of downland that still remain provide a delightful environment in which to walk or ride, picnic or play, botanise or look for butterflies, hang-glide or fly a kite. Downland has already lost its 'wilderness' role. But now, ploughing is gradually stripping the downs of the opportunities they have offered for other kinds of recreation. Alkham is a downland village in East Kent where this process is as clearly visible as it is anywhere. Stretches of easily accessible rough downland made Alkham a delightful place in which to live – until 1978. Tucked away two miles behind the White Cliffs of Dover, the Alkham Valley was a small gem of the kind with which England's countryside used to be so generously studded. Now, stripped of the main things which gave it its character, it stands as a small monument to the ravages of agricultural change.

The sides of this dry chalk valley rise gently to a height of 140 feet; a B road cuts a serpentine course along the valley bottom, following its twists, turns, ups and downs. Here, as in most of our chalk country, the graceful curves of the underlying rock are most apparent in winter when the sun casts long shadows down the valley sides and over their sensual dips and swells. The village of Alkham, nestling at the bottom of the valley, is a neat cluster of flint or red-brick-and-tile cottages dominated from higher up the hillside by a small flint church.

Like many of our other English villages, Alkham owed much of its charm to the countryside that framed it: until 1978, the village was virtually ringed by rolling chalk downland interspersed with oak and ash remnants of the Wildwood, much of it designated by the Nature Conservancy Council as a site of special scientific interest. The existence of so much rough down, scrub and wood within easy walking distance was one of the village's main attractions. Tussocky, hummocky grass with numerous anthills, interspersed with bushes of wild rose, wayfaring tree, bramble and hawthorn, made the hills behind the village a favourite playground for village children; many older people made these hills the start of a circular walk up around the village. On the opposite, more gentle side of the valley it used to be possible to walk for miles through a belt of rough chalk downland lying between farmland in the valley bottom and woodland on top. This belt of downland provided good blackberrying land and plenty of flowers, birds and butterflies; one length of it was always known as 'Paigle Meadow' because of the creamy drifts of cowslips ('paigle' is an old Kent word for this flower) that used to grow there.

All this is now but a memory, however. In 1977 the main farm at Alkham changed hands and the new owner cleared away virtually all the natural vegetation clothing the valley sides on his land. The downland was ploughed up, bushes, scrubland and hedgerows were bulldozed away, trees were felled, and one whole wood was removed. Other woods would have followed had not Dover District Council protected them by imposing tree preservation orders. Public footpaths, too, were affected. Public rights of way are theoretically sacrosanct, but this has not meant immunity for Alkham's footpaths. Where fields with rights of way across them are ploughed up, farmers are supposed to send a roller in afterwards to reinstate the path. This was not done for what was arguably Alkham's loveliest path, however, and local people used to wandering through a leafy lane now have to struggle across ploughed earth if they still feel it is worth taking the walk. Not many do. What was a particularly attractive flint-based track leading north from Alkham bounded by hedges and bordered with primroses, violets, bluebells, campion and many other flowers, is now almost impossible to find. The whole area has been made into one large field, the wood and hedges have gone and the dip in which the track ran has been filled in.

Sunny Hill is just one of the areas on which stretches of downland were ploughed up. This steep, rounded hill facing southwards across the valley was a particularly favourite spot for blackberrying, picnicking or playing hide-and-seek, all of which activities could be pursued on an aromatic carpet of wild thyme, marjoram and wild carrot, eyebright, rock-rose and harebell, pyramidal and spotted orchid. Butterflies –the chalkhill blue, common blue, brown argus, adonis blue and brimstone – would dance among the flowers, while children played hide-and-seek among the bushes of wild rose, wayfaring tree, hawthorn, blackthorn and gorse. By 1980, Sunny

Hill had become a bare white chalk slope. Though ploughing seems to have yielded little agricultural benefit, it has destroyed the down's attractions.

Archie is now retired, but he used to walk over Sunny Hill twice a day to and from his work at a bakery in Dover. He described to me what it was like. At 4.30 in the morning, he could hear but not see skylarks ascending and nightingales singing. Ghostly white barn owls would float across the meadows, while vixens screamed from the woods around. By early afternoon, when he returned from work, it was a different world: the chirping of hundreds of grasshoppers was the dominating sound. Flowers and butterflies were everywhere. Sometimes he would see an occasional adder or grass snake, rabbits cropping the turf or one of the many tawny kestrels that hovered in the sky.

Many of the villagers of Alkham are still upset by what has been done to their environment. The clerk to the parish council complained bitterly to me: 'The law simply hasn't caught up with the fact that things can be done so quickly and on such a large scale. If a picnicker digs up a cowslip root he can be prosecuted (under the Conservation of Wild Creatures and Wild Plants Act, 1975). But if a farmer ploughs up a whole field of cowslips we can't do anything about it.'

The farmer who has made the changes remains unrepentant. Indeed he is busy carrying out similar 'improvements', with the help of Ministry of Agriculture grants, in another part of the North Downs near Maidstone. To him the countryside around Alkham before he took over was 'derelict' and a disgrace to the locality. He feels his actions have improved the standard of the area and made it more agriculturally civilised. It is a view. But nobody else had a chance to challenge it.

What has happened in the Alkham Valley has occurred in many other similar areas of chalk downland. The dry valleys of the Yorkshire Wolds, perhaps our least appreciated chalk hills, look like being the next victims.

William Marshall, a traveller in 1788, considered the Yorkshire Wolds 'the most magnificent assemblage of chalky hills this island affords. The features are large. The surface billowing but not broken; the swells resembling Biscayan waves half pacified.'[8] In Marshall's day, each of the villages lying in the dry valleys or dales that cut through the hills was surrounded by a large arable field cultivated in a fixed rotation by the villagers; beyond this was another 'outfield' cultivated occasionally and then a large area of sheep walk, clothing the steep dale-sides, which was never tilled. Towards the end of the eighteenth century, however, more and more of these sheep ranges went under the plough, and by the nineteenth century the Wolds were almost entirely arable, dominated as they are today by big, regular fields, wide, straight roads, and isolated farmsteads with their characteristic L-shaped shelter belts. So unlike the Wiltshire or Sussex Downs for instance, the Yorkshire Wolds were never used by city-dwellers as recreation areas over which to wander freely. The only rough grassland left was and is the downland that clothes the steep sides of the dry valleys. Up till now, these downland slopes have been used as rough grazing for the sheep or beef cattle that many farmers have kept as a sideline alongside their main business, barley-growing. The steepness of the valley sides has meant that they have resisted the plough, and their rough downland turf provides oases for wild creatures in what would otherwise be a wildlife desert. On these dalesides, ecologically isolated from England's main chalkland massif, a unique flora has evolved: the sheep's fescue and brome grasses are spangled with the intense red blooms of bloody cranesbill, together with flax, early purple orchid, lady's smock, purple milk-vetch and gorse.

Since about 1975, however, sheep and beef-cattle rearing have become much more profitable than hitherto, and the improved financial incentives, coupled with the development of new techniques for reseeding steep-sided slopes with rye-grass, have led many farmers to take stock-rearing more seriously. So they have fenced off the rough dales, killed the natural grasses and flowers with herbicides like Paraquat sprayed from four-wheel-drive or crawler tractors; then they have drilled ryegrass seed into the old dying turf with special cultivators fitted with narrow knife blades that cut slots into the earth and drill the seed into these slots in a new technique called 'slit-seeding'. While this has been going on, the Ministry of Agriculture has been actively encouraging farmers to reseed the dales through for instance a series of demonstrations in 1980 to show farmers new grassland renovation techniques developed mainly on the Ministry's string of experimental farms, to discuss the 'improvement' of the dales and to make farmers aware of the Ministry's farm capital grants for fencing and reclamation. A local Ministry official told me in 1980 he was convinced that all 4,200 acres of the downland dales in North Humberside would have been improved by 1990.

If the elimination of our last stretches of chalk downland turf is allowed to proceed unimpeded, this unique habitat will be only a memory by the end of this century. Our children's children could expect to see cowslips nodding on chalk downland or the stately bee orchid growing wild only in the artificial confines of a nature reserve.

8

Moors

The great, rough, open sweeps of heather and grass moorland that clothe the moors of the north and west have an appeal quite different from that of the more intimate landscapes of the lowlands. But those who are attracted by the moors are among the most passionate enthusiasts for the countryside. Tom Stephenson, for example, has spent most of his eighty-four years campaigning for the protection of moorland, mainly as Secretary to the Ramblers' Association. It was a clear, frosty day in 1906 when he first felt the lure of the moors – at the age of thirteen, on Lancashire's Forest of Bowland moorland massif after climbing up from the industrial towns below. 'It was just wild country,' he told me, 'nothing at all. And the great attraction was that so easily you lost any sense of industrialisation or civilisation: you felt you were alone in the world.'[1]

In spite of contemporary attitudes to the moors, they are not entirely 'natural': most of them were covered in forest after the Ice Age, and they are now open moorland only because this forest was cleared over the centuries to provide sheep runs and timber for fuel and building. But at least the moors were not ploughed in the recent past. As a result, many of our moors are particularly rich in archaeological remains; and these relics of ancient man seem, paradoxically, to enhance the moors' feeling of remoteness from present-day civilisation. In the foothills of the Cheviots, for example, round barrows, fortifications and Bronze Age cup-and-ring carvings of unknown function form a distinctive motif within the pattern of the landscape. The North York Moors are so thick with thousands of barrows and cairns, Bronze and Iron Age hut clusters, dykes and defences of all kinds, standing stones and stone circles that the archaeologist Jacquetta Hawkes has described this area as 'a single monument to prehistoric man, one of those small areas where his handiwork is often still dominant over that of his descendants ... They [the remains] are all there, part of the moorland scene, tales of a day when man fitted himself into a countryside, embellished it a little, but did not hack it into alien shapes.'[2] Much the same has been said of Dartmoor, which is so rich in antiquities that, it has been estimated, only 50 per cent of them have so far been discovered. As on the downs, however, ploughing is removing the archaeological interest of the moors. And even where scheduled monuments are left untouched, they cease to create the same atmosphere of lonely timelessness that is perhaps the most distinctive feature of our moors once the open landscape in which they stand has been tamed.

The incentives for agricultural 'improvement' are even greater on our moorlands than they are in the lowlands. The Pennines, the North York Moors, the Lake District, Dartmoor, Exmoor and Bodmin Moor (as well as 90 per cent of Scotland and Wales and 50 per cent of Northern Ireland) fall within what the EEC defines as 'less favoured areas'. On top of the usual tax concessions and price guarantees, farmers in these areas are eligible for capital grants at higher rates than those available elsewhere (70 per cent for field drainage and 50 per cent for conversion of open moorland to ryegrass lots, for example). What's more, they are also receiving about £94 million a year in the form of 'livestock compensatory allowances', which entitle hill farmers to an automatic annual payment of £35 for every cow they rear and £5.50 each for most of their sheep. Thus in 1974–75, grants and subsidies accounted for the remarkable proportion of three-quarters of the total net farm income of Britain's hill and upland farms.[3]

There are two main reasons for the EEC policy of support for agriculture in the hills and mountains of Europe. The first is to stem depopulation: subsidies to farming are seen as a way of keeping people in the hills. The second reason is, ironically, conservation. Conservation is important because tourism provides many more jobs and better economic prospects for these areas than does agriculture or forestry.[4] And traditional farming is considered the best means of safeguarding the landscape in hill country.

In Britain, the Ministry of Agriculture chooses to administer the funds involved in ways that make nonsense of the EEC objectives. Instead of helping to conserve upland landscape and communities, EEC grants are speeding the destruction of both. The Ministry of Agriculture is using EEC funds as a replacement for Britain's own post-war programme of support for hill farmers – a programme that was stopped when we entered the EEC. And the emphasis in British hill farm support has traditionally been on food production, not conservation. The British Government began to subsidise hill farming immediately after the war. Acts of Parliament in 1946 and 1951 set the pattern of taxpayer support to the hills for the next quarter-century: there were to be special 'headage' payments for sheep and cattle kept by farmers in designated upland areas, and higher rates of farm capital grant than elsewhere. The policy was based on the idea that Britain needed to retain an army of farmers in the hills as a reservoir of food-producing land that could be called upon if the wartime food blockades were ever repeated. Meanwhile, in peacetime, special support would enable farmers to increase food production from the hills – an end that seemed after the war desirable enough in itself.

It has however always been accepted that hill farming can never contribute more than a small fraction of our total food production. Although hill and upland farms account for one quarter of Britain's farmland, they produce only one-twelfth of the country's agricultural output.[5] No matter how much money we plough into the hills, the basic limitations of climate and soil will always prevent the hills yielding crops on a scale similar to that achieved on the lowlands. Nonetheless, the policy operates as if our lives depended on securing every extra ounce of food that can be wrung from the hills, whatever the cost. It is possible to produce wheat on the North York Moors, but it costs about three times as much to do so as it does on the wheat prairies of America's Mid-West. To achieve the Ministry's unnecessary objective, the unwitting taxpayer is undermining prospects for the economic development of the hills in areas other than agriculture (such as tourism). And he is destroying a source of recreation that ought to be seen as an important asset for the nation as a whole.

The process can be seen as clearly as anywhere in the Exmoor National Park. Exmoor's expanses of wild, open moorland have traditionally been freely accessible to walkers. This is the main reason why the area was made a national park in 1954. However, between 1947 and 1976 more than 300 acres of open moorland have been squared off and converted mainly to inaccessible ryegrass fields *each year*. A total of 12,000 acres of moorland – one-fifth of the total on Exmoor – has now disappeared. The Exmoor Society declared in 1979: 'Unless a halt is called *now* to the reclamation and enclosure of wild and open moorland (both grass and heather) there will be so little left that Exmoor's continued existence as a National Park will be an expensive farce.' Agricultural 'reclamation' is even now biting into the central core of unenclosed moorland – the 'critical amenity area', as it was named in 1968 – which has now been reduced to about 40,000 acres. Between 1,000 and 1,500 acres of this moorland were ploughed up between 1968 and 1977; at least 650 acres of this total was ploughed up with the help of Ministry of Agriculture grant. At present levels of agricultural support, it would be profitable to improve two-thirds of the critical amenity area moorland that remains. If this happens, and a further 26,000 acres goes under the plough, Exmoor's sense of remoteness and hence its function as a wilderness will be memories. So will its wildlife. Six of Exmoor's moorland plant species have already become extinct through agricultural change since 1930, according to the Nature Conservancy Council. Fifty of Exmoor's wild moorland plants are rare in England, says the Conservancy. It is a basic law of ecology that the greatest diversity of plants and animals is always to be found in the largest blocks of semi-natural vegetation, so the chances of survival of these fifty scarce species will be steadily reduced if the moorland shrivels any more.[6]

Such benefits as accrue from the conversion of Exmoor's open moors to ryegrass pastures will be felt mainly by the few individual farmers who happen to own the land involved. The benefit to the nation at large will be negligible. When Lord Porchester asked the Ministry of Agriculture to estimate how much potential food production would be lost if constraints were imposed on land reclamation in the 'critical amenity area', the Ministry said that the loss would be equivalent to 0.05 per cent of total UK production in 1975 of beef and veal, 0.3 per cent of mutton and lamb, and 0.2 per cent of wool. For this we are sacrificing not only an amenity we may want to use ourselves, but also, eventually, revenue from tourism which could far exceed the economic value of agricultural improvement. To the EEC, too, the cultivation of the moors entails serious losses. Not only does the EEC have to provide the grants that make 'improvement' possible; if the extra output adds to the vast EEC surpluses, then the Common Market has to buy it up and dispose of it.

What is lost when the moors are ploughed up – whether they be those of Exmoor, Dartmoor, the Peak District, the Yorkshire Pennines or the Cheviots of the Border Country – is by no means only the subject of an enthusiast's obsession. The moors have made themselves an integral part of our cultural heritage partly through the inspiration they have given to artists. The moors have played a vital role in the work of sculptors like Henry Moore and Barbara Hepworth, painters, poets, and of course a whole series of novelists. The classic moorland work is perhaps Emily Bronte's *Wuthering Heights*, which is set in the moors of the West Riding. Here the contrast between the rough vitality of the moors and the tamed, enclosed fields of the valleys is personified in the book's two main characters, Heathcliff and Edgar Linton. *The Hound of the Baskervilles* and *Jamaica Inn* are two other tales that would be inconceivable without their moorland backcloth.

Even if not everybody seeks out the hills for philosophical musing, few people remain completely untouched by some aspect of the beauty and interest of England's moors. The spell which the moors wield over their devotees and our artists is also felt by more casual visitors. On Ilfracombe promenade in August 1978 I asked a few people how they felt about Exmoor. A nursing sister told me it was the moors' aura of history that appealed to her: 'They've been there untouched for hundreds of years; people have been fighting battles over the same moors.' An electricity board showroom manager with whom I spoke loved the natural life of the moors; a Chinese student relished the sense of freedom – 'it broadens your heart' – a retired miner from Rotherham the individual heather plants; a young factory girl the peacefulness of the moors. But the colours of the moors were the most generally popular feature to the holidaymakers I talked to. The attractions of the moors for our artists are understandable. There are few more breathtaking sights anywhere in the world than Dartmoor in August, aflame with a mosaic of golden gorse and purple heather, ripening moor-grass and the russet hues of dying bracken. And quite apart from their intrinsic charms, the moors are also a vital ingredient in the whole landscape mix of England. Their rough open spaces provide a contrast with the gentle patchwork of fields and hedges below that emphasises the pastoral intimacy of our

Hedgerows, like these near Childe Okeford in north Dorset (above) provide the framework of the English countryside, but over the last 35 years, a quarter of our hedgerows have been removed. New machines, like this flail cutter (below), are chopping many of our remaining hedges down to a height of a few feet. (Chapter 3)

The traditional deciduous woodland of England, like this beech wood near Bradenham in the Buckinghamshire Chilterns (above), is gradually disappearing. The trees are being uprooted to create more farmland and to enable new farm machinery to operate more easily (below). One third of England's small woodlands have been cleared away since the war. (Chapter 5)

Field drainage programmes, like this pipe laying operation (above), are transforming much of the English landscape. When excess water has been removed, farmland can be exploited more intensively, but landscape features and wildlife often disappear in the process. The bleak monotony of this scene in the Somerset Levels (below) characterises many drained landscapes. (Chapters 9 and 22)

England's countryside is a living history book. Our moors, downs and woods are littered with relics of man's earliest activities, like this Bronze Age burial

mound on Malham Moor in North Yorkshire.
Remains such as these are usually swept away in the
process of agricultural intensification.

Improved field drainage imposes new burdens on England's lazy, winding streams and rivers, like this tributary of the River Frome near Dorchester (above). To overcome the problem, many rivers and streams are being 'canalised', that is straightened and deepened so that water will flow faster through them. As in this canalisation scheme on the River Yeo near Sherborne in Dorset (below), riverside trees and bushes are normally removed in the process. (Chapter 9)

Downland, as on the scarp face of the South Downs behind Cocking in West Sussex (above), is one key element in the variety of England's landscape. However, agricultural intensification is robbing the downs of their interest and character, as woodland and downland turf are relentlessly ploughed up. The Alkham Valley, in the North Downs of Kent (below), reflects what is becoming the typical face of England's downs. (Chapter 7)

The Common Frog – a species that was taken for granted as an abundant inhabitant of the English countryside only fifteen years ago. Now, as pump drainage of marshes has gathered pace and ponds and dykes have been filled in, the frog population has been decimated. Soon, the frog may become an animal we have to go to a nature reserve to see, along with many other familiar creatures of the traditional English countryside. (Chapter 17)

typical lowland countryside.

The wildlife of our moors is quite different from that of any other habitat in England. Our moors harbour some of our most spectacular birds, like the raven, the king of aerial acrobats, the merlin, our smallest bird of prey, the buzzard, the short-eared owl, the hen harrier and the world's most spectacular falcon, the peregrine. All these birds are at the end of food-chains: the merlin, for instance, preys on meadow pipits, which in turn live off the craneflies in the rough grass and heather. And when the moors are ploughed, the moles, voles, meadow pipits, wheatears and dunlins on which they feed disappear. The rare creatures of the moors are replaced by those that are found anywhere else in Britain.

Finally, the 20,000 young people who take to the moors every year in the course of qualifying for their Duke of Edinburgh's Award are just one other group whose requirements highlight the value of moorland. The organisers of the Awards scheme told me that 'wild country' (defined by them as the national parks of England and Wales and the Highlands of Scotland) provides the best environment for testing young people's endurance, orienteering skills, and ability to get through unexpected difficulties.

But perhaps the most important function our moors fulfil is that of providing a 'wilderness'. The relatively uniform vegetation of the moors, the wind, the vastness of their open spaces manage to conjure up a sense of timelessness and distance from civilisation. England's moorlands somehow manage to provide an environment that feels remote from man's works, and, for a growing number of people, access to such an environment meets a vital psychological need. The reason for this need is far from clear. Unlike the gregarious bee or the solitary fox, Man seems to be both a herd animal and a loner. Since the dawn of the Romantic Era, however, it has been the human individual who has been placed on a pedestal in the West. Those attracted to wilderness landscape seem to be seeking a context for the pursuit of their individual identity away from the herd. To do this they need to get away from the environment their fellow men have created for the group to a place as devoid as possible of what is obviously human handiwork. A kaleidoscope of other living things is also unhelpful: what seems to be sought is a blank canvas on which individuals can commune with themselves or their Maker.

There seem to be seven conditions all, or nearly all, of which landscape *must* meet if it is to arouse the enthusiasm of wilderness seekers in this country. These conditions are: wildness, openness, asymmetry, homogeneity, height, freedom for the rambler to wander at will and the absence of what is obviously human handiwork. In England today, the moors meet these conditions far more completely than any other form of landscape.

Current moves to carve up the open moors into square lots, to replace the heather and harebells, the gorse and the bracken with enclosures of the barley or ryegrass that can now be found in a hundred other types of countryside, or to blanket the rough moors with conifer plantations, destroy completely the fragile sense of wilderness of the moors. Enclosure for agriculture destroys the freedom to wander at will: but it also destroys the point of it. The sense of timelessness evaporates when the silence broken only by the wind sighing in the heather and the cries of curlew and buzzard gives way to the drone of farm machinery. When the wide, rough, open spaces have been turned into a food or timber factory, many walkers find them little less oppressive than the manufacturing complexes of the cities. Indeed, those who love the moors as 'wilderness' tend to find the rape of the hills more offensive than the fouling of man's own nest.

Thirty years ago, two forms of wilderness environment other than upland moor existed in England: rough, unenclosed chalk downlands, and coastal marshlands. Unfortunately, however, these two types of country have been enclosed and turned over to intensive agriculture so energetically that the remnants that survive are no longer extensive enough to provide a sense of remoteness. The onslaught on our open moors by agriculture and forestry is depriving us of more than a wildlife habitat, a living archaeological museum and an environment for outdoor activities. Christopher Brasher once wrote that 'a nation that expands into all its wild land is a nation that has lost its soul'. It may not be easy to define the importance of wilderness, but it is real. And we should think before we deprive our children of it.

9
Wetlands

Wetlands present the most obvious of challenges to the farmer intent on agricultural intensification. Anything that is wet can be drained – at a price. And here, as elsewhere, technology and the unwitting taxpayer work together for the farmer's gain. At present, electrically powered pumps which can artificially lower water tables are striding into our wetlands under the direction of the water authorities which work to improve conditions for farmers largely with Ministry of Agriculture money. Already, land drainage has converted thousands of acres of marsh and water meadow into uniform expanses of farmland dissected by dykes. It is something that has been going on for a long time. The Lincolnshire and Cambridgeshire Fens, the Ancholme Levels north of Brigg in Lincolnshire and the Hull Valley were all once extensive wetlands, but they had all been at least partially drained before the last war. The agricultural revolution now under way, however, is spreading the process to virtually all the wet areas, large and small, that remain – the flood plains of river valleys, mosses and mires from Shropshire to Northumberland as well as our most extensive remaining wet meadow areas –the Yare marshes that border the Norfolk Broads, the Pevensey Levels near Eastbourne, and the Somerset Levels. I do not, however, intend to complete this survey of threatened landscape features with another grisly tally of national devastation. Instead, to give as clear an idea as possible of just what agricultural change means on the ground, I have decided this time to use a close-up rather than a wide wide-angle lens. In this chapter, I am going to look in detail at what is happening to just one wetland area – our largest surviving wetland, the Somerset Levels.

The Somerset Levels

Stand on Burrow Mump, a 300-foot, solitary, grassy knoll six miles south of Glastonbury, and below you stretching away northwards to the Bristol Channel lies one of the most artificial yet most alluring of England's landscapes. The Somerset Levels are 170,000 acres of low-lying marshy meadowland created in the flood plains of eight rivers which converge as they meander towards the Bristol Channel. Divided up not by hedgerows but by water and duckweed-filled dykes or 'rhynes', they provide summer-pasture for cattle and produce great quantities of milk.

This unique area is cut off from the rest of England by four ranges of hills – the Mendips ridge to the north and east, the limestone hills of Dorset to the south, and the Blackdown Hills and the Quantocks to the west. If the land surface dropped by a mere ten or fifteen feet the whole of the Levels would turn into a shallow bay of the Bristol Channel (which is what they were until Neolithic times). Today, the flatlands are studded with hills topped by quirky, isolated villages with queer-sounding names like Mulcheney, Meare and Westonzoyland, and pierced by the long, low ridge of the Polden Hills. Long, straight roads, bordered on both sides by willows, run across the plain; lesser, narrow roads lead off them on erratic courses through right-angle bends to hamlets lost in orchards and alder thickets. And from the roads, the Levels themselves stretch away to the hill ranges on the horizon. Their vegetation varies in colour and texture tremendously: the deep, rich green of the meadow grass is set off by the soft, light shimmering greens of the willows, aspens, poplars and alders that grow in little clumps and on the banks of the rhynes. The plants that grow in the rhynes – reeds, sedges, yellow flags, purple loosestrife, water lilies, water violets, frogbit and kingcups – as well as the orchids, cowslips, meadowsweet, campions and ragged robin of the meadows splash the whole area with colour.

The Levels provide a home for the otter as well as for more common, though in many areas fast diminishing, species like frogs, toads, newts, sticklebacks, voles, shrews, field-mice, glow-worms and dragonflies. Birds here are everywhere: herons, kingfishers, snipe, geese, swans, duck, bittern, curlews, warblers, woodpeckers and nightjars. But despite their variety and life, the Levels are a deeply peaceful place. Their miles of watery marshes, transformed from one day to another by the vagaries of cloud, mist and sunset, but always spacious and isolated, are calm and relaxing in all their moods. However, both the landscape and the wildlife of the Somerset Levels are under threat from drastic land drainage and flood alleviation schemes.

For hundreds of years farmers have been at war with the rivers of the Levels. Often swollen by the frequent rain, they wind their way across the plain only to be forced back into their courses by the rising tide of the British Channel. Floods are regular, though they have brought benefits as well as inconvenience. Silt and the rotting remnants of ancient forests have produced a deep peaty soil which in summer, when the water is low, provides rich pasture. Farm holdings in the Somerset Levels cover 160 acres on average. Most embrace two distinct kinds of land: a stretch of free-drainage 'upland' on an island of higher ground or on the slopes of the hills that penetrate and surround the Levels, and an area of Level below. The purpose of the drainage schemes being installed on the Levels is to make them as versatile as comparable land in eastern England has become. (The Lincolnshire Fens, for example, were once much like the Levels.) Before drainage, a Level in Somerset is used as summer grazing for cattle: natural grass pasture doesn't mind getting its feet wet and can stand several weeks of flooding. But the more nutritious artificially developed strains of ryegrass, with which farmers are anxious to replace the naturally occurring species, are more sensitive: they perish if they are exposed to water for more than a few days. Cereals too are easily spoilt by flooding. On top of this, intensive grazing and cereals now demand huge quantities of herbicide and fertiliser, and a flood washes them away. The benefits of drainage to the farmers on whose land the schemes are installed are considerable. Profits were increasing by about £100 an acre in 1979 from £450 per acre for dairy farming on natural grassland to £550 per acre for dairying on reseeded ryegrass. The financial benefits to the taxpayer and consumer are less clear: the purpose of about 90 per cent of the land drainage and flood alleviation schemes being implemented is to boost production of milk – a commodity of which the EEC enjoys a large structural surplus both as skimmed milk powder and as butter.

As elsewhere in England and Wales it is not the farmers themselves who are draining their land. The task is being handled for them by the local water authority. Our eight regional water authorities were created in 1973 out of the old river authorities and boards. They have functions relating to water supply, sewerage disposal, the maintenance of water quality and land drainage. About half their members are appointed by the Minister of Agriculture, the rest by local authorities in whose areas they lie. In practice, farmers and landowners form a high proportion of the members appointed from both sources, particularly on the authorities' land drainage committees, since both the Minister and local authorities are required under the Water Act 1973 to select people to sit on these committees who have a practical knowledge of agriculture or land drainage. No practical obstacles stand in the way of their natural inclinations. Land drainage schemes carried out by water authorities are funded at a higher rate than the capital grants to farmers: the Ministry usually pays 80 per cent of the cost. In 1979-80 the Ministry of Agriculture gave water authorities an estimated £21 million by way of grants for land drainage capital projects.

At present, land drainage schemes in the Levels are of two main kinds: river canalisation and pump drainage.

River canalisation schemes

The Wessex Water Authority has drawn up detailed plans for seven river 'improvement' schemes in Somerset alone. The Authority puts their total cost at about £6 million.[1] A typical scheme carried out in 1979 and 1980 involved the canalisation of the 2½-mile stretch of the river Yeo between the villages of Bradford Abbas and Thornford near Sherborne in North Dorset. The Wessex Water Authority drew up this scheme after local farmers claimed that the dredging the Water Authority had been carrying out in Sherborne Lake, near the Yeo's source, was exacerbating flooding a few miles downstream, and that the particular stretch of river between Bradford Abbas and Thornford had not been properly cleared of vegetation to facilitate water flow since the last war. The Water Authority first suggested that an embankment should be built on either side of the river to contain any flood water. However, the farmers objected to this idea because it would have restricted the yield from a 150ft wide stretch of land on either side of the river between the two embankments. So instead, the Authority decided to try and make flood water drain away more quickly by deepening the river, widening it and staightening out some of its meanders – a course of action which found much more favour with the farmers, partly because it actually increased their effective land. In the course of this operation, 100 trees have been felled and uprooted, and a further 400 cut back, mainly alders and willows. Herons used to nest in some of these; otters used to live here too, but local people have not seen them since the scheme got under way. Children can no longer swing from ropes over the waterside trees on which they used to play because the river is much deeper and therefore more dangerous; some of the banks have now been cut so steep by the excavators that the Water Authority has had to fence them off and put up warning notices. For years this stretch of river was a favourite walk for people living in the two nearby villages of Bradford Abbas and Thornford. They used to walk their dogs there, watch birds or fish ; now, as a local resident told me, 'It's like the Suez Canal'. The Water Authority plans to replant over 300 trees to make up for those lost – not alongside the river but at other sites nearby. This plan depends however on the release of the necessary land by the farmers who requested the scheme. Even if all these trees are planted, they will not restore a recreation and wildlife resource which is now severely damaged. Nor will any amenity benefit be felt for many years to come.

Altogether, the scheme cost £145,000; 80 per cent of this, or £116,000, was paid by the Ministry of Agriculture in the form of a grant to the Water Authority; the rest was paid by the Water Authority itself; the landowners who are to benefit have not had to pay anything. As a result of the operation, five acres of what used to be unproductive agricultural land can now grow cereals and an area of three square miles which was already given over to cereals and dairy cattle has become more productive. Unfortunately, of course, as the products involved are in surplus in the EEC, the taxpayer's generosity has cost him a further penalty.

In this, as in similar water authority schemes for agriculture, the community at large has no say in what is done. Neither the county, the district nor the two parish councils in whose areas this stretch of river lies were consulted about the proposals; the county and district councils were contacted by the Water Authority only about public services for which they are responsible that were being affected. The only organisation that was officially consulted, the Nature Conservancy Council, referred the matter to the Dorset Naturalists' Trust. The

Trust suggested that the flood water should be contained by the erection of embankments either side of the river – the plan which the farmers originally rejected. Had it been adopted instead, the river would have been conserved in its existing state, and much of the appearance and wildlife population of the river would have been preserved. So would the trees.

The trees at Bradford Abbas went either because they were growing on the bank that was cut back, or because they stood in the way of the giant excavators used in the scheme, or simply because they had been growing alongside meanders which were eliminated. Suddenly isolated in the middle of fields, they clearly threatened to obstruct farmers' attempts to exploit to the full the extra land that the drainage scheme was creating. So they went too.

Pump-drainage schemes

Pump drainage is, however, more common than canalisation. Electrically-powered pumps are installed, which artificially lower the water level in the rhynes by between three to five feet and then pump up into a main drain or river. About half of the rhynes in an area covered by a pump-drainage scheme are filled in; the others are widened and deepened. Pipe drains are laid under fields which draw water into the rhynes, thereby lowering the water table in the fields. Deprived of the water they need to survive, the characteristic plants of the water meadows soon die. Wild plants like buttercups which might otherwise develop in place of these other species are killed with weedkillers like Paraquat. Cereals or a specially formulated grass monoculture, usually Italian ryegrass, are then sown into the ground by drilling. Or, if the water table is sufficiently low, the whole area can be ploughed (including the areas which used to be water meadows and many of the rhynes, which can be filled in). Barley, carrots, sugar beet or any other arable crop can then be put down.

The ecological effects of this process are far-reaching.[2] First, all the plants of the rough meadows, the orchids and marsh marigolds, ragged robin and cuckoo flowers, that grew amongst the grasses are eliminated. Then the population of butterflies, spiders and other small creatures that depended on the wild plants are decimated. Virtually the only remaining wildlife is soon confined to whatever drainage ditches have been left. But soon wildlife in the surviving rhynes suffers too.

For once the land has been put down to ryegrass or barley or whatever, farmers start applying vast quantities of fertiliser and pesticide. These chemicals upset the ion concentrations in the water. And if the plants and animals that live in the rhynes are not killed by this, they are wiped out directly or indirectly by the herbicides rained onto the rhynes to keep what are now main drainage channels free of any vegetation that might possibly impede the fast flow of water along them at times of heavy rainfall or flood. So dykes once alive with meadowsweet and yellow flag, water lilies and frogbit, are turned into nothing more than open chemical sewers. The new agricultural regime has only one use for the rhynes – land drainage – and, within reason, it doesn't matter from the farming point of view what is in the rhynes so long as it is soluble. The cattle that used to get refreshment from these rhynes are, under the new system, watered from concrete troughs in the fields, if they have not been put indoors.

Birds are just one group of animals whose populations are greatly affected by pump drainage and river canalisation, since the habitats to which centuries of evolution have adapted them are taken away. A study in 1978,[3] compared the populations of breeding birds in two areas on the Levels virtually identical but for the fact that one (West Sedgemoor, east of Taunton) was 'natural', consisting of rough meadows used as summer pasture and drained by rhynes, whereas the other (Witcombe Bottom near Langport) was pump-drained in 1977 (at a cost of £184,000). The main characteristic species of the Levels were all present on the undrained area, but only four of them were present on the drained area; all but one of these were far more scarce. These were the figures:

Species	West Sedgemoor No. pairs	Witcombe Bottom No. pairs
Lapwing	13	5
Snipe	16	0
Curlew	1	0
Redshank	4	0
Skylark	28	15
Grasshopper warbler	2	0
Sedge warbler	11	0
Meadow pipit	16	0
Yellow wagtail	1	4
Reed bunting	15	1

Dr Norman Moore, the chief scientist at the Nature Conservancy Council, said in 1977: 'Unless steps are taken to lay down a strategic plan for development which provides for the maintenance of habitats, the Somerset Levels could become as devoid of wildlife as the East Anglian fens.'[4] But to turn the Somerset Levels into something like the East Anglian Fens is precisely what the promoters of land drainage in the Levels are seeking to do. 'Lincolnshire Fens in Somerset' was the title of an enthusiastic article in 1975 in *The Somerset Farmer*, the journal of the local branch of the National Farmers' Union. It was written by a local farmer called Ralph Baker who in 1980 was chairman of the regional land drainage committee and a member of all three local land drainage committees (Avon and Dorset, Somerset and Bristol Avon) of the Wessex Water Authority.

The present state of the Lincolnshire Fens demonstrates the implications of Ralph Baker's dream – a dream for the Somerset landscape. The Fens have been stripped of all functions other than profitable food production. They stretch for mile after mile, devoid of any obsservable natural life. The traditional sounds of the English countryside, birdsong and the chirping of grasshoppers, are absent here: the silence is broken only by the wind as it blows dust from the peaty soil with no hedges or trees to break its passage. The variety of the old countryside has gone: everything is exactly the same, a great emptiness of ploughed earth or sugar beet or barley as far as the eye can see. With the trees have gone the colours of autumn, and with the hedgerows the bright, glossy berries that bring colour to our countryside in winter and provide food for birds. Robbed of their sense of place, the Lincolnshire Fens are now just a production line for food products.

Agricultural change has not just taken away the animals and plants: it has taken the people too, as machines have taken the jobs once done by men. There are too few people to form real communities.

In Somerset, thousands of acres of the Levels have already been pump-drained and new schemes are being installed all the time – this despite cutbacks in other areas of public expenditure; the fact that the extra food to be produced is often already in surplus; the concern of the Nature Conservancy Council (less than 200 acres of the Levels are secure as nature reserves) which sees another arm of government, the Ministry

of Agriculture, doing things which it continually tries, un-
successfully, to prevent; and the destruction of the unique
landscape beauty of this secluded land. The drainage in 1979
of Stockmoor, an area of low-lying land on the southern
outskirts of Bridgwater, demonstrates clearly what is going
on.

In 1973 the farmer who owns Stockmoor complained to his
local internal drainage board of the damage his land had
suffered after a particularly bad summer storm. (Internal
drainage boards are associations manned mainly by farmers
and responsible for the maintenance of minor watercourses.
They receive about £4 million from the Ministry of Agriculture
every year for this purpose.) The Stockmoor farmer was
anxious to reduce flooding and improve drainage to permit
more profitable beef and dairy farming and to make arable
farming possible. The Wessex Water Authority stepped in,
and drew up plans for a pump-drainage scheme. The costings
were carried out in 1977 and the scheme was installed in 1979.

The main financial benefit of the scheme to the farmer has
arisen through a lengthening of the grazing season and
opportunities for more intensive farming. The total benefit
to him was estimated to be £41,000 every year in the unpublished cost-benefit analysis carried out by the Water
Authority in 1977. In addition, the capital value of the land
covered by the drainage scheme will have increased substantially. Only a small area of land is involved, however: the
watertable is being lowered over about three square miles and
an area of less than one square mile will flood less frequently
than it did before.

The farmer who is receiving these not inconsiderable
benefits had to pay nothing at all towards the cost of the main
feature of the scheme – the installation of three pumps at a
cost of £153,000. Eighty per cent of this cost is being borne by
the Ministry of Agriculture; the remainder by the Wessex
Water Authority. There are three other lesser costs which the
farmer at Stockmoor is helping to pay, however. Intensification of farming will increase his maintenance costs by £1,000
a year. The huge quantities of fertiliser he will have to pour
onto his land in order to sustain the high output he is aiming
for will cost £50,000 over thirty years, but he can claim 20
per cent of the cost of this from the Ministry of Agriculture.
Installing pipe drains under the fields will cost £43,000, of

which the Ministry of Agriculture pays half and the farmer the other half.

The only thing that holds the Wessex Water Authority back from canalising virtually the entire lengths of the Rivers Yeo, Isle, Tone and Parrett as well as installing hundreds more pump drainage schemes throughout the Levels and north Dorset is drainage problems further downstream. Certainly shortage of taxpayers' money does not seem likely to inhibit this particular form of public spending however savagely the axe may be falling in what may seem more defensible areas. The Yeo, Isle and Tone are all tributaries of the River Parrett, which flows into the Bristol Channel at Bridgwater Bay. But before it reaches the sea, the Parrett meanders in great loops often above sea level for 35 miles across the Somerset Levels. As soon as it gets too full, it floods into the low-lying pastures of the Levels. To prevent the water in the newly canalised stretch of river at Bradford Abbas from rushing down and flooding other farmers' fields further down the Yeo or in the Parrett, the Water Authority has had to build two walls projecting out from the banks into the river at the end of the 'improved' section. When the water comes rushing down, these walls retard the flow by creating floods over fifty acres of farmland to a depth of up to three feet. So the scheme has not eliminated flooding; indeed it has increased the area over which flooding occurs and its depth. The difference is that the new floodwater is supposed to drain away more quickly. To eliminate the need for flood barriers such as these and to enable many more canalisation and pump drainage schemes to be carried out, the Water Authority has drawn up plans for the installation of a tidal barrage in the Parrett near Bridgwater at a cost of £13 million. This scheme threatens to make north Dorset and half of Somerset unrecognisable by the end of the century.

Quite apart from environmental considerations investment in schemes like those at Bradford and Stockmoor is a dubious investment for a hard-up country like Britain. No real examination of the costs and benefits of drainage in the Somerset Levels has ever been attempted. But just such an inquiry was launched in Sussex in 1978. This happened when a Sussex wetland, Amberley Wildbrooks, became the site of the only water-authority pump drainage scheme ever to be the subject of a public inquiry. And the outcome posed a real challenge to the assumptions behind all such schemes.

Amberley Wildbrooks: costs and benefits examined

Amberley Wildbrooks are a 1,000 acre miniature version of the Somerset Levels. The Wildbrooks are the centrepiece of a sliver of land running between Pulborough and Arundel that is one of the few surviving reminders in the area of the pre-war rural landscape. Walled in by the South Downs and the river Arun, which snakes its way in great loops southwards to the sea, the area consists of wide, peaceful, dyke-drained grazing pastures best seen under a gentle spring rain on foot or by bicycle: the pastel-green meadows belong to lapwings and kingcups, redshanks and ragged robin, cattle and horses and an endless variety of grasses of all kinds of hue and texture, checkered with the occasional stretch of reed-bed or tangled, swampy woodland.

The Wildbrooks themselves were probably a lake in medieval times and now consist of rich alluvial grazing pasture for dairy cattle. They are criss-crossed by a fine network of watercourses in the south. In the north, swampy woodland grows on the only remaining natural peat bog in south-east England outside the New Forest. The brooks are one of the key wildfowl haunts of bird-watchers in southern England and they are also a lovely place for a stroll. Thick with dragon-flies, grasshoppers, butterflies and snails as well as the flowers and birds, the Wildbrooks are dominated at their southern end by the half-ruined, battlemented walls of Amberley Castle which rise sheer from the flat meadows on a little cliff.

In 1977 the Southern Water Authority, at the request of local farmers, asked the Ministry of Agriculture for a grant to install a £340,000 system of electrically-powered pumps which would lower the water-table throughout the Wildbrooks and reduce the frequency of winter flooding. This would have enabled farmers to go over to intensive dairying and arable production instead of using the land merely as summer grazing for dairy cattle. It would also have meant that the character of the area would have been completely transformed, as trees and copses were felled, dykes filled in and the rough, natural pastures ploughed up and reseeded with a single species of more nutritious grass or with barley. Far more fertilisers and pesticides would have been used, and these would have had a very damaging effect on the plant and animal life of the dykes.

The villagers of Amberley, who have always considered the Wildbrooks an integral part of the village, were shocked by the proposal. They no longer depend on the Wildbrooks as they once did for reeds to make baskets and to thatch roofs, for cranberries for food and peat for fuel. But local people still use the Wildbrooks for a host of activities that matter to them: bird-watching, tadpoling, or an evening stroll, for example. The villagers spearheaded a campaign to get John Silkin, the then Minister of Agriculture, to hold a public inquiry into the scheme. Mr Silkin agreed, and appointed an inspector from the Department of the Environment to examine the Southern Water Authority's plans and to advise him on whether the £245,000 Ministry grant for which the Water Authority would have been eligible should be paid. At the inquiry, in March 1978, the Amberley Society was able to demonstrate that the Wildbrooks are a well-used, well-loved amenity not only for local people but for many others from beyond the vicinity. Fourteen bird-watching societies, for example, had visited the Wildbrooks forty-three times during the three years before the inquiry, said the society. Contributions to help the Amberley Society fight the drainage scheme had come from places as far afield as Hong Kong, Central America, New Zealand and Germany, as well as all over Britain. The West Sussex County Council, the Nature Conservancy Council, the Royal Society for the Protection of Birds and the Council for the Protection of Rural England also energetically opposed the Water Authority's plans, arguing that the Wildbrooks were of special scenic and wildlife importance.

Mr Silkin's inspector recommended that the grant should be refused, partly because the scheme had not been shown to be cost-effective and partly because of the impact the lowering of the water table would have on the natural history of the Wildbrooks. The inspector ruled out the compromise solution the Southern Water Authority had put forward after their original plan to pump-drain the whole of the Wildbrooks had run into opposition. Under this plan, 800 acres would have been drained, but 200 acres, consisting mainly of swampy woodland in the north, would have been left undrained as a 'conservation zone'. The inspector pointed out that important plant and animal habitats occurred across the whole site and not just in this 200 acres; and such an area would have been too small to support the populations of wintering wildfowl for which the Wildbrooks were particularly important. The Water Authority was criticised for failing to take conservation considerations into account adequately when drawing up its plans. In July 1978 Mr Silkin refused the grant.

The method by which the Southern Water Authority carried out their cost-benefit analysis for the Amberley Wildbrooks pump-drainage scheme, which is the same as that used for all pump-drainage schemes, came in for heavy criticism at the inquiry. It was shown by John Bowers, a lecturer in economics at Leeds University and the expert witness called by the Council for the Protection of Rural England, to be defective in three main respects. First, the Water Authority had not examined alternative, cheaper means of achieving increases in productivity – for instance, by providing better technical advice to farmers or by reorganising farm holdings. (Oddly sized patches of independently owned land are a major obstacle to improvement programmes.) Second, the Water Authority had examined only the private, not the social benefits of the scheme. 'Where society foots the bill it is the returns to society that matter', said Mr Bowers. 'It is therefore vital to distinguish social costs and benefits from the private costs and benefits of individuals.' Because most EEC farm produce has to be subsidised by both consumer and taxpayer, the value to society of agricultural improvement only becomes clear when these subsidies are deducted. The Water Authority had calculated the financial benefits from drainage by interviewing farmers on the Wildbrooks to determine their existing practices, to find out what changes they would make if drainage were carried out and to estimate the extra profits. But the Authority failed to adjust their figures to reflect the workings of the Common Agricultural Policy. Once Mr Bowers did this, the social benefit of the project was found to fall short of the costs of the drainage project by £46,000. So quite apart from the amenity and conservation costs of the project, the project failed its cost-benefit test. Mr Bowers' third objection was that the Water Authority totally ignored the costs that would have been incurred. 'At the local level the beneficiaries of drainage are a very few farmers and at a very optimistic assessment one or two farm workers. Two-thirds of the benefits accrue to just three farms. The costs fall on an entirely separate group, prominent among whom are Amberley residents.'

The inspector said he considered that the Water Authority's asessment had been based on too many assumptions, and that the calculations submitted on behalf of the objectors were more authoritative and realistic; therefore he preferred the latter. Mr Silkin agreed that the probable agricultural benefit of the scheme in relation to its cost was questionable.

The unlearned lesson

Since the Amberley inquiry, the Ministry of Agriculture has amended its guidelines to water authorities on the assessment of drainage schemes only marginally. Authorities are now expected to include on the debit side of the equation the capital costs to farmers changing the form of their holdings, or the type of farming carried out, for instance a switch from dairying to potato growing. But the Ministry has not changed the approach to accommodate the basic criticisms made at Amberley. On the issue of deductions from benefit estimates to reflect agricultural subsidies, the Ministry says that it is impossible to take this into account in individual cases. Mr Bowers did, however, and it can certainly be argued that an estimate, however rough, would be more useful than the pretence that this factor does not exist. If, on top of this factor, a modest price was put on the value to the community of the landscape and wildlife that is being destroyed, there is little doubt that the cost to the community (as opposed to the lucky farmers) of the drainage schemes currently going ahead in the Somerset Levels and elsewhere would outweigh the benefits by a substantial margin.

Nonetheless, the schemes go on, sparing not even the most valuable corners of our countryside.

West Sedgemoor is a 130-acre finger-shaped level five miles long, seven miles east of Taunton. Not all the remaining 17,500 acres of the Somerset Levels that have not yet been pump-drained are identical in their wildlife value. A high water-table and uneven fields combine to make West Sedgemoor one of the most important wildlife sites on the whole of the Levels, providing a refuge for 80 per cent of the wildlife species of the whole of the Levels. So important was this place as a haven for creatures increasingly being driven out of other Levels by land drainage that the Nature Conservancy Council considered it a 'prime area' for nature conservation.

In 1978 two farmers applied to the Ministry of Agriculture for grants to help finance the installation of their own private pump-drainage scheme to lower the water-table over forty-four acres of West Sedgemoor, about a third of the level. The Nature Conservancy Council pleaded with the Ministry to withhold aid in this particular instance. Fearing that grant would nonetheless be given, the Royal Society for the Protection of Birds asked the farmers concerned to sell them the land they intended to drain. But the farmers refused. And in 1979 Jerry Wiggin, Parliamentary Secretary at the Ministry of Agriculture, approved the farmers' application for grant. 'If the Ministry of Agriculture is prepared to sanction the drainage of the best site in the richest part of the remaining levels, what hope is there for the rest?' asked the Nature Conservancy Council in a statement. The answer seems to be that there is very little hope indeed.

Conclusion to Part Two

The erosion of these seven landscape features is changing the balance of the English landscape insidiously but drastically. In place of the varied intimacy of our traditional patchwork quilt of fields, hedges and woods, a new uniformity is emerging. The kind of countryside we are getting is the kind in which the people of Kansas or the Central Asian steppes live without complaint. But those people were never blessed with the good fortune to experience the rural glory of our demi-paradise. And those of their number who visit our countryside and see what is happening sometimes find it hard to understand why one of the world's unique treasures is being yielded up so easily.

PART THREE

Toothless Watchdogs

Britain's world-famous town and country planning system is widely considered the most sophisticated and effective mechanism in the world for curbing the inherent tendency of powerful private interests to override public interest in land. So what has it been doing to safeguard our landscape heritage from the systematic onslaught launched by modern agriculture on the English landscape?

The answer is almost nothing. The planning system does not attempt to reconcile the different priorities of food production and landscape or wildlife conservation in cases where the two interests conflict.

For farming and commercial forestry happen to be the two industries uniquely privileged by exemption from the controls imposed on the rest of society through the town and country planning system. They are effectively above the law as it applies to other activities which affect the environment. As some compensation for this hole in the planning apparatus, we have a scheme for the designation of certain areas as being of special landscape importance. Although such a scheme could never have protected the countryside completely from something on the scale of the present agricultural revolution, the most important form of designation – national park status – could have been of some value. In fact, however, our national parks are at present contributing even less than they might to the struggle against agricultural change. For most of them are geared up to fight the wrong battles in the wrong places.

Farming and Forestry – Above the Law

The system of planning permission introduced by Clement Attlee in the 1947 Town and Country Planning Act is still the basis of our planning system and the central means whereby ordinary people are able to influence the shaping of their environment.

This system reflects the long tradition in English land law that possession of freehold does not confer absolute ownership of land. All land in England is owned by the Crown: freehold is merely a form of tenure which happens to confer a particularly wide range of rights over the land held. Other rights have always existed alongside those of the freeholder, like common land rights (which may include a right to pasture animals or collect wood), the right to fish, the right to quarry minerals, or the right of passage across private land (public footpath rights). In the United States, in contrast, absolute ownership of land does exist. There is no network of public rights of way across private land, a much cruder and less effective planning system and heavy reliance on acquisition as the only available means of asserting the public interest in land. Ever since our 1947 Town and Country Planning Act was passed, the right to develop land has been vested in the state. This means that anybody who wishes to make the changes in land use defined as 'development' – even on land over which he possesses the freehold – has first to apply to his democratically elected local planning authority for permission to go ahead. The definition of 'development' is wide-ranging: it embraces 'the carrying out of building, engineering or mining operations in, on, over, or under land or the making of any material change in the use of any building or other land'. But although this covers the erection of a new porch on a suburban semi, it leaves out the whole vast area of farming and forestry operations.

The present position is, then, that if somebody wishes to divide his house into two flats, build or extend a factory, convert his house to an office, convert his hotel to a factory, his sweet shop or supermarket to a garage, put up an advertisement hoarding or let out his field as a caravan or camping site for more than twenty-eight days of the year, to take typical examples of activities that are 'development', he has first to convince representatives of the local community that his proposal will not unduly disadvantage other people. Planning authorities have to publicise all the planning applications they receive and details of every application are freely available for inspection by members of the public so that they may, if they wish, make their views known to their local authority before a decision is reached. If a local council refuses planning permission or makes permission conditional, the applicant can appeal to the Secretary of State for the Environment, who may hold an inquiry into the situation and, if he wishes, overrule the local authority. If a landowner has a planning application rejected or is granted only conditional approval he can sometimes force the local authority to buy the land. He has only to be able to show that the land has become incapable of reasonably beneficial use in its existing state to be entitled to serve a purchase notice on the authority. If the authority refuses to comply, he can again appeal to the Secretary of State.

This system is designed to allow people the freedom to do what they want with the land they 'own' unless their plans are materially harmful to the rest of the community. But in practice the system gives the interests of people other than the freeholder far less of a hearing in the countryside. A farmer may convert rough moor, heath or down to wheat prairie, clear away hedgerows and trees, put streams underground, and drain and enclose marshes without even notifying, let alone seeking the views of, the rest of the community. Yet other people's interest in such uncultivated marginal land may involve anything from wildlife, history, archaeology or landscape to recreation. Even building operations for farming are given special exemption: farmers and foresters have to apply for planning permission to put up only very large buildings, that is, those with a ground floor area of more than 5,000 square feet.

Why farmers are above the law

Farming was exempted from planning control in 1947 because it hardly occurred to anybody to include it. At the time, planners and conservationists saw agriculture as something that needed to be protected rather than as a potentially destructive force. Before the war, enormous quantities of good agricultural land had been buried under bricks and mortar. The built-up area of London, for instance, quadrupled during the first forty years of this century. And less fertile land was being left uncultivated because it couldn't yield an adequate return. During the 1930s, conservationists regarded farming as the ailing guardian of the landscape and were anxious to see it reinforced. Vaughan Cornish, a leading member of the Council for the Preservation of Rural England, was typical of conservationists of the 1930s and 1940s. He considered agriculture 'the least changing of industrial pursuits' and said that 'the unspoilt parts of agricultural Britain have a beauty which is unique in the history of civilisation'.[1] Cornish, like his fellow conservationists in the CPRE, believed farming could pose no threat to the beauty of the English scene: farming conserved the landscape; threats came from those activities the CPRE wanted controlled – ribbon housing development, mineral excavation, the building of factories, offices and seaside bungalows and the erection of unsightly advertisement hoardings. Wartime ploughing had changed some landscapes dramatically, including the Downs of East Sussex and Wiltshire. But these changes were seen then as local and temporary. And in such a climate, the failure to provide for control of farmers' activities in the countryside seemed quite unremarkable.

Even if agriculture had been considered a serious threat to the beauty of the countryside, efforts to subject it to planning control would probably have been overruled: a nation which had experienced the U-boat campaign in the Western Approaches would not have been anxious to see its legislators obstructing domestic food production.

But of course, things are no longer as they were in 1947. Since then it has become increasingly clear that modern farming practices do threaten many of our best-loved landscapes. As a result, the countryside conservation movement has started to press for some check on what farmers do. A system of advance notification of agricultural change has been proposed, for example.[2] Under this scheme farmers would have to inform their local planning authorities before removing important landscape features. The authority would then have the opportunity of asking the farmers to desist, and of trying to secure agreements whereby farmers would drop destructive plans in return for compensation. This, and other similar moves, have, however, got nowhere. Although the justifications for the immunity of farmers have disappeared, no steps to change things are being taken.

One reason is that our urban-based society feels it does not understand the countryside. We tend to believe that the people who are best equipped to decide what goes on there are the farmers who run it. Farmers benefit from a prejudice built into England's cultural tradition which insists that the countryside breeds more wholesome people than the towns and that, therefore, farmers are the best custodians of the countryside we could possibly wish for. This idea is fostered by everything from breakfast cereal commercials and children's books to radio and television series like 'The Archers' or Angela Rippon's 'In the Country'. Gerald Wibberley, the Ernest Cook Professor of Countryside Planning at the University of London, explains the background to this attitude.

> The uncritical belief that human character fashioned by rural, and particularly by agricultural, experience was somehow vital to the development of a healthy nation, was fostered in the rapidly growing industrial climate of nine-teenth-century Britain. So much of the literature of the time bewails the passing of rural Arcadia and its replacement by the dark satanic mills and hateful conditions of the industrial city.[3]

It is not only that many of us believe that the countryside tends to nurture a superior kind of person, however: farmers do actually embody qualities many people admire. Apart from the inherent worthiness of food production as an activity, farmes do 'real work'. They are sturdy yeomen who are their own boss and they do not go on strike.

In fact, of course, agriculture is now as much of an industry as manufacturing, involving cash-flow calculations,the use of machines rather than men – and massive subsidy from the taxpayer. But people are still reluctant to accept this. The National Farmers' Union in particular constantly exploits the arcadian mystique in which agriculture is bathed. After all, it is true that farming created what is arguably the loveliest landscape our planet has ever seen. In its main statement on agriculture and conservation, *New Agricultural Landscapes*, published in 1975, the Union declared:

> The farmer, being totally dependent for his livelihood upon the environment, is more closely concerned than anyone else with the well-being of the land which he farms. ... There is no reason to suppose that the efficient development of agricultural activity leads to a decline in landscape quality, indeed it can be reasonably contended that just the opposite is the case. ... The best guarantee of a continuing attractive rural landscape, in all the rich diversity in which it exists in England and Wales, is a stable, buoyant and productive agriculture, cooperating willingly with the rest of society in perpetuating the best features of our rural countryside. ...

If this last argument held good then we might expect East Anglia, which is the most prosperous agricultural part of England, to be the most beautiful. Its prairie-style landscapes do not, however, embody what most people would consider the typical charms of rural England. The NFU behaves as if those who dispute the right of farmers to decide the fate of the countryside can be dismissed as ignorant and naïve. It implies that these people, coming from towns, lack understanding of the mysterious intricacies of farming. What they seek to preserve is a temporary fashion in landscape. The kind of argument in which the NFU delights is this one, taken from a *Farmers' Weekly* leading article in 1978: 'Landscapes will change as they have done to meet the needs of succeeding generations. And future conservationists will inherit something new and interesting to protect.'

It was the introduction of the annual review of farm prices in 1945 that made possible the rise of what is now one of England's most influential pressure groups: the National Farmers' Union. Founded in 1908 to meet the threat of unionisation among farmworkers, it was, before the war, relatively small and insignificant. Now, with a staff of three hundred, the NFU is part of the constitution of rural England. In terms of resources, it towers over the pressure groups that oppose it.

Under the 1947 Act, the Ministry is required to consult the representatives of the farmers before fixing prices, and the final settlement has to be broadly acceptable to both parties. Throughout the year the Ministry is engaged in detailed negotiation with the NFU, which represents about 80 per cent of English farmers. Since 1973, when prices for most farm products have been fixed in Brussels, these discussions have become little more than fact-finding exercises. But over the years,the NFU has taken advantage of its negotiations with Whitehall to build up a close relationship with the Ministry which now goes far beyond the price review. The Union now has a hand in almost every step the Ministry takes. Fortunately for the NFU, the Ministry of Agriculture has more freedom than the majority of government departments and government agencies in the way it operates because it has relatively little legislation on which to base its work. What it has is mostly old. The Ministry's powers to provide grants for drainage, for example, have survived virtually unaltered since 1930, when they were widely framed. This situation has enabled a lot of policy-making to go on beyond the public gaze and without too much public accountability. Furthermore, the Ministry of Agriculture has remained separate from the Department of Trade and Industry and the Minister himself has invariably been given a seat in the Cabinet. The Ministry is a large one with about 13,600 employees in local and regional offices as well as in Whitehall. Thus although farmers and farmworkers together make up only one per cent of the population of the UK, on average one civil servant looks after the needs of every 21 farmers. Entry into Europe does not seem to have diminished the NFU's power: its Brussels office keeps a close eye on EEC activities affecting farming; Sir Henry Plumb, who was president of the Union between 1970 and 1979, is chairman of the agricultural committee of the European Parliament.

Publicity is one of the NFU's particular strengths. In 1975, it issued 162 national press notices, held 12 major press conferences, sent out 800 press releases to local newspapers and placed 200 special articles.[4] But its real successes lie in the extent to which it has infiltrated the media that handle this prodigious outflow. The NFU has a nationwide network of seven Regional Information Officers, each one a trained and experienced journalist sent into his region to ensure that NFU views are properly put across. Fair enough. But in some regions, the NFU man has a considerable advantage over the representatives of other pressure groups. He does not have to put his views to a local radio or television journalist: he prepares or presents the programme itself. In an article in its journal *Landworker*,[5] the National Union of Agricultural and Allied Workers reported that NFU officers were preparing or presenting several different local radio and regional television farming programmes in 1979. It is easy to see how resource-starved minority progamme departments may be tempted to turn to readily available sources of specialised expertise, even if these sources are committed to a sectional interest. The same kind of thing happens elsewhere along the uneasy interface between public relations and journalism. But the apparent success of the NFU in this field demonstrates that the organisation and effort that go into promoting the farmers' cause have results far beyond anything achieved by other interests operating in the countryside.

Meanwhile, farmers match their grip on the media with active involvement in politics. The Maud Committee, reporting in 1967, found farming to be the dominant occupation among rural district councillors, accounting for 35 per cent of all rural district council members in England and Wales.[6] Local government reorganisation, in 1974, might have been expected to destroy the dominant position of farmers because it combined the old urban districts, county and non-county boroughs with rural districts. But the only study carried out in this area since reorganisation – covering Suffolk – indicates that there has been only a slight reduction in the numbers of farmers on district councils in Suffolk; they have also retained the key posts in the county council.[7] Sociologists at Essex University estimated in 1978 that the proportion of farmers on Suffolk County Council was 16 per cent, while on the two district councils they studied the proportions were 35 per cent in Mid-Suffolk and 11 per cent in Suffolk Coastal. (In 1971, the last year for which figures are available, farmers comprised just 1.2 per cent of the population of Suffolk.) Farmers enjoyed something approaching a monopoly over key positions on the county council, reported the sociologists: the chairman and vice-chairman of the council were both farmers; so too were the chairmen of the planning and education committees and the leader of the majority Conservative group.

Any pressure group seeking to exploit the pastoral strand

in our cultural tradition could expect a reasonable response. When the group involved is as powerful as the NFU – a giant among pressure groups, comparable in terms of power only to the BMA, the TUC or the CBI – it is easy to see why any attempts to curb what farmers do to our countryside have been kept at bay.

Planning and the countryside

The control of new development through the system of planning permissions is only one of the two pillars of the system of town and country planning set up in 1947. The other is a mosaic of structure plans (originally called development plans) which lay down land-use policies for every square inch of England and Wales. Local planning authorities are required by law to draw up plans indicating the projected size and location of population and economic growth in their areas and zoning areas for different uses – industry, housing, shopping and so on. They also have to set standards for the design of new buildings. Structure planning gives members of the public an opportunity to influence the broad policies shaping the future of their areas. County councils are required by law to publish an outline of their plans in advance, together with the survey data on which their thinking is based, and they are required to encourage people to make representations about these matters and to give them the opportunity to do so. Once the structure plan itself is published, the Secretary of State for the Environment subjects it to a public examination at which private individuals and groups are free to question the thinking behind the plan as well as the actual policies it advances. Finally, the Secretary of State announces which of the local authority's policies are to be modified to take account of the views expressed at the public examination.

Not unreasonably, however, since planning authorities are virtually powerless to control changes on farmland, structure plans say little about the 70 per cent of England's land surface that is farmed, even though many members of the public are expressing concern about the impact on the countryside of the present agricultural revolution. At best, areas of land are allocated in structure plans as places where priority should be accorded to conservation. However, local authorities are powerless to impose this priority in the face of agricultural change, as their only weapon – the planning application process – is not available for use against farmers.

There are just a handful of minor constraints available to local planning authorities seeking to curb farmers' plans to transform the rural landscape. Unlike the imposition of planning controls over building, however, these measures require authorities taking advantage of them to pay out large sums in compensation for profit foregone because improvements are blacked. Mainly because of the compensation requirement, these powers are little used.

The 1947 Town and Country Planning Act nationalised development rights in undeveloped land – but not other rights. As a result, freeholders own only the existing use rights of their land. So if a local authority refuses an industrialist or householder planning permission for development which would have increased the value of his property, it does not have to pay him compensation. Nor does he have to pay a betterment levy if his land gains in value through a planning decision. Both compensation and betterment were dropped from our planning system in its early days since it proved impossible to administer either fairly. But when they were part of planning practice, compensation and betterment went hand in hand.

Where agriculture is concerned, however, such planning as exists follows neither the old model nor the existing arrangements in built-up areas. At present local planning authorities may impose three minor constraints over farmers' activities. In all three cases, they have to pay the farmer compensation for lost profit or increase in land value; but betterment is not collected from the farmer who is released from these constraints. On the contrary, the taxpayer provides the farmer with a grant to help him help himself. So while the community subsidises the destruction of the countryside, it takes hardly any share of the increase in profits and land values that its subsidies make possible (since farmers pay less income tax than other people and no rates). Should it seek to persuade a farmer to refrain from making changes, for instance from changing the use of his land from woodland to farmland, or from rough downland over which the public have *de facto* access rights to intensive cropland with no access, it has to give him still more cash.

Of the three modest constraints available, the most widely used is the tree preservation order. Local planning authorities

can control the felling of trees and woods if they consider
their removal would have a significant impact on the environment and its enjoyment by the public. But in practice, very
few tree preservation orders are used to protect woods from
agricultural change. Although most trees and woodlands lie
in the countryside, the vast majority of orders have been
made over single trees or groups of trees in towns. The cost of
compensation is not the only reason why rural local authorities have fought shy of the tree preservation order. As significant a deterrent is the complicated administrative procedure
that has to be gone through. Simply to make a tree preservation order, a local council has to advertise a draft order and
a plan of the area concerned. If objections are lodged, a public
inquiry may be held and the Department of the Environment
may decide against the local authority. But if this does not
happen, and an order is made, the planning authority's consent will have to be sought before felling can take place.
When a landowner seeks permission to clear a wood covered
by an order, the council can refuse him permission. But he
can then claim compensation from it in respect of 'disaf-
fection' – which includes the loss of revenue from, say, growing
barley on the land after felling and not merely the losses
accruing from unsold timber. In Somerset, where the County
Council has made more orders to protect woodlands threatened with clearance for agriculture than most authorities,
council officials consider eighteen months is the minimum
period it is safe to allow for the compensation wrangles that
almost always follow refusal of permission to clear. However,
if a landowner clears trees in defiance of a tree preservation
order, the fine he will incur is paltry; and when he has paid it,
planning authorities have no power to force him to replant
the wood. To make matters even worse, planning authorities
cannot apply tree preservation orders at all to the 20,000
acres of woodland scattered through England which are subject to 'dedication' schemes, under which the Forestry Commission agrees to pay the landowners for managing their
woods under plans the Commission has approved. When all
these factors are considered, it is easy to see why so few tree
preservation orders have been made in the countryside.

The second minor constraint on farmers' freedom involves
farm buildings. However, here too farmers' freedom to transform the countryside is enormous. Whereas a householder

needs planning permission before he can put up a garage, a farmer can put up any building without needing to apply for planning permission so long as the building is no more than 5,000 square feet in ground floor area nor more than 40 feet in height, at least 100 yards from another building and 80 feet from a metalled road. Five thousand square feet is equivalent to the size of a netball court or two and a half tennis courts. In that area a farmer can cram four or five tower silos (they are specially designed to reach a height of 39½ feet). In theory a farmer can in any one year cover all his land with large buildings, each one up to 5,000 square feet, so long as he spaces them 100 yards apart. He can pack them even more closely together without the need to submit a planning application, but in this case he has to wait two years between putting up one building and another close to it.

Planning authorities do have the power to require farmers to seek permission for the erection of buildings of less than 5,000 square feet by exercising powers vested in them under Article 4 of the Town and Country Planning General Development Order 1977. But these 'Article 4 Directions' have to be approved by the Secretary of State for the Environment before they can come into force. And if a planning authority refuses permission for a farm building covered by a Direction, or grants it subject to conditions, the farmer can claim compensation.[8] The Article 4 Direction, bringing under control (at a price) buildings that would automatically be under control (free of compensation) if they were used by any industry other than farming and forestry, is, like the tree preservation order, little used mainly because of the cost of compensation. In the first six months of 1979, for example, only two Directions were made in the whole of England, one covering ten acres, the other four acres, both in the Breckland District of Suffolk.

The third planning constraint on agricultural change arises from the only amendment ever made to our town and country planning system deliberately designed to control the impact of the post-war agricultural revolution on the countryside. It is a requirement that farmers responsible for open moorland in certain limited areas of national parks should give their planning authority six months' notice before they plough up rough moorland or 'improve' it in some other way. Despite fierce protests from the National Farmers' Union, Section 14 of the Countryside Act 1968 empowered the

Secretary of State for the Environment to impose an order over areas of moorland in national parks. Farmers seeking to 'improve' moorland in park land covered by an order must first notify their national park authority. In spite of the extreme tentativeness with which these orders have been used, all they do is to provide the authorities involved with six months in which to try to prevent the proposed 'improvement' if they wish to do so. The authorities have no power to impose a moorland preservation order, so any attempts to prevent reclamation have to depend on persuasion, and the future of the area of moorland at issue still rests in the landowner's hands. If the planning authority does manage to dissuade him from ploughing, it is the landowner, not the planning authority, that is in the position to name terms.

Three courses of action are open to national park authorities learning of plans to improve moorland which they see as conflicting with the interests of the community as a whole, whether under the few Section 14 orders that have been made or through voluntary notification schemes that exist over parts of Exmoor and the North York Moors National Parks. First, they can attempt to persuade the Ministry of Agriculture to withhold grants for the improvements; second, they can seek a special agreement with the landowner requiring him to undertake not to improve in return for compensation; third, they can seek to persuade the owner to sell them the land. (These courses of action are, of course, also open to local planning authorities responsible for any area of countryside which object to plans to reclaim uncultivated land. The examples of agreements I mention below occur in national parks not because agricultural change is doing more damage to the countryside inside national parks than it is outside – the reverse is true – but because national park authorities have always been provided with much more money for conservation and recreation provision than other countryside planning authorities and because national park authorities are usually in a better position than other planning authorities to hear about land 'reclamation' schemes before they go ahead.)

The first option – persuading the Ministry of Agriculture to withhold grant – is, of course, not in itself sufficient to prevent improvement taking place. The owner can go ahead at his own expense. But in any case persuading the Ministry to withhold grant is almost impossible, however strong the conservation case may be. A planning authority has persuaded the Ministry to withhold a grant probably on only one occasion: the authority was the North York Moors National Park Authority, which persuaded the Ministry to withhold grant for the improvement of thirty acres of Lockton Moor, which forms part of the moorland backbone of the Park and is very popular with visitors. In 1977, the tenant applied to the Ministry of Agriculture for grant to help finance the reclamation of thirty acres in the centre for the moor. The previous owner had made an agreement with the park authority not to plough this area. When the National Park Authority heard of the application for grant, it asked the Ministry of Agriculture to withhold the money, and the Ministry agreed.

The second available means of preventing the reclamation of marginal land is the negotiation of an agreement with the landowner. Local planning authorities have general powers to enter into agreements with landowners or tenants in order to restrict or regulate the development or use of the land either permanently or during a period prescribed by the agreement.[9] When this involves the restrictions of agricultural improvement, financial compensation is normally provided. Two kinds of problem tend to arise, however. There are cases in which a farmer enters an agreement secure in the knowledge that he never had any intention of carrying out the improvement for which he is being compensated. He knows he can terminate or renegotiate the agreement at any time; meanwhile he is getting money for nothing. Other farmers who are genuinely being fettered may exact a premium price for their consent. The planning authority, dependent on agreement, can only pay up or give up. As farmers usually demand that the payments be indexed, the planning authority that enters into such agreements commits itself to unknown sums of money. But the agreements do not usually guarantee conservation for anything more than a year: the owner is free to terminate or renegotiate the agreement, which in any case lapses with a change of ownership.

The recent experience of the Exmoor National Park Committee in seeking to safeguard heather and grass moorland against agricultural improvement – measures which would destroy the sense of wilderness which distinguishes the park – has highlighted the scale of costs that public bodies have to incur if they wish to conserve uncultivated land against agricultural change.

The advance notification procedure for moorland ploughing led to the conclusion of a management agreement over a
spectacular stretch of the heart of Exmoor, the Glenthorne
Estate, in 1979. The owner has agreed to leave 150 acres of
moorland unploughed and to re-route the part of the South-
West Peninsula long-distance footpath that runs across his
land through a more attractive part of it. In return for his
agreement not to plough, an operation that would have enabled
him to expand his flock of sheep, the Park Committee is
paying him £3,000 every year. The amount will undoubtedly
rise in 1984 when the agreement is reviewed, and every three
years after that. But even if the park authority can afford to go
on paying out the necessary amount of money, the agreement
will not necessarily mean that the moorland is conserved for
all time: either side is free to terminate the agreement at any
time. Forty thousand acres of moorland in the heart of
Exmoor have been designated by the park authority as a
'critical amenity area'; the authority feels that if this moorland is fragmented through conversion to intensive farmland
the whole point of designating Exmoor a national park will
have been removed. Yet to conserve this area through
management agreements like the one just concluded at Glenthorne would require compensation payments of £840,000
every year, adjustable upwards with inflation. Exmoor
National Park Committee's budget for 1978–79, including
the payment of staff as well as the cost of landscape conservation measures, was less than half this amount. So management agreements are not going to protect this national park
or any other substantial tract of open country threatened by
agricultural change.

The only other course of action open to local authorities
anxious to prevent agricultural change they oppose is to buy
the land in question – if the owner is willing to sell. While the
cost of this approach is of course even more fearsome at first
glance than those of management agreements, at least it does
not involve local authorities in writing blank cheques. One of
the few cases of purchase for conservation arose in 1974 when
the North York Moors National Park Authority learned of
plans to plough up 1,800 acres of Levisham Moor. This is a
high, wild piece of moorland crowned by ancient earthworks
in the southern part of the park that is visible for miles around
and enjoys splendid views over other parts of the park:

summer Sundays usually see well over two hundred cars parked at the main viewpoint. By 1974, Levisham Moor had become almost completely encircled by arable and ryegrass fields and the park authority was very anxious to preserve one of these last remaining stretches of open access land in the southern part of the park and one that is easily reached by people without cars (through the North York Moors railway) as well as by motorists. But their attempts to enter into a no-ploughing agreement with the Moor's owners fell down, and they were faced with acquisition of the whole 2,100-acre estate at a cost of £80,000 as the only means of saving the Moor. Since 1976, when it bought the estate, the park authority has never had enough money to buy any other stretches of moorland to prevent ploughing.

The Nature Conservancy Council, the government agency charged with safeguarding the interests of science in land use, has no more powers than a local authority to control the main force for change in the countryside – agriculture. As a result, even those sites it considers of special scientific interest are being destroyed. So far 3,535 areas in Great Britain covering 5.3 per cent of the total land area have been specially selected and designated by the Nature Conservancy Council as Sites of Special Scientific Interest. Most SSSIs embrace the best remaining examples of particular wildlife habitats; others provide a home for rare animals and plants, while others contain interesting geological or physiographical features. Unfortunately, however, this designation, introduced in 1949, affords the areas concerned protection only against development. As a result, many of these sites are altered or even completely destroyed by farming and forestry activities every year. A survey in 1977 of the outcome of threats to SSSIs on the Isle of Wight, for example, showed that 90 per cent of proposed agricultural improvements to SSSIs actually took place, compared with 29 per cent of development proposals. The types of SSSI destroyed through agricultural improvement were chalk grassland, chalk heathland and meadowland. The author of the report, Jennifer Tubbs of the Nature Conservancy Council, says: 'Grasslands are exceptionally vulnerable because there is no forum in which to pursue an objection to reclamation if the owner rejects conservation arguments.'[10]

At the moment, the Nature Conservancy Council has to

rely on persuasion to conserve Sites of Special Scientific Interest. Section 15 of the Countryside Act 1968 enables it to make agreements with landowners under which the owners agree to refrain from carrying out certain operations on the SSSIs, usually in return for compensation. No powers of compulsion exist. The Section 15 agreements are not binding on the land, only on the owner with whom they are made. Thus in Wiltshire – a county in which Mrs Tubbs discovered that five SSSIs had been destroyed since 1951, 33 damaged and a further ten threatened, all by agricultural reclamation or forestry operations – a new owner has recently refused to accept the agreement signed by his predecessor and has ploughed up the meadow grassland SSSI in question. Farmers do not even bother to tell the Conservancy their plans for their SSSIs: a letter sent to all SSSI owners and tenants in Wiltshire in 1975 asking what their intentions were on future management elicited replies from only 2 per cent. Without any effective means of stopping undesirable changes, the Nature Conservancy Council is virtually powerless to control the erosion of these important reservoirs of plant and animal life.

So the Conservancy, like local planning authorities, has to rely on land purchase if it wants to make absolutely sure that any site threatened with agricultural change is conserved. And as such changes as the conversion of woodland to farmland or the drainage of marsh are highly profitable, land purchase can involve the Conservancy in extremely large sums of money – like the £1¼ million it had to pay in 1979 to stop the agricultural 'improvement' of 6,000 acres of coastal marshland in the estuary of the river Ribble in Lancashire. The Ribble marshes are one of our few remaining extensive areas of coastal marshland – that is, areas of mudflat and salting lying between high- and low-water mark that are neither totally land nor sea. Coastal marshland used to be a common feature of many parts of our coast, but 'reclamation' of the land for intensive agriculture as well as for factories and power stations has cut the range and number of coastal marshland sites dramatically. These marshes, peopled if at all only by sheep grazing freely, provide as near a wilderness as one can find in many of the areas in which they occur, such as the Thames Estuary, Morecambe Bay or the Wash. But when the Conservancy Council heard of plans to drain the Ribble marshes it was the potential impact on wading birds that gave the Council most cause for concern.

In 1978 a Dutchman bought the Ribble marshes with the specific intention of putting a sea-wall round them, draining them and then eventually putting them down to a crop; potatoes, sugar beet and barley are all successfully grown on reclaimed coastal marsh in Norfolk and Lincolnshire, for example. When the new owner refused to give the Conservancy an assurance that no work would be undertaken that would destroy the nature conservation interest of the area, and prepared to convert the marshes to intensive farmland, the Conservancy asked him to let it buy the site (previous offers from the Royal Society for the Protection of Birds had been turned down). When the owner seemed once more unwiling to sell, the Conservancy said it would attempt to make a compulsory purchase order on the site, and under this threat the owner agreed to sell (at a much higher price than that he had paid for the site a year before). With a 1978/79 budget of only £6 million, there is clearly a limit to the number of purchases on this scale that the Conservancy can make.

Purchase of land to stop a particular change of use, when ownership is not really what the conservation interest requires, is therefore an enormously expensive way of using a sledge-hammer to crack a nut – the exact opposite of the flexibly specific planning permission system governing changes to the urban environment. Compensating farmers for refraining from ploughing up moorland in national parks is pretty much as hopeless a financial proposition as it would be to try to prevent speculators from building office blocks in London by paying them not to – a perfectly accurate urban parallel for the Canute-like operation into which planning authorities like the Exmoor National Park Authority as well as the Nature Conservancy Council have been forced.

To make matters even worse, there have been signs that payments by planning authorities to landowners to secure conservation could be undermining traditional attitudes governing landowners' obligations towards the rest of the community. In the past, many landowners seem to have seen the conservation of attractive landscapes and the provision of public access as things which the public were entitled to expect of them as duties incumbent on those privileged to own land. The case of the Roaches in the Peak District demonstrates how attitudes are changing.

Every weekend in the summer large numbers of climbers visit the Roaches near Leek in Staffordshire, one of Europe's finest outcrops of millstone grit. Until 1977, the Roaches were part of the 3,000-acre estate of Sir Philip Brocklehurst, who, in his later years, allowed any number of climbers onto the crags while the general public were allowed to wander at will over the heather moors below – an oasis of moorland tightly pressed in by 'improved' grass farms. Sir Philip used the moor for rearing and shooting grouse while wild deer and even wallabies roamed freely in the heather and bilberries. When the estate was sold, it was split up and two local farmers bought the 1,134 acres lot containing the Roaches for £53 an acre. They promptly fenced in the moor, supplemented the grouse with large numbers of sheep, and put up notices on the rockface announcing 'Rock Climbing Prohibited: Trespassers Could be Prosecuted'. They said they intended to plough and reseed the moor, but eventually told the Peak Park Joint Planning Board that they would be willing to sell them the land instead – if the price was right. The Board finally bought nearly 975 acres of the Roaches late in 1979 for £185,000 (£189 an acre).

Local planning authorities then, including those responsible for national parks, lack the power rather than the inclination to prevent the destruction of uncultivated land. But there are two organisations which do have more direct and easy-to-administer powers to curb undesirable agricultural change: the Ministry of Agriculture and the Forestry Commission. Unfortunately, they have the power, but they lack the inclination.

Although the Ministry of Agriculture's power to withhold grants for improvement schemes on conservation grounds would not always be enough to block the scheme in question, withholding grant would choke off many plans. The problem, as we have seen, is that the Ministry refuses to withhold grant.

Parliament has required that 'in the exercise of their functions relating to land under any enactment every Minister, government department and public body shall have regard to the desirability of conserving the natural beauty and amenity of the countryside' (section 11, Countryside Act 1968). But the Forestry Commission is no more exercised by this

responsibility than the Ministry of Agriculture. No group of
trees amounting to more than 825 cubic feet of timber (about
ten mature oaks or fifty small trees) can be felled in any one
quarter, for any purpose, unless the Forestry Commission
has granted permission. The Commission may refuse felling
licences or grant them subject to conditions not only 'in the
interest of good forestry' but also 'in the interest of the
amenities of the district' (section 10, Forestry Act 1967).
However, out of a total of 1,945 applications for felling licences
in the year ended 31 March 1979, a mere five were refused,
and of these only one was turned down on amenity grounds.
Although the Commission points out that it tries to persuade
the applicant to withdraw or modify his proposals where
these are unacceptable, and that only where these efforts are
unsuccessful does it resort to the refusal of a licence, it is clear
that the felling licence system is not a serious obstacle to
landowners wishing to clear away woodlands that stand in the
path of agricultural 'progress'.

A landowner is entitled to compensation if a felling licence
is refused, but this is not the main reason for the Commission's
inertia. The Commission argues that the felling licence system
does not absolutely prevent the destruction of woodland
because if a landowner is intent on clearing trees over which a
licence has been refused he can clear it progressively by felling
timber up to the 825 cubic feet limit each quarter. The
Commission argues that it is therefore up to local authorities
to preserve woods if this is considered desirable in the interest
of amenity by imposing tree preservation orders. While it is
true that the loophole exists, however, the refusal of a felling
licence would create a sufficient inconvenience to deter some
undesirable woodland clearance. The Commission has never
tried to get the 825 cubic feet upper limit reduced so that it
can regulate felling more closely.

The reluctance to take action to conserve some of the
beauty or wildlife value of the countryside on the part of these
bureaucratic organisations springs from attitudes rooted deep
in the official mind. The presumption remains that the needs
of agriculture must have priority over all other claims on land
use in the countryside, no matter what damage farmers may
cause nor how great the food surpluses created as a result.

11

The Education Experiment

The government agency entrusted with responsibility for the conservation of the countryside and the enhancement of facilities for enjoying it is the Countryside Commission. This body replaced the National Parks Commission in 1968 but was required to deal with the whole of the countryside and not merely the national parks, like its predecessor. The Countryside Commission is the arm of government on which the citizenry could be expected to rely to combat excesses of agricultural change. So what is the Commission doing?

The Countryside Commission certainly recognises the dangers posed by farming and can claim to be doing something about them. 'Education' is the corner-stone of its plan of action. In policy statements in 1977 and 1979[1] it put forward the view that farmers should be persuaded to change their ways through a programme of education in the landscape and wildlife implications of their actions.

This approach to the conflict between agriculture and conservation goes back to the 1950s. As early as 1953 the Council for the Protection of Rural England was pleading with farmers to refrain from ploughing archaeological relics on the South Downs. In both 1954 and 1955 the Council for the Protection of Rural England organised conferences on downland ploughing in an effort to bring together farmers, conservationists and various arms of the government machine. The same problems that are now reaching overwhelming proportions were even then being clearly identified. 'Ruined nature can sometimes be retrieved, but antiquity does not repeat itself, and we would appeal to our friends the farmers . . . to pay heed to some of the other interests concerned when bringing marginal land, such as hitherto uncultivated downland, under the plough. These include ancient monuments, nature conservation, rights of way and so on', pleaded the representative of the Council for British Archaeology. A West Sussex County Council planning officer told the 1954 conference that the ploughing of rough downland in the South Downs was one that had worried his Council for several years and would have been attacked by them earlier if ploughing had been classified as 'development'. He pointed out that the Ministry of Agriculture was giving grants to farmers to plough up the same tracts of rough down that the Nature Conservancy was attempting to conserve as sites of special natural history importance. There was much talk about the need to harness farmers' innate goodwill towards the countryside and to coordinate the Ministry of Agriculture's policy on grants with conservation. Sir Herbert Griffin, who was then Secretary to CPRE, told the conference that the NFU had said its members 'were sympathetic and willing to do anything they could to help prevent damage to archaeological sites and places of scientific interest.'

Since the 1954 conference, farmers in East Sussex have succeeded in converting virtually all the rough downland turf into barley prairie. With the roughland have disappeared hundreds of archaeological remains that had lain undisturbed for centuries. Forty per cent of the 660 most important archaeological sites in rural Sussex were being ploughed up in 1976, including an Iron Age hillfort and the remains of a Romano-British village, for instance.[2] This is just one demonstration of the sad fact that our considerable experience of efforts to educate farmers into a heightened awareness of the value of landscape suggests strongly that this approach by itself is quite inadequate. Countryside conservationists of the 1950s can be forgiven for placing so much faith in education. They were not so aware as we are today of the speed of agricultural change or of the intensity of the financial pressure for the reclamation of uncultivated land. Today, however, the Countryside Commission has no such excuse. Yet nearly thirty years on from the 1954 conference, the slogans are the same.

The Commission's aim, promoted zealously by its Land Management Advisor, Keith Turner, is to 'change permanently the outlook of all in the farming industry'. To this end, the Commission has employed experts to draw up detailed plans showing ways in which agriculture and conservation could be combined on ten 'demonstration farms'; the Commission hopes other farmers will visit these establishments and follow the practices pursued on them. Together with the National Farmers' Union, the Country Landowners' Association, the Ministry of Agriculture, the Forestry Commission and the Nature Conservancy Council, it is also publishing a series of leaflets designed to provide practical advice to farmers wishing to plant trees or conserve natural features. The Commission is also encouraging tree planting by providing grants to landowners, commissioning research and financing the appointment of local authority 'project officers' in certain counties: the Commission is providing these officers with funds which it makes available to landowners seeking to improve landscape and recreation opportunities.

It is certainly true that valuable work is carried out on the education front not only by the Countryside Commission but also by several other organisations. The Farming and Wildlife Advisory Group, for example, set up in 1969 mainly by the NFU and the Royal Society for the Protection of Birds, organises about fifteen one-day events every year in England at which farmers and conservationists are invited to see and discuss plans and proposals drawn up to reconcile conflicts between agriculture on selected farms. The National Farmers' Union helps finance the Association of Agriculture, a primarily educational organisation, although in this case it is school-children who are being told about farming mainly in the hope that they will respect farming and farmers. In 1978 the NFU announced proudly that it had circulated its members with a leaflet entitled *Caring for the Countryside*, which exhorted farmers to retain special features on marginal land, plant trees, dig ponds and take care in the design and siting of new farm buildings.

Showing farmers how to conserve features and explaining to them how failure to conserve them damages the landscape are of course worthy enough objectives. But in the face of the present commercial pressures the Countryside Commission's emphasis on education needs to be backed up by many other, more forthright measures. Reliance on educating farmers alone is inadequate for three reasons. First, education takes a long time, and in the conflict between modern agriculture and conservation, time is not on the side of conservation. Another thirty years of huge economic incentives for the maximisation of food production, coupled with the exclusion of farming operations from our planning machinery, will mean the end of the English landscape. The Countryside Commission admits that its education effort since 1968, when it was set up, has had very little effect in conserving features on the ground so far. It says that its new education campaign will take at least twenty-five to thirty years to change attitudes throughout the farming industry. The problem is that once all this effort has been expended there may be little countryside left to conserve. Certainly the only tracts of countryside with natural features remaining will by that time, on current policies, tend to be those which have been specially bought for conservation or which for reasons of ownership are unlikely to be thwarted by agriculture at all.

The second weakness of the education approach is that in a straight clash between the interests of conservation and farmers' economic interests the latter are bound to prevail unless something more than education is imposed. Keith Turner says many features could be saved by the Ministry of Agriculture's farm advisors 'simply . . . putting in a word or two at critical times of decision – when that old meadow is to be drained . . . when that copse or green lane is threatened with destruction'. But these activities are not indulged in for fun: they bring with them huge financial rewards. What's more, all the other 'education' with which farmers are bombarded – from the advertisements in *Farmers' Weekly* to contacts with salesmen, other farmers and the Ministry of Agriculture's pest control and other advisors – runs directly counter to conservation but happens to chime with farmers' commercial instincts. So educating farmers in conservation is a singularly uphill task. It is an unfortunate fact of life that no form of farming obviously benefits from the retention of rough land.

The third major weakness of 'education' as a means of protecting the countryside is that it has to assume that farmers are somehow worthier, more altruistic beings than the rest of us. The Countryside Commission wants farmers to have the freedom to decide where and when the activities they wish to carry out for economic reasons should be modified or abandoned in the interests of the rest of the community. But no one would place the same burden of responsibility on those in charge of road-building, quarrying or nuclear power station construction. Why should agriculture be a special case?

The answer is mainly tactical. No technical problems stand in the way of planning safeguards to embrace farming. It is the power of the farming lobby that leads the Commission and others to conclude that Parliament would never extend planning controls to agriculture. So the fate of the countryside will always remain in farmers' hands, it is argued. And this means conservationists' main objective must be to avoid upsetting farmers, for fear they might withdraw the few concessions they have made.

Recognition of the status quo is reflected in the first piece of countryside legislation of the 1980s. The Thatcher Government's Wildlife and Countryside Bill would leave the encroachment of agriculture and forestry on the landscape uninterrupted.[3] The Bill is expected to extend the consultation period within which management agreements to conserve moorland in national parks can be made; and to require the farmers responsible for about 2 per cent[4] of our Sites of Special Scientific Interest to give advance notification of any plans to damage their wildlife value. The real issues would remain untouched by the Bill.

What all this means is that our farmers' freedom to shape, use and change 70 per cent of our land surface as they choose is likely to remain unimpeded. While the Countryside Commission is ineffective and the public believes farmers know best, the only changes in the way we administer the countryside that seem likely to take place are those that have the backing of the NFU.

The NFU has been able to remain independent of the main political parties over the last thirty years because of the absence of party political differences on the conflict between agriculture and conservation. In this world of comfortable consensus, the views of civil servants take on a new significance, and, as it happens, those civil servants with most responsibility in the field of conservation and agriculture have recently made their views known.

A group of civil servants set themselves up as the Countryside Review Committee in 1974 and abolished it in 1979 after publishing five papers covering all the main areas of public policy towards the countryside. The names of the members of the Countryside Review Committee were secret, and its activities beyond the public gaze.

The Review Committee paper that dealt most clearly with agricultural change was called *Food Production and the Countryside* and was published in 1978.[5] Its main recommendation was that the role played by the Ministry of Agriculture's local advisors should be widened. Instead of advising farmers only on ways of increasing productivity and profit, as they do at present, these advisors should be trained to advise on conservation too. It is undesirable, argued the CRC, that farmers should receive often conflicting advice on what to do with their land from different arms of government (such as the Nature Conservancy Council and the Ministry of Agriculture). The Committee recommended that advice should be co-ordinated better, and proposed that the Ministry of Agriculture should be the body that synthesised a government attitude since it is well-manned and enjoys the confidence of farmers and landowners. Similar conclusions emerged from the Advisory Committee for Agriculture and Horticulture, a special committee set up in 1973 to advise the Ministry of Agriculture on a range of issues. This committee's report, entitled *Agriculture and the Countryside*, was published in 1978,[6] and accepted in principle in 1979 by the then Minister of Agriculture, John Silkin, who did point out that implementation would have to await the removal of public expenditure constraints. If and when more money becomes available, a widening of the role of the Ministry of Agriculture's local advisors to embrace conservation is likely to be presented as the Government's means of meeting the requirements. The NFU is likely to encourage the Ministry of Agriculture to accept this proposal, since the NFU is bound to see it as a means of heading off demands for much more radical change.

A policy merely widening the knowledge of farmers' advisors while the farmers themselves remain free to behave as before springs naturally enough from the two central assumptions on which the Countryside Review Committee worked. Firstly, in lowland England 'agriculture is *without question* the prime use', it says (my italics). Secondly, it contends that no real conflict between agriculture and conservation exists at all. It says its policies 'would harmonise with the idea of *consensus*, on which great importance was placed in *The Countryside –Problems and Policies*' (the CRC's first paper, my italics again). Any controls over the removal of particular landscape features would be merely negative, says the Committee; so what is needed is 'a positive and creative attitude towards change' and 'a voluntary and flexible policy, based on advice, education and financial inducements'.

An obvious problem with this reliance on education and

persuasion from the Ministry of Agriculture is that this Ministry is virtually bound to accord a lower priority to conservation than to agriculture in almost any circumstances. The Ministry of Agriculture is built around the idea that the countryside exists for the maximisation of food production. It is hard to see how the basic philosophy of a sixty-year-old department can be changed overnight. After all, for some years now, the Ministry has had certain powers – and indeed certain duties – to protect the countryside, and it has hardly lifted a finger in this cause. Under Section 11 of the Countryside Act 1968, the Ministry is required to 'have regard to the desirability of conserving the natural beauty and amenity of the countryside' in the exercise of its functions. But the Ministry has never even carried out a serious study of the impact on the landscape of the agricultural revolution it is helping to fuel. The Ministry has even refused to let the public know the facts about the administration of farm improvement grants, for example. The Ministry's lack of interest in conservation can be sensed in the readiness with which it devolves consideration of the conservation interest to other people and organisations whenever it is forced to take that interest into account to some extent. The Ministry relies completely on the water authorities to examine the impact of their own activities on the landscape when, for example, large-scale land drainage schemes are being planned.

A second difficulty with reliance on officers of the Ministry of Agriculture to sort out conflicts between agriculture and conservation is their lack of accountability. Questions in the House to the Minister of Agriculture are not much of an opportunity for people to influence the fate of a particular hedgerow or stream. If any organisation is to adjudicate between competing claims on land use in the countryside, elected local planning authorities are better placed by far to fulfil this function fairly and impartially. Not only are they accountable to an electorate, but their committee meetings are public, their activities are reported in the press, and the system they operate for dealing with planning applications and for drawing up plans are celebrated for their fairness and for the opportunities they afford interested parties to have a say.

Strict accountability on the part of decision-makers is particularly important in countryside conservation since 'conservation' is a term open to widely varying interpretations. The

conservation of wild creatures, historical sites, recreation
areas and, more particularly, natural beauty is based on principles quite alien to the men who operate the Ministry's local
advice service: at present, their minds are geared to weighing
up the financial costs and benefits of land improvement
schemes, advising farmers on disease control in animals or
recommending the best means of disposing of farm effluent.
The conservation of landscape requires a different frame of
reference. The basic assumption has to be that although conservation cannot be costed in money terms and although
people's preferences for different landscapes will vary to some
extent, nonetheless it is possible to work out a consensus
view on what is a beautiful landscape which can be a consideration in land-use decision-making. The selection over the
last thirty years of national parks, areas of outstanding natural
beauty and, in individual counties, areas of great landscape
value, could not have been made without such an assumption.
But because even the conservation of wildlife involves some
value judgement, land-use decision-makers have always tried
to avoid building conservation into their equations. Planning
authorities preparing structure and local plans know, however, that they cannot afford to ignore important considerations
which happen to be difficult to quantify. There is provision
for public participation and comment at all the main stages in
the drawing up of these plans, and this helps concentrate the
minds of planning authorities on the implications of their
plans for wildlife, landscape, archaeology and recreation.
Ministry of Agriculture officials, however, tend to tell you
that the Ministry cannot be concerned about the beauty of
the countryside because that is a matter of taste. The authorities to which the Ministry turns when it is forced to explore
conservation considerations take the same view.

For example, the Yare marshes have long been widely recognised as possessing special landscape beauty: they have been
included in proposals for a Norfolk Broads National Park
since the Hobhouse Committee reported in 1947. In 1977
the Anglian Water Authority employed a firm of consultants
called Rendel, Palmer and Tritton to carry out an assessment
of the feasibility and desirability of installing a barrier across
the river Yare at Yarmouth in order to reduce the frequency
of flooding. The scheme would enable farmers to transform
about 20,000 acres of the Yare marshes from rough grazing

pastures threaded by drainage dykes and dotted with lines of trees and small woods to intensive cereal and dairy farming lands on which most natural features would be eliminated completely. But the consultants confined their assessment of the environmental impact of the scheme to the local visual impact of the barrier itself and the impact of land drainage on the wildlife of the marshes. They ignored the likely impact of the drainage scheme on the landscape, pointing out that the environmental effects of their plans were unquantifiable, their values being determined differently and subjectively by each individual.[7] Water authority officials pointed out to me that beauty lies in the eye of the beholder and some expressed the view that they personally felt the Yare marshes had no landscape beauty. The Countryside Commission has, however, told the Water Authority that the rapid and extensive agricultural change that would follow the installation of a flood barrier would involve 'a significant loss to the character and the attractive diversity of this unique landscape'.[8]

So a plan to resolve conflict between farmers and conservation by educating the Ministry's local advisors would in fact be of merely cosmetic value in arresting the rape of the countryside. Such a move would merely aid the forces of destruction in a propaganda war which is already getting under way, as farmers sense the beginnings of a real protest about what they are doing. Almost every farmer I have ever talked to has claimed to be 'a conservationist'. But what does this really mean? What it can mean is that when explaining his activities to the outside world a farmer will claim to have left a woodland uncleared 'as a haven for wildlife', when in reality the poverty of the soil was the main factor; other areas much more important to wildlife may have been cleared away without compunction. There is a real danger that the CRC's approach would actually help farmers cover up the damage they are doing to our environment. The unfortunate truth is that introducing the same new agricultural practices slightly more circumspectly will not eliminate the problem.

The NFU and CLA have proposed that a new Ministry, a 'Ministry of Rural Affairs', should be formed out of the Ministry of Agriculture and the countryside conservation corner of the Department of the Environment. This proposal was rejected by John Silkin in 1979. But the farmers' and landowners' pressure groups are continuing to support it energetically, and it is still very much on the political agenda. It may seem that this proposal would meet the objection that the Ministry of Agriculture is too firmly committed to farming to take on conservation functions. But because the remnants of the Ministry of Agriculture would vastly outweigh the other elements in manpower and functions, a new Ministry would probably be as ineffective in conservation matters as the present Ministry of Agriculture. And it would be the more dangerous because the farming interests which would dominate it would be able to operate from behind the disguise of their new inoffensive-sounding title.

12

Graffham Down: Victim of the System

Graffham Down on the South Downs north of Chichester was until recently one of the gems of the Sussex landscape. Its unhappy fate demonstrates as typically as anything the impotence of the community in the face of agricultural change. The Down, together with the adjacent Woolavington Down, forms a wedge-shaped strip of land covering about 120 acres along the crest of the escarpment and overlooking the villages of Graffham and East Lavington, 600 feet below. From the tip of the wedge, which lies up a track from Graffham church, the Down runs eastward for about 1¾ miles broadening to a maximum width of about half a mile. The South Downs Way (one of the long-distance paths designated by the Countryside Commission) runs alongside it, and there are numerous other public footpaths and bridleways crossing the area.

Two swathes of rough chalk downland turf up to 40 feet in width, labelled on maps of 1795 and 1806 as Graffham Down and Lavington Down and used for several decades of this century as gallops for racehorses, snaked through the woodland and scrub that covered most of the area, offering a rare reminder of what the South Downs used to offer. And by the mid-1970s, Graffham Down had become one of the few remaining examples of traditional downland landscape in the whole of the South Downs. Agricultural 'improvement' and conifer afforestation had eliminated many other stretches of rough open downland along the ridge of the Downs from Beachy Head to Harting south of Petersfield. Approached from the little villages of Graffham, Duncton or East Lavington at its foot, Graffham Down still offered the heady blend of experiences celebrated and taken for granted by downland enthusiasts like Kipling, Belloc and W.H. Hudson. After a few steps along a chalky, buttercup-lined track out of the village the walker would find himself in a different world. First, he would climb up through the cool greenness of a beech wood hanging on the steep northern slope, with the few shafts of sunlight that filtered through the dense leaf canopy and up through the understorey of hawthorn, hazel and yew picking out the ground covering of dog's mercury. The only sounds would be bird song (led by willow and wood warblers) and the rustle of the wind tossing the beech boughs high up in the sky. But, after a 500 ft climb, he would emerge into the quite different surroundings of the summit. First the beech would give way to ash, and then the ash would merge into that characteristic chalk medley of spindle tree, dog-rose, the wayfaring tree, clematis and whitebeam, bramble, black-thorn and dogwood, alternating with open grass down. The relatively restrained chorus of the beechwoods would give way at the top to what was sometimes an almost deafening concert featuring blackcaps, greater and lesser whitethroats and always, overhead, the song of skylarks, filling the sky. In high summer, clouds of blue and brown butterflies would fly up from stretches of thyme-scented turf edged by woods of yew, oak, silver birch and sweet chestnut. The rough, grassy rides, carpeted with wild flowers, made Graffham Down a favourite spot for walkers on the South Downs Way, who now encounter very little downland turf along the eighty-mile route: most of the path now runs through intensive farmland.

The rough turf on Graffham Down had probably existed for hundreds of years, maybe thousands. And this lack of disturbance in the vegetation cover would have made it a treasure-trove of archaeological remains: certainly any arch-aeologist excavating there would have expected to find Iron Age, Roman or medieval lynchets at the very least, inter-spersed among the mapped but unexcavated upstanding arch-aeological features: three tumuli and a cross-dyke (a single bank and ditch, probably dating from the Iron Age).

Naturalists were in no doubt about the value of this speci-men of a disappearing habitat. Early spring on Graffham Down saw the appearance of cowslips and the early purple orchid. These were followed, as spring passed into summer, by such flowers as the common spotted orchid, the bee orchid, self-heal, pink centaury, ragwort, marsh agrimony, viper's bugloss, and the rock-rose; and then in July and August by harebells, lady's bedstraw (white and yellow varieties), knapweed, autumn gentian, St John's wort and various kinds of thistle and tall, yellow daisy-like flowers. It used to be possible to walk along the gallops and pick fifty different kinds of wild flower. Butterflies, attracted by the brightly-coloured flowers, included the small tortoiseshell, the meadow brown, the marbled white, the white admiral, red admiral, chalkhill blue, common blue and gatekeeper. Badgers, foxes, stoats, weasels, roe and fallow deer all frequented the woods. Nightingales, tree pipits, seven species of warbler, woodcock, turtle-doves and three species of woodpecker were among the birds which bred regularly on the down, many of them concentrated in what was one of the few remaining suitable habitats on the crest of the downs. In autumn and winter the down was home to fieldfares, siskins and redwings from Scandinavia and the occasional buzzard.

The butterflies, the flowers, the wild animals, the birds, the seclusion of the woods and the peace of the downland made Graffham Down an unusually splendid place to ramble, ride, picnic or play. But to the farming community Graffham Down merely constituted uncultivated marginal land, unused capacity for food production. In 1978, a Dutch farmer who believed he could exploit this wasted opportunity bought the land on top of the down. And between August 1979 and July 1980 he cleared away most of the natural features on the site and ploughed up the land he had cleared. The woodland scrub and down where nightingales had sung and badgers scuttled became an expanse of barley prairie, like so much of the rest of the South Downs. Its appeal as landscape and its value for wildlife, and humans seeking recreation, have been obliterated. Efforts were made to save Graffham Down. It is instructive to see why they failed.

The proposal to plough up the down came to light because of a statutory requirement that any person seeking to fell more than 825 cubic feet of timber (the equivalent of ten oaks) in one quarter year must get consent from the Forestry Commission. In December 1978, Mr J.M. van de Vegte, the farmer who had bought the land, applied to the Commission for a licence to chop down 809 trees covering 120 acres of this land so that he could grow cereals on it (120 acres is about one and a third times the size of St James's Park). These trees were in three blocks: there were two smaller areas of very old oak at the foot of the scarp on the edge of East Lavington village and a larger stretch of oak, ash, chestnut and silver birch woodland and scrub on the crest of Graffham Down.

If the site had all been open downland, there is no reason why the plan should have become public knowledge before it was carried out. Felling licences are treated quite differently from applications to planning authorities for development. The details of a planning application are regarded as a legitimate matter of public interest. Local planning authorities are legally obliged to list all planning applications on a public register and to make available details of applications, including plans, to any member of the public who wishes to see them. Most local newspapers publish a summary of planning applications, so ordinary citizens, as well as the amenity societies which regularly inspect planning registers, have a chance to learn of changes proposed in their neighbourhood. These procedures enable any objectors to make their views known to the planning authority well before the meeting at which the application is to be considered. However, removal of trees, copses and woods is another matter. The Forestry Commission which administers felling licences is mainly concerned with timber as a crop. It is not legally obliged to publish felling licence applications, or to give members of the public details if they learn that an application has been made. The Commission does, however, consult local (usually district) councils on those felling licence applications which it considers could have a serious impact on amenity.

In the case of Graffham Down, this procedure meant that certain local residents did come to learn about Mr van de Vegte's plans. A district councillor, who had seen the application at a district council meeting, telephoned a constituent who she believed would be concerned. This constituent and a friend, both of them living in Graffham, drew up a memorandum explaining the recreation and wildlife importance of Graffham Down and sent it to the county and district councils. In addition, the local parish council, the Society of Sussex Downsmen, the Sussex branch of the Council for the Protection of Rural England, the Sussex Ornithological Society, and a number of other local residents, all made their anxieties known to the local authorities. But by the time the protests were under way the district council had already considered the application once and decided against trying to block it completely.

Chichester District Council relies for specialist advice on nature conservation, landscape conservation, forestry and archaeology on West Sussex County Council, which employs specialist advisors in all these fields. The county council's attitudes in these areas are determined largely by the approach to different areas of the county set out in its structure plan. The West Sussex Structure Plan, prepared after several rounds of public consultation and approved by the Secretary of State for the Environment in 1980 after a public examination, is quite clear-cut in the priority it accords to landscape and nature conservation in the Western Downs. 'There is an *exceptionally strong* presumption against development and changes of land use and management which would be harmful to the visual quality and essential rural character of Areas of Outstanding Natural Beauty', says the plan (my italics). The Council says that throughout West Sussex it will 'oppose land use changes which will be ecologically harmful'. In addition, it divides the county into four zones according to the relative priority that conflicting rural interests should be accorded within each zone. Graffham Down is bang in the middle of an area in which the Council says landscape and wildlife should have priority over other demands.

If the county council means to conserve anything in West Sussex, it might have been supposed that it would want to conserve Graffham Down.

But West Sussex County Council made no written objection to the Forestry Commission. It remained similarly inactive when Mr van de Vegte applied to the Ministry of Agriculture for a grant to clear the land in question, although the Ministry is required to have regard to the desirability of conserving the natural beauty and amenity of the countryside when considering grant applications. Both the Ministry of Agriculture and the Forestry Commission rely on local authorities to inform them of any amenity reasons why they should withhold felling licences or provide grants. In fact, one of the county council's planning officers attended a site meeting with Mr van de Vegte's agent, and officers of the Forestry Commission and district council. After the site meeting the district council was informed that the county council had no objection to Mr van de Vegte's plans for felling, so long as he retained the thin strip of trees and bushes running alongside the South Downs Way on the southernmost edge of the site together with rough cover over the site's scheduled ancient monuments.

At the site meeting, the district council planning officer had requested that Mr van de Vegte be refused permission to fell trees on an area of about four acres and that he be required to replant another area of about twenty-five acres, in both cases for amenity reasons. Both these requirements were incorporated by the Forestry Commission into the felling licence. However, when the position was reported to the District Council's Development Control Committee, members expressed considerable concern. They asked the Forestry Commission to defer a decision on Mr van de Vegte's application until district councillors had had a chance to look at the site. After a site inspection, this committee became even more concerned, particularly about the gallops. But the only way in which it could have stopped the gallops being ploughed would have been by acquiring the land. Even supposing Mr van de Vegte had been willing to sell, such a purchase would have cost the council at least £30,000 – a prohibitive figure, especially at a time of public expenditure restraint. (It could have tried to get a management agreement over the gallops to prevent ploughing, like those the Exmoor National Park Committee has secured to prevent the ploughing of rough moorland (see page 113), but in the long term this would have proved even more expensive than purchase.) The council ended up requesting Mr van de Vegte to leave the gallops unploughed. He refused.

The district council decided against objecting to the tree felling proposals. In the end it was satisfied with the steps being taken to mitigate the loss of the trees. Had the district council felt differently it would have been in a stronger position than it was in opposing ploughing – at least on paper. Two courses apart from acquisition would have been open to it. It could have urged the Forestry Commission to refuse a felling licence; but the Commission almost never refuses a licence on amenity grounds. Or the district council could have imposed tree preservation orders; but in this case it would have had to pay equivalent compensation itself – once more, this would have been prohibitively expensive.

Concessions like those secured from Mr van de Vegte are far from watertight. Even if the owner who makes the agreement sticks to it, a new owner may not want to. And the trees which are supposed to remain on Graffham Down could be gradually removed without a felling licence by clearing trees constituting a little less than the minimum quantity for which a felling licence is required each quarter until all the trees had been cleared.

The case of Graffham Down shows as well as any how countryside of high amenity value can be reclaimed for intensive agriculture without any real resistance being put up. The position of the farmer involved is perfectly understandable. His brother, Frans van de Vegte, wrote to me:

> My brother intends to farm in England as well as possible. This is the reason why we asked the Ministry of Agriculture if it would be worthwhile to clear the land on the Downs. After being told that this particular area should be quite suitable for growing corn, we applied for a clearing licence. We fully understand that it is very important to maintain landscape beauty and valuable timber reserve. Therefore we have offered to leave some borders and to replant a certain area. We understand that people who were opposed to this clearing have had every opportunity to discuss the matter with the Authorities before we obtained this clearing licence.

This is quite true: the objectors took such opportunities as were open to them. They never had a hope of succeeding and the fault lies in the system by which land use in the countryside is determined. The pursuit of profit from the exploitation of uncultivated land is now an impressive force. But the interests ranged against it are virtually powerless. At Graffham, those local people and organisations which saw their amenity threatened approached the institutions which appeared to be in a position to do something – their local councils. In fact, however, in spite of theoretical responsibilities, both local authorities failed to put up much of a fight. It is usually so. Rural amenity just does not rank high enough among the many priorities with which local authorities have to juggle. Had the Sussex councils wanted to make more of an effort, however, they would have quickly found that they were just not capable of resisting the landowner's designs on Graffham Down. The powers of the town and country planner were denied to them. And such steps as they were entitled to take would have been ruled out because of their cost. This impotence gives local authorities another reason to accept agricultural change without protest. If we are to have any chance of rescuing England's landscape, administration of the countryside will have to be revolutionised.

13

The National Parks

Apart from the development control machinery, the national parks system is the main protection that might have been expected to save at least some of our countryside from agricultural change. At present the national parks of England and Wales are ten areas specially selected for priority protection and spending on account of their particular beauty and the opportunities they afford for recreation. Together they cover 5,250 square miles. There is no doubt that our national parks system could help protect landscapes threatened by agricultural change. So far, however, it has done little in this direction. Its most striking weakness has been that the areas of farmed lowland countryside most at risk (like the South Downs, the Dorset Downs or the Vale of Herefordshire) are excluded from the parks system, which concentrates on upland England.

Our national parks cover a higher proportion of our land surface than those of other countries – about 9 per cent of England and Wales, compared to about 0.5 per cent in Poland, for example, or 2 per cent in France. The National Parks Commission, set up in 1949 and replaced by the Countryside Commission in 1968, designated ten parks between 1950 and 1956; none have been added since. They are, in order of designation: the Peak District, the Lake District, Snowdonia, Dartmoor, the Pembrokeshire Coast, the North York Moors, the Yorkshire Dales, Exmoor, Northumberland (consisting of the Cheviots and part of Hadrian's Wall), and the Brecon Beacons. Their location is shown on Map 1.

Up till now, Britain's national parks system has been unique. In all other countries in which national parks have been established, the parks are relatively small areas of wild, spectacular scenery bought by the Government as museum pieces. Government ownership makes it possible for all economic activity (apart from catering for visitors) to be excluded. But Britain's national parks are not museum pieces. Our system aims to conserve some of our finest tracts of countryside while allowing people to live and work in them at the same time. We have not tried to keep the appearance of our parks exactly as it was when they were designated. Instead, normal life goes on insofar as economic activities (from the building of roads, houses and factories to the afforestation of hillsides or the ploughing of moorland) which would impair the beauty of the parks, their wildlife interest or the opportunities they provide as national playgrounds, are supposed to take second place to conservation and recreation.

Potentially, a sophisticated mechanism for conserving the beauty of large areas of exceptional countryside, national park designation is superior to the crude tool of state ownership which can only ever be applied to small areas. We came by our parks system because it happened to be set up two years after the nationalisation of development rights had introduced an effective town and country planning system for the control of new development. Both our planning and our national parks systems flow naturally from our tradition of the less-than-absolute ownership of land. The absence of such a tradition in the United States, where national parks started in the 1870s, led that country to rely on state or federal ownership of land as the only means of conservation.

The effectiveness of development control in national parks is enhanced by the allocation of this responsibility to special national park authorities, rather than the local district councils which administer it in the rest of the English countryside. One-third of the members of these park authorities are nominated by the Secretary of State for the Environment to represent the conservation and recreation needs of the nation as a whole, if need be, in defiance of the local claims which may be made by the other two-thirds of its members, who are drawn from local authorities. Only 0.5 per cent of the population of England and Wales live in national parks, and the interests of these people are often different from those of the mainly city-dwelling people in whose name the parks were created.

This system has kept at bay changes which might have destroyed the sense of remoteness and peace and quiet for which people value the areas our national parks cover. The successful opposition to plans to put a motorway through the heart of the Peak Park in 1977, to mine copper in Snowdonia in 1972, to extract potash from the North York Moors in 1979 and to afforest a large area of moorland in Exmoor in 1957 all

Map 1. Existing National Parks and Areas of Outstanding Natural Beauty

National Parks

Areas of Outstanding Natural Beauty

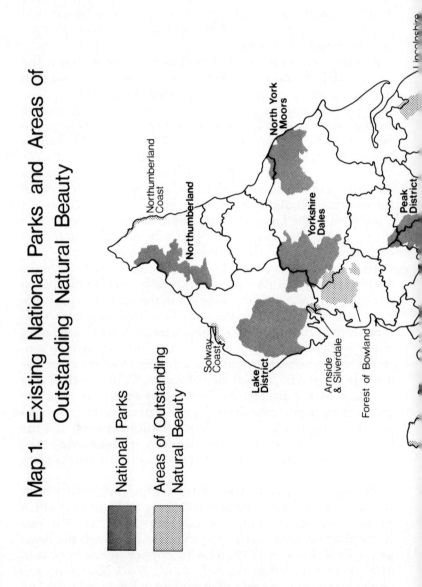

Northumberland Coast

Northumberland

Solway Coast

Lake District

Arnside & Silverdale

Forest of Bowland

Yorkshire Dales

North York Moors

Peak District

Lincolnshire

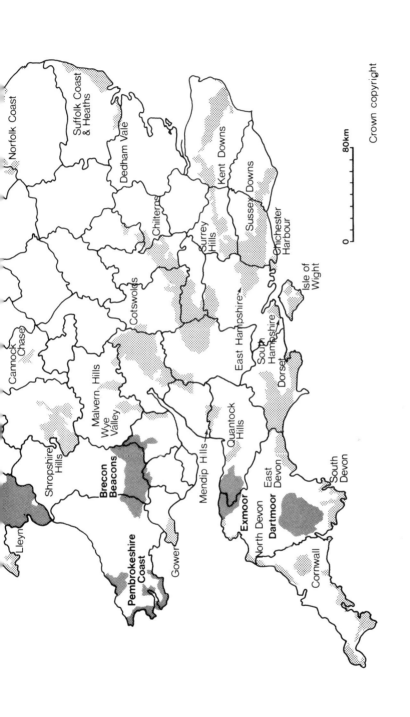

Norfolk Coast

Suffolk Coast & Heaths

Dedham Vale

Chilterns

Surrey Hills

Kent Downs

Sussex Downs

Chichester Harbour

Isle of Wight

Cotswolds

East Hampshire

South Hampshire

Dorset

Cannock Chase

Malvern Hills

Wye Valley

Mendip Hills

Quantock Hills

Shropshire Hills

Brecon Beacons

Gower

Exmoor

North Devon

East Devon

Dartmoor

South Devon

Cornwall

Lleyn

Pembrokeshire Coast

80km

0

Crown copyright

relied heavily on the national park status of the threatened countryside. It is most unlikely that the proposals of British Nuclear Fuels Limited and the North West Water Authority to extract water from Wastwater and Ennerdale in the Lake District and that of the Department of the Environment to run a bypass round Okehampton through a corner of Dartmoor would be discussed in such depth if national park land were not involved.

Throughout the last thirty years, our national parks have received the lion's share of government spending on conservation and recreation in the countryside: in 1977–78, for instance, the government and the Countryside Commission gave our parks over £4 million out of a total spending on conservation and recreation in the countryside of England and Wales as a whole of just under £8 million. Since the only means of impeding damaging agricultural change presently available to planning authorities involves considerable cash outlay, the national park authorities have been in a far better position to take this kind of action than the local authorities responsible for the rest of the countryside. And the park authorities have taken a number of other positive initiatives. Since the designation of 556 square miles of the Peak District in 1950, for example, the park authority has secured public access through access agreements with landowners and through the acquisition of land over a total of 76 square miles of open moorland from which walkers were previously barred; it has acquired 800 acres of woodland scattered through the Park to preserve them; it has sponsored special Sunday bus services from towns and cities around the Park into its heart for the benefit of local people without cars; and it has established eight visitor information centres. The limits to planning power have prevented even our national park authorities from saving many beautiful landscapes from agricultural change. Woodlands in the Lake District, hay meadows in the Yorkshire Dales, cliff roughland in the Pembrokeshire Coast Park and open moorland on the North York Moors and Exmoor have been some of the notable casualties in National Parks. But their extra resources have enabled them to do a great deal more than local councils outside.

Their real importance in the struggle against agricultural change has, however, been negligible. And that is basically because the parks exclude the countryside that is most threatened – the farmed countryside of lowland England. Instead, our national parks enshrine only three types of countryside: moors, mountains and, to a lesser extent, dramatic coastal scenery. There is certainly no chalk downland, fen country or lowland heath in any of our national parks nor are there any sizeable stretches of coastal marshland. Our lowland vales are nowhere specifically protected by national park status. Our most distinctive tracts of lowland landscape can perhaps be listed as follows: the South Downs, the Norfolk Broads, the Chiltern Hills, the Somerset Levels, the Cotswolds, the Weald, the Dorset Downs, the Malvern Hills, the Exe Valley in Devon, the Thames Valley and the Golden Valley in Herefordshire. All of these areas are gravely threatened by agricultural change yet none has been accorded the protection of national park status. Meanwhile, our national parks do embrace some threatened moorland, particularly on Exmoor and the North York Moors. But they include much larger areas not threatened by any form of change. The mountains of Snowdonia, the Brecon Beacons and Kielder Forest in Northumberland, for example, repose contentedly in the protection they do not need, while lowland England is ravaged.

The bias towards upland areas in the selection of our national parks conflicts with the intentions of Parliament when it passed the legislation setting up the national parks system. The Attlee government's 1949 National Parks and Access to the Countryside Act required the selection of national parks to be based on two criteria: the 'natural beauty' of the areas concerned, and 'the opportunities they afford for open-air recreation, having regard both to their character and to their position in relation to centres of population'.

But if this suggests that Parliament intended our national parks to play an important recreation role for city dwellers, only two parks came to be designated close to conurbations: the Peak District and the Yorkshire Dales. Most of our parks are located in the remote corners of England and Wales.

A complex of reasons lie behind the peculiarly biased selection of our national parks. The first is a preference for wild rocky country on the part of the people who have dominated countryside policy-making in England and Wales this century. By far the most influential of these was John Dower, an architect and planning consultant and founder member of the main pressure group for national parks, the Standing Committee on National Parks of the Councils for the Preservation of Rural England and Rural Wales, who was appointed by the government in 1945 to consider the form Britain's national parks might take following twenty years of mounting pressure for the creation of such parks in Britain.[1] Dower confined his search for national parks to what he called 'wild country', which he defined as mountain, moor, forest and rough heath. Although Parliament rejected this restricted view, it was Dower's definition, incorporating the crucial words 'wild country', rather than Parliament's, which was remembered. And to this day, Dower's definition is still the one most often quoted by the countryside establishment. The reason Dower gave for confining his search for national parks to wild countryside was that it is only in such country that the public wants widespread access or can be given it satisfactorily. This approach clearly ruled out most of lowland England, where access is largely confined to public rights of way and where freedom to wander exists over only relatively small stretches of rough wood, down, heath and marsh.

The attitude of the establishment was compounded by the influence of the North American example. The USA and Canada had blazed the national park trail, and the parks they had created were all of a certain type. In *Travels with Charley in Search of America* (1962), John Steinbeck puts the position in a nutshell:

> I must confess to a laxness in the matter of National Parks. I haven't visited many of them. Perhaps this is because they enclose the unique, the spectacular, the astounding, the greatest waterfall, the deepest canyon, the highest cliff, the most stupendous works of man or nature . . . . It is my opinion that we enclose and celebrate the freaks of our nation and of our civilisation. Yellowstone National Park is no more representative of America than is Disneyland.

Finally, the post-war pressure for priority for food production served to inhibit the designation of the lowlands as national parks. The war had demonstrated in particular the agricultural potential of the hitherto unimproved chalk downlands of eastern, southern and south-east England. In the uplands, agricultural prospects looked much bleaker, as at that time the acid and poorly drained moors of the north and west were thought to be beyond the reach of agricultural improvement.

In spite of these pressures, two lowland areas, the South Downs and the Norfolk Broads, were proposed for designation as national parks by a committee appointed by the Government to consider Dower's proposals. The Hobhouse Committee, which reported in 1947, adhered to most of Dower's prescription, but argued that there should be at least one park easily accessible from each of the main centres of population and that the parks should cover a wider variety of landscape than Dower had suggested. 'There is merit in variety,' said the Committee, 'and with the wide diversity of landscape which is available in England and Wales, it would be wrong to confine the selection of National Parks to the more rugged areas of mountain and moorland, and to exclude other districts which, though of less outstanding grandeur and wildness, have their own distinctive beauty and a high recreational value.'[2] But when the National Parks Commission was established by Parliament in 1949 and charged with selecting the parks, it adopted ten of the Hobhouse Committee's twelve areas but rejected the two the Committee had proposed for the lowlands – the Broads and the South Downs.

A Committee appointed in 1971 under the chairmanship of Lord Sandford to review national parks did express concern at the landscape and regional imbalance they embodied. It recommended that when selecting parks in future the Countryside Commission 'should examine more diverse types of landscape, provided that they are of the highest quality, than the rugged uplands which dominate our existing parks with the partial exception of the Pembrokeshire Coast Park'.[3] The Commission should seek to 'redress, to some extent at least, the existing uneven geographical distribution of the national parks, none of which is close to the large populations of the south and south-east of England'.

The Countryside Commission responded in 1977 by asking for public reaction on the suitability of national park status for the Norfolk Broads. But this proposal was later shelved because of opposition from the local authorities concerned. The Commission is not at present scouring the lowlands for other candidates for national park status, and shows no likelihood of doing so in future.

There is at present no sign at all that the national park system will contribute anything to the rescue of lowland landscapes threatened by agricultural change.

The Cinderella countryside: Areas of Outstanding Natural Beauty

Our National Parks and Access to the Countryside Act 1949 did introduce another type of landscape designation besides national park status. It became possible to designate a stretch of countryside an 'area of outstanding natural beauty'. As it has turned out, AONBs have embraced a much larger proportion of lowland than upland countryside: many of our best-known landscapes are AONBs, including the Cotswolds, the Dorset Downs, the Malvern Hills, the Chilterns, the Wye Valley, the High Weald and Dedham Vale. A total of thirty-three AONBs, covering 9.6 per cent of the land surface of England and Wales, have been designated by the National Parks Commission and the Countryside Commission, which took over this function in 1968.

The National Parks' and Countryside Commission's reasons for bestowing national park status on some areas while denying it to other areas that meet the criteria Parliament laid down do not stand up well to scrutiny. In practice AONBs have been established in places like the Cornish coast, where an attempt at national park designation failed, or places considered unsuitable for national park designation for one reason or another. The main objection of this kind raised has been an absence of large areas of open, unenclosed roughland. This point emerged clearly when Reginald Hookway, the Director of the Countryside Commission, spoke to me in 1978. He said:

> In terms of scenic significance, AONBs are not in any statutory or policy sense regarded as second-rate. They are meant in scenic terms to be on a par, but they are different.... National parks are recognised in particular for the opportunities they can offer for extensive enjoyment of open country. That is the distinction between the two.

In fact, this distinction, although clearly related to John Dower's restriction of national parks to land consisting wholly or predominantly of wild, open country, finds no basis in legislation. And in spite of Mr Hookway's emphasis on the landscape importance of AONBs, they are denied the special planning and administrative arrangements provided for national parks. Mainly because of this, they have become the second-class citizens of the world of protected landscape.

Since there are no national parks in lowland England, the lowlands have lost out.

The AONBs looked like a damp squib from the beginning. It was not until 1955, when all ten national parks had been selected, that the first AONB was designated. Neither the National Parks Commission nor the Countryside Commission has ever issued any detailed advice to local planning authorities on the way in which AONB designation should be reflected in planning and development control policies on the ground. And in practice, designation has done nothing to protect the landscape involved from the greatest threat confronting it – agricultural change. Indeed in a policy paper in 1978 the Countryside Commission demonstrated its remoteness from the conflict between modern agricultural methods and the conservation of landscape when it declared that one of the main policy objectives for AONBs should be 'the careful and sustained improvement of agriculture'. Lack of official interest in AONBs helps explain why these areas have even been denied the one specific sanction against agricultural change that has so far been devised. This is advance notification of moorland ploughing, which can be required in national parks but not AONBs, although the latter face a far graver threat from ploughing than the almost entirely upland national parks.

There is very little positive planning in AONBs compared with what happens in national parks. Unlike the parks, AONBs have no authority to administer them with one-third of its members representing the national interest; they have no equivalent of the national park officer and the national park plan. And they get much less money from central government than the national parks. Each national park authority receives a block grant from central government (the national park supplementary grant); any spending on AONBs has to be done by local authorities out of the rates or the rate support grant. Planning authorities throughout the country-side may seek grants from the Countryside Commission for certain specified activities, but AONBs do not receive a particu-larly large slice of the funds available for this purpose.

The local authorities in whose hands the AONBs' destiny lies do not make up for the Countryside Commission's lack of enthusiasm. Studies on development control in AONBs indi-cate that AONB status does not in itself lead local planning authorities to redirect pressures for development. If an authority does happen to pay special attention to conservation in a designated area, the studies suggest that it would probably have done so even if the area had not been designated. A study on development control in the East Devon AONB showed that the chances of getting planning permission to build a house were higher inside the AONB than outside it.[4] And although the boundaries of the Cornwall Coast AONB, for example, were carefully drawn to encompass only the most spectacular parts of Cornwall's coastline plus Bodmin Moor, the number of planning applications granted within the AONB was only slightly smaller than the number granted outside, according to a study by Cornwall County Council of the period between 1970 and 1974.[5] Fewer than 13 per cent of all permissions granted within the AONB had any conditions attached to them. The developments permitted were all in the open countryside outside settlements and, says the County Council, were 'in many cases isolated and visually prominent'.

So although the AONBs are supposed to be equal in status to the national parks, although they are in the front line of attack by modern agriculture and although many have to serve the same recreation role as some of the national parks, they have never received the money, the staff, the legislative protection and the other forms of special treatment enjoyed by the national parks. They are little more than lines on a map, areas shaded one colour because somebody happened to think they were important, but the designation having little real effect on what actually happens.

The future of national parks

In the uplands, at least, our national parks system has proved a clear success story. Large and important areas of countryside have been conserved and made accessible to tens of thousands of people who would never otherwise have gone near them. Like green belt, but unlike many other planning concepts, national parks have won the understanding and approval of the public. Yet, after three decades, change is in the air. Though complaints about the present system are few, the case for 'reform' of our national parks now seems to be taken for granted. In September 1979, the Countryside Review Committee proposed that national parks and AONBs should be completely replaced, and a government review of national park administration promised for 1981 provides an opportunity for action. If the changes now being considered puzzle those impressed by the success of the existing parks, they nonetheless have advantages both for those responsible for administering our landscape conservation system and for those who have been prevented by the present system from pursuing profitable activities.

The Countryside Review Committee's proposals flow from the idea, which first emerged in the 1960s, that the wildest heartlands of our existing national parks deserved more stringent protection than the rest of the parks. In 1973, when this idea had become familiar, the journalist Jon Tinker proposed that small 'wilderness areas' should be established in the wildest parts of Britain's national parks: 'wilderness area' would then replace 'national park' as the highest accolade that could be bestowed on landscape.[6] Tinker's proposal foreshadowed a recommendation from the Sandford Committee in 1974 that 'national heritage areas' should be established within these areas, most of which would lie in the wildest and more remote parts of our existing national parks, no development would be permitted without Parliament's approval and the movement of vehicles would be strictly limited. This thinking reflects recent interest in the national parks system of the United States and France, which concentrate on preserving islands of completely untouched, museum countryside largely through state ownership. The Countryside Review Committee has noticed that if this fashionable approach were adopted here, then many of the troublesome and messy conflicts that arise within our existing parks could be avoided. For such conflicts arise mainly because Britain's present parks embrace large areas of countryside used for many purposes other than as museum pieces. The presence of a block of people representing the national interest on national park committees and boards, alongside local authority representatives, is seen by the Review Committee as another cause of friction. And this, too, would disappear under their plan.

The Committee's proposals, published in 'Conservation and the Countryside Heritage',[7] would replace the existing national parks and AONB machinery with another two-tier system. 'First-tier areas' would resemble the national heritage areas or wilderness areas. They would cover only a small proportion of our land surface – between one and two per cent – although they would be found within what had been AONBs as well as national parks. 'Essential characteristics might be,' according to the committee, 'superlative landscape quality, near absence of population and capability to regulate access.' The sort of areas the committee seems to be thinking of are core areas of our existing designated areas like the mountainous heartlands of Snowdonia and the Lake District, and the central moors of Dartmoor and Exmoor (though clearly not the whole of the 'critical amenity area' which is around 40,000 acres). In the lowlands they might include the saltmarshes at Blakeney and Cley in the North Norfolk Coast AONB, and core areas of the Quantock Hills, the Mendip Hills, the Chilterns and the North Downs. Under the new system our existing national parks and AONBs would become 'second-tier areas'. The current administrative arrangements for our national parks (based on one-third national representation) would disappear: the parks would be handed over to local authorities with the Countryside Commission in charge of the first-tier areas. The existing fairly large staffs that run our national parks would be replaced by a chief officer, presumably with a small supporting staff, and they would be administered by a special executive committee of the local authorities in whose areas they lay. These committees would have 'appropriate delegated powers' and would have to prepare a management plan. The new system would then abolish grade one status over about 4,200 square miles (80 per cent of our existing national parks) and replace it with grade one protection for the remaining 20 per cent plus some countryside outside.

Unfortunately, the approach reflected in the Committee's scheme has little to offer the countryside threatened by agricultural change. The areas it would protect most stringently are almost always areas least in need of protection. If any of our countryside is still completely unthreatened by agricultural change or, for that matter, anything else very much, it is the core areas of our national parks. Yet under the Committee's plan, the second-tier areas would inevitably suffer the consequences of second-class status – indeed the Committee says they would act as 'buffers' for the core first-tier areas. In Dartmoor, for example, relegation would probably be the fate of the wooded, shady valleys of the rivers Dart and Bovey, the foothills of Dartmoor with their delicate balance of rough moorland and gentle, green fields plus much of the open moorland, all of which areas are probably as well loved by visitors as the remote tops and moors of the very centre. Such a change in status would almost inevitably weaken resistance to development on the part of local authorities. The Countryside Commission's attitude to second-tier countryside would also inevitably be different from its present attitude to the national parks. At the moment it is opposing plans to route the Okehampton bypass through the outskirts of the national park: it would be hard to see it bothering with developments like this if only second-tier countryside were involved.

Perhaps the clearest indication of the irrelevance of the first-tier area as a form of protection is the emphasis the Committee puts on the absence of conflict within the first-tier areas. In justifying its proposals, the Committee points to the conflicts within our existing national parks, both the tension inherent in the administrative system which takes the planning of the parks out of the total control of local government and gives the committees and boards which run our parks one-third national representation, and the conflicts that arise when major proposals for development are put forward within the parks. But while conflicts may be troublesome and messy, many of our finest landscapes would now be much the worse if battles had not been fought over them. If there is no conflict in our countryside, there is no role for conservation.

The Committee's plan is reminiscent of national park systems on the Continent and in the United States. During the last three or four years, British conservationists have become more and more familiar with the French experience in particular.

Each of the six national parks in France contains a core area which is normally uninhabited, unfarmed and without roads. Fishing, hunting, forestry, building and the gathering of plants are prohibited. Surrounding each core area is an envelope of land through which run access roads to the core and which contains tourist accommodation and information centres. The core areas of the French national parks cover in all only 0.5 per cent of the land surface; their outer envelopes 1.5 per cent. Mr Hookway writes: 'The French have produced a sort of two-tier system of national park, and I must say that I think a number of people in this country are beginning to be attracted to that concept.'

But there is one crucial respect in which Britain differs from the other countries whose national park systems are now being admired: we have the National Trust, an organisation that has no counterpart abroad outside Scotland. In France, for instance, no voluntary body acquiring land for conservation existed until 1977 when the Conservateurs des Espaces Littoraux was established, modelled on the National Trust's Enterprise Neptune. Voluntary National Trusts exist in the United States, Australia and New Zealand, but they confine themselves almost entirely to the preservation of buildings.

The National Trust of England, Wales and Northern Ireland is one of our largest landowners, holding 400,000 acres of land. Virtually all of this is inalienable, which means that it cannot be compulsorily acquired by government departments, local authorities or any other agency without Parliament's approval. Once the government has approved a Trust proposal for inalienability, it fights off challenges vigorously, wherever they come from. Only once in the last seventy years has the parliamentary procedure for removing inalienability been invoked. Effectively, National Trust land is already our 'core' countryside. The Trust already owns many of the areas that might be expected to emerge as first-tier areas. For instance, it owns 23 per cent of the Lake District National Park; our most outstanding stretches of sand dune, like Whiteford Burrows in the Gower, Braunton Burrows in North Devon, parts of the Northumberland Coast and Murlough in County Down; fen country like Wicken Fen; and stretches of dramatic coast in Cornwall, North Devon, the Isle of Wight and Yorkshire. Virtually all of a thirteen-mile stretch of the North Norfolk Coast – an area mentioned by Mr Hookway as a likely area to emerge as a first-tier area – is already protected through ownership by the National Trust, the Royal Society for the Protection of Birds and the Norfolk Naturalists' Trust. First-tier designation of areas already owned by conservation organisations – and the Committee does envisage that first-tier areas would often cover such land – would bring extra funds that could be used to manage the areas in question. But it could afford them little extra protection over and above what they receive at present. The benefits of extra money would also have to be set against the harm first-tier designation could do to the areas designated. Because of a combination of small size and wide publicity the first-tier areas would inevitably attract many more visitors per square mile than do the present national parks with the result that the actual countryside included within the first-tier designations could be physically harmed by the sheer impact of visitors. Most of the areas that might be expected to be designated are fragile and easily susceptible to damage by visitors. Because these areas in question would be so small, the people who would have to manage them would have little room to redirect visitors away from the areas that were being eroded. The second-tier areas acting as 'buffer zones' would certainly not protect the tiny first-tier areas completely: in some areas, like North Norfolk, the second-tier areas would also be small. Even if they were large, our experience over the last ten years with 'country parks', established in many places to decoy people away from fragile landscapes, has shown that recreation management is very hard to achieve in the absence of complete prohibition. Buffer-zone countryside would not have the virtue of being in the first-tier area; everybody would want to go there, and it would inevitably be eroded.

A move in the direction the Countryside Review Committee suggests would at least seem to be meeting the most important criticism of our national parks system: the concentration of all the parks in the uplands and the denial of national park status to any lowland countryside. A move towards first- and second-tier areas would increase the proportion of lowland England enjoying grade one protection; and, as second-tier areas, the AONBs would probably have more money and coordination than they do at the moment. But in spite of appearances, the micro-surgical approach would do little for the lowlands; and there is no suggestion that the protection afforded to second-tier areas against agricultural change – the main threat to them – would be any greater than it is to the AONBs at present. What are needed, rather, are measures which will enable agriculture to coexist with traditional landscapes over wide areas.

Of course, our existing landscape designation system is not without its defects. But these could be corrected without the creation of new forms of designation.

Local people sometimes feel their concerns are not adequately represented on national park committees and boards. But this concern would perhaps be best dealt with through the co-option of more district councillors into the local

authority contingent on national park authorities in place of
the existing majority of county councillors, many of them
living outside the park areas. There is no doubt that the most
glaring defect of our existing national parks system is the
absence of any national parks in lowland England. The
Countryside Review Committee acknowledged this problem
by drawing attention to the anomalous position of AONBs: it
bemoaned the fact that the AONBs which it said are supposed
to be equal to the national parks in terms of landscape quality,
have been treated as second-class national parks. Whereas the
parks have special administrative arrangements, AONBs
have none set down by law. Unfortunately, however, the
Committee's solution was not therefore to suggest that
national parks be designated in the lowlands, perhaps out of
some of the existing AONBs, but to throw out the baby with
the bath-water and use the discrepancies between the ways in
which the two types of area are treated as a justification for
abandoning both.

The truth is that AONBs have failed, but the national parks
succeeded. The proposed new system would neatly duck the
challenges which the national parks have been meeting. Ironically, while we toy with the Americans' approach to national
parks, they are taking a much greater interest in our parks
system, as they struggle to protect more familiar landscapes
nearer to population centres. Our national parks system is
one of the real triumphs of post-war rural planning. What we
need is the expansion of the principles it embodies to our
threatened lowlands, rather than its replacement with a system
which would do little to meet the problems which actually
exist.

Conclusion to Part Three

Our apparently sophisticated system of landscape protection, then, is having virtually no impact on the problem of agricultural change. It lacks any means of constraining farmers seeking to exploit their exemption from the town and country planning system to launch operations which will damage the landscape.

Any administrative solution to the problem of protecting the English countryside from agricultural change would have to involve a major reorganisation.

PART FOUR

Economics

When pressed, farmers defend their activities in the countryside by appealing to the usefulness of what they do to the rest of the community. Aesthetic considerations are all very well, they argue, but do we really want to place difficulties in the way of so vital an industry? In the end, they like to imply, the hard-headed realist must always support the farmers against the conservationists because agriculture is so obviously in the public interest. Most of us are predisposed to accept a thesis that sounds unarguable, so much so that it is rarely questioned. In fact, however, the material costs and benefits involved are not what they may seem. A glance at the economics of agriculture reveals that much of what farmers are doing is of very doubtful benefit to the community by any standard at all. At the same time, conservation may yield cash benefits to the nation of far more importance than most of us would imagine possible.

The Farmers' Case

The argument for the sacrifice of our countryside to agricultural change is that we need the extra food produced. It is an argument that plays on fear of the ultimate calamity that can befall a society – starvation. So profound is this fear, so entrenched the belief that no policy designed to improve food supplies can be wrong, that the argument has gone unexamined since the end of World War II, when our present agricultural system was devised. In British politics today nobody really asks whether we actually need the extra food we are expending taxpayers' money to produce. Yet the truth is that we do not. Indeed, over-production of food has become the most serious problem of the European Economic Community, costing the UK's consumers and taxpayers alone well over £1 billion a year. The world today is a very different place from that in which our agriculture policies were devised in 1945.

The Government's current policy on agriculture is set out in two White Papers. *Food from our own Resources* (1975)[1] puts forward a strategy for increasing domestic food production by 2½ per cent a year – in line with the proposals of the National Farmers' Union. Explains the White Paper: 'Most benefit is likely to come from higher output of milk (with its byproduct the beef from the dairy herd) and sugar beet. Cereals and sheepmeat should also make a significant contribution.' *Farming and the Nation* (1979)[2] updates this strategy, with developments such as the ending of the transitional arrangements accompanying Britain's accession to the EEC, but leaves the strategy unchanged in its essence.

Both White Papers affirm the same reasons for the expansion of domestic agriculture. The 1979 document says:

> The case for devoting resources to agricultural expansion rests essentially on three factors: the likely price and availability of imports; the argument for greater self-sufficiency as insurance against unexpected scarcity and high prices in

a world of rapidly growing population; and the likely effect on national income and on the efficient allocation of resources of the measures needed to procure higher agricultural output.

Let us examine the validity of these arguments.

'Price and availability of imports'

An argument based on this (and the second) factor runs as follows. The world's population is increasing and has been doing so at a time when the world price of food has been increasing too. So we can expect food imports to cost Britain more and more money. Much of the food we have been importing could be produced at home. Increased domestic production will guarantee us supplies at lower prices.

It is certainly true that world food supplies fluctuate at the whim of the weather, and because of this there are times when the case for unlimited expansion of domestic food supplies can seem appealing. *Food from our own Resources* was published at such a time. When it appeared in 1975, the world had just been hit by a sharp but temporary disruption in food prices. Between 1972 and 1974 our food import bill had risen steeply. The White Paper points out: 'Over the decade to 1972 expenditure on food rose at an average rate of about 5 per cent a year. Between 1972 and 1974, however, expenditure rose at the rate of 15 per cent a year as a result of the exceptional increases in the prices of basic food materials.' The White Paper reviewed this experience and concluded that as the world's granaries were unlikely to be fully replenished, high cereal prices could not be expected to fall in the United States and Canada, which account for two-thirds of world cereal exports. The 2 per cent annual growth in the world's population would keep prices up.

In fact, however, the price rises of 1972–74 were not created by a savage god visiting famine on helpless mankind. Rather, ironically, they were the outcome of the over-production of agricultural produce which now causes so much trouble in the developed world. About 80 per cent of world grain trade is controlled by the United States; about 90 per cent of that trade takes place between the developed countries only. This trade is artificially balanced so as to keep prices at such a level that the farmers who produce the grain as well as the people involved in processing and transporting it get a reasonable profit every year, whatever the weather. During the 1960s the United States amassed large surpluses of wheat that could not be sold on the world market at a profit. The US Government dealt with this situation by paying farmers to withdraw land from production so that the resulting shortage would push up the price. Other producers followed suit, and during 1968 and 1970, the four major cereal-producing nations of the world (the USA, Canada, Australia and Argentina) took a third of their grain-growing area out of cultivation in response to 'over-production'. If these countries had continued to grow grain at a constant rate, they would have produced 90 million more tons of wheat between 1969 and 1972 than they actually produced, according to Susan George, the author of *How the Other Half Dies: the Real Reasons for World Hunger*.[3] This tactical, artificially engineered retrenchment then happened to be accompanied by the partial failure of the Peruvian anchovy catch, which increased demand for alternative sources of protein, such as US soya bean. At the same time there were widespread but unexpected purchases of grain by the Soviet Union (the world's main grain importer), of which the US Government was unaware until very large amounts of grain had been sold. So this unlikely chain of events has its roots in the dread of *over*-production rather than the insufficiency of world agricultural output. In any case, the set of circumstances that occasioned it could not recur. Since 1974 Soviet purchases of US wheat have been regularised through an agreement that Soviet purchases above a certain level must be notified to the United States Government. The US is also pushing for the establishment of a global cereals storage system. So much for the world food price hiccup of 1974, which remains the best example the agriculture lobby can point to of the horrors from which they wish to make us safe. In 1978, North American wheat prices were 13 per cent lower than 1975 despite inflation.

We are now better protected from world price increases than we were before 1975. We now purchase half the grain we used to buy on the world market from the EEC. But we have paid an enormous price for protection against what is now a minimal danger. Our present situation is that of a man paying an annual insurance premium greater than the value of the goods insured.

'Insurance against unexpected scarcity'

Far more emotive, however, than the argument about price is
the argument about supply. Our agriculture policies were
forged in the aftermath of the U-boat campaign in the Western
Approaches, and at that time the strategic case for self-
sufficiency seemed unarguable. Today the self-sufficiency
argument is still the lynch-pin of the case for maximising food
production. Tax a farmer with the apparent senselessness of
our present farm support policies and the chances are that he
will resort ultimately to the argument that his efforts and
those of his kind are the *only* ultimate guarantee of an adequate
diet for the population in the face of an unexpected inter-
ruption in supplies from overseas. Is such an insurance policy
not worth a little taxpayers' money and, perhaps, a little
damage to the landscape as well? It is an awesome argument
calculated to make those who are unsure of their facts back
off. But when it is examined it fails to provide any real justification for the policies pursued in its name.

There will always be fluctuations in food supply caused by
the weather, disease, or rises in costs, whatever methods a
country institutes to secure its food. Our task as a nation is to
assess the risks and the costs of offsetting those risks and then
settle upon the degree of protection compatible with a proper
balance between the two. This is the calculation that has not
been made. If it were, no one would consider for a moment
that the threat posed to our food supplies at present justifies
the destruction of our countryside, let alone the vast sums of
money squandered on excessive but over-priced food output.

There is no contemporary equivalent of the U-boat campaign to destroy our access to food imports. But if there were,
we certainly would not starve to death. The entire nation
could be fed adequately from existing farmland, so long as we
were prepared to accept a modified diet, which in the supposed
crisis we presumably would be. Calculations by the Centre for
Agricultural Strategy of the University of Reading, by Professor
Kenneth Mellanby, the former director of the Monks Wood
Experimental Station of the Nature Conservancy Council,
and by Dr Kenneth Blaxter FRS, the director of the Rowett
Research Institute, Aberdeen University,[4] have shown that if
all Britain's food imports were cut off, we could produce
enough food to feed ourselves without even cultivating

hitherto uncultivated land (as we did during World War II). And although we would not be able to sustain the rich diet most of us enjoy at present, we would never be able to achieve this however much more marginal land we ploughed up or however many more fertilisers and pesticides we pumped into the soil now. For in order to incorporate large quantities of meat and other forms of animal protein like eggs in our diet we now have to import £548 million worth (1979 figure) of feedstuffs and turn over most of our arable land to growing grain to feed animals. Of all farmland in the United Kingdom *only 8 per cent provides for man directly*. Nearly all the remaining 92 per cent is devoted to feeding livestock. Barley, for instance, our main cereal crop in terms of tonnage produced, covers about 5,799,550 acres in the UK. Of the 10 million tons produced in 1978, 6 million went to fatten animals and a further 2 million tons were exported. If the economy were under siege, we would have to cut off the animal intermediary and devote most of our lowland countryside to producing food we could consume directly ourselves. Under the regime Dr Blaxter has worked out, the mass production of pigs and poultry would be suspended and a small number of these animals would be fed on by-products of other agricultural processes. Our beef herd would contract as less meat would be eaten. But the dairy herd would be expanded as milk would become even more of a staple food. Dairy cows would, however, be fed solely on grass. Both potato and sugar beet acreages would be expanded by 70 per cent and oil-seed rape would be grown widely to produce margarine and cooking oil. Some sheep would remain in the hills and, in the absence of imported feed mixtures, battery chicken production would give way to free-range hen farming. All of this would be possible without any further destruction of the landscape to improve agricultural output, and indeed the contribution of such extra output would not make much difference in these crisis conditions.

Ironically, the present agricultural revolution is in one important sense reducing our security from external disruption. Technological advance has made our agriculture dependent on imports of oil and fertiliser which are, if anything, more susceptible to supply disruption than imports of food would be. Most people would perhaps consider oil supplies more likely to be jeopardised than supplies of lamb or butter from New Zealand or wheat from North America or Australia. At the moment, of course, much of our oil comes from the North Sea, but when this oil runs out in the 1990s dependence on imports of one of the most coveted commodities in the world is likely to be the Achilles' heel of a mechanised agricultural industry.

So the unpalatable truth for the farming lobby is that what little life there is in the strategic argument for domestic food production works against the logic of the present agricultural revolution, not for it.

'The likely effect on national income': the balance of payments

The third reason the Government put forward in 1975 and 1979 for subsidising domestic food production was 'the general benefit to the balance of payments' of extra agricultural output. Perhaps because the first two arguments seem less pressing this third point is often relied on most heavily nowadays. Peter Walker, the Minister of Agriculture, made much of the 'contribution' farming may make to the balance of payments when he spoke at the Conservative Party Conference in 1979:

> One area of expansion available to us in the immediate future is British agriculture. We are net importers; we are small exporters. We can reduce our imports and increase our exports. Ten per cent increase in British food production is £700 million on the balance of payments. That is why I say to you today that the prosperity of British agriculture makes political sense, makes economic sense, makes European sense, and it is for that reason that the Government will give it the priority it deserves.[5]

It is of course true that an increase in food exports and a cut in food imports would increase any surplus or reduce any deficit on the balance of payments. It is equally true that state subsidies to manufacturing industry of the kind lavished on agriculture could achieve a far more dramatic effect of this kind, though they would presumably not go down so well with the Conservative Party Conference. The real question is, of course: does it make sense in either case to subsidise output to rig the balance of payments? There cannot have been many people at the Conservative Party Conference who really supported that principle. And any who did were living in the past. The reasons why it used to be thought so important to maintain a balance of payments surplus no longer apply. A balance of payments deficit does, it is true, lead to a fall in the value of the pound, and in the 1960s this was something to be avoided. In the oil-rich 1980s it is something which the authorities would clearly like to bring about, but cannot. The flood of North Sea oil into our economy has made Britain fall victim to what economists called 'the Dutch disease': a much higher exchange rate than is good for us. An over-high pound makes our exports too expensive overseas. But it makes imports cheap – so we buy foreign goods instead of British goods. This phenomenon has become one of the major problems of the British economy and is an important contributory factor in our record level of unemployment. Industrialists have been begging the Government to bring the exchange rate down, but no way of doing this has been found that would not contribute to inflation – except leaving the oil in the North Sea, which the Government cannot afford to do. In these circumstances, pushing up the exchange rate further with subsidised agricultural exports is the last thing the economy needs.

A starving world

One thought that may occur to some people is that we owe it to our fellow human beings in parts of the world stalked by the spectre of famine to produce as much food as we possibly can. In fact, however, the argument about food production in Britain has little to do with the world food question. If we produce more, this will not make the hungry of the Third World any better off. It might even make them worse off. The reason for world hunger is not a shortage of cultivable land, which would be reduced, however slightly, by an increase in production in Britain. In fact, the world has all the physical resources and technical skills necessary to feed a much larger population than it supports at present. The reason why food supply falls short is that poverty prevents Third World countries from exploiting successfully the opportunities open to them. Many of these countries lack the foreign exchange they would need to buy even minimum amounts of fertiliser, pesticide, tractors and so on. On top of this problem, such resources as exist, including land itself, are often concentrated in a few hands which do not use them efficiently. If we wish to help the hungry Third World, what we have to do is to provide aid to improve agriculture in Third World countries themselves, not produce more butter, cheese and beef in Britain. Indeed, excess production in the developed world can increase the problems of the Third World. When excess production leads to dumping, as it does all too often in the EEC, the effect is to disrupt the efforts of the developing countries to get their own agriculture industries off the ground. Unpredictable floods of produce undercutting their infant industries are the last thing they (or those who put up their capital) want to see.

If we in Britain were to plough up all our remaining tracts of marginal land and the EEC were to sell the Third World the extra food produced at discount price, this would do them more harm than good.

If we really wanted to help alleviate world hunger, there are of course steps we could take. We could provide Third World countries with cash aid to buy fertilisers and pesticides and to reclaim land. At present, only 10 per cent of the world's land mass is producing crops, according to calculations by Susan George. She believes that an extra 2.7 million square miles could be brought into production with relative ease and that 'with an altogether reasonable investment, a reasonable world could increase its present farming area by about 50 per cent . . . without going to ecological extremes'.[6] The Food and Agriculture Organisation of the United Nations has shown that a simple campaign to eliminate the tsetse fly in Africa could reclaim an area of nearly three million square miles in 35 African countries, which could support about 140 million head of cattle.[7] It is measures like these, rather than varying the amount of food Britain contributes to the EEC surplus stockpiles, which might genuinely help the world's hungry. This is an enormous subject, but it has little to do with the issue of food production in Britain. Except, perhaps, that the diversion into overseas aid of the funds we put into agricultural support might suggest itself as a productive step.

Waste

The pursuit of the objectives underlying Britain's agriculture policy need not entail the destruction of our countryside. The removal of landscape features is not the only way in which food production could be made more efficient. It is merely the way that is most convenient to farmers. It is convenient because up till now there has been no real obstacle to this approach. Efficiency could easily be improved in other ways if different pressures were imposed. Every year in Britain a large amount of food is wasted – on our farms, in the processing industry and in our kitchens. Not all this wastage could ever be eliminated, but savings could be made here instead of through the destruction of landscape features if we wanted to save the countryside without sacrificing any food output.

The Ministry of Agriculture itself recognises that the present scale of waste is excessive. Its chief scientist, Dr H.C.Pereira, wrote in 1974:

> There is no doubt that the amount of food available substantially exceeds that required, indicating a measure of over-consumption plus wastage. Only a small part of this difference represents domestic food supplies consumed by pets; the 5.6m dogs and 4.2m cats in the UK have been estimated to consume supplies equivalent to those required by 2m people, whereas the present food supplied for 56m people would, if even half the estimated waste could be eliminated, feed some 7m more.[8]

At the moment, however, the Ministry is making virtually no effort to reduce this waste. Instead, it pours taxpayers' money into the reclamation of marginal land.

Dr Robin Roy, of the Open University, in a study on food wastage carried out in 1976,[9] estimated that we waste 35 per cent of all the food produced in Britain. And in 1978 the Ministry of Agriculture estimated that food wastage could be costing the UK £2 billion a year.

Dr Roy discovered that the main losses occur first in harvesting and storage on our farms; losses after food has been bought by the housewife or caterer are secondary. Poorly designed or adjusted machinery and unskilled operators are the main reasons why crops like sugar beet, potatoes and carrots, for example, are wasted. Dr Roy reports a survey by the British Sugar Corporation that revealed that 8 per cent of the sugar beet crop on average is left in the ground after harvesting; in many cases the loss is over 16 per cent and in one case the Corporation studied it approached 50 per cent. More than 20 per cent of potatoes are so damaged during harvesting that they do not reach the required standards for marketing, according to a survey by the Potato Marketing Board. Twenty-four per cent of the carrots stored on our farms and between 25 and 45 per cent of winter cabbages and cauliflowers are lost. So is between 25 and 75 per cent of the energy content of stored hay and silage, says Dr Roy. Straw burning, of course, represents a colossal waste. At the end of the system, only between 5 and 10 per cent of the edible food bought by housewives is thrown away as kitchen and plate waste. So farmers could do a lot to increase the quantity of food available without ploughing up more marginal land. What would make them do this would be pressure or incentives of exactly the kind that are now leading them to destroy the countryside.

There are a wealth of ways in which wastage could be reduced if anyone wanted it reduced. The development of more sophisticated harvesting equipment and improvements in the training of operators would help, as would the development of better food storage and the feeding of more waste food to farm animals. The Royal Commission on Environmental Pollution, reporting in 1979,[10] recommended that the Ministry of Agriculture should give priority to the development of more efficient ways of applying pesticides to farmland. At the moment, in some cases more than one million times as much pesticide may be applied as is needed to kill the pests. As our farmers spent about half a billion pounds on pesticides in 1979, relatively straightforward changes in this field could save them considerable amounts of money.

On a world scale, any conceivable increases in UK food production, however achieved, are completely dwarfed by the savings that might be achieved by reducing waste in the Third World. Colossal quantities of food are wasted in some countries whose populations lack the most basic nutritional requirements simply because these countries cannot afford even basic pesticides. Food lost on the stalk through pests and disease in the poor countries of the world is estimated at about one-third of the actual harvest, according to Susan George.

15

The Tourism Bonanza: Conservation as a Cash Crop

The complexity of the economics of the countryside becomes instantly apparent when the implications of agricultural change for the tourist industry are considered. (Not, of course, that they are considered when the fate of the countryside is being determined, since agricultural interests hold sway). Tourism is one of Britain's strongest and fastest-growing industries. Spending by tourists from overseas rose from £190 million in 1965 to £3,131 million in 1978. And there is evidence that many of these tourists come to see our countryside as much as anything else. Opinion polls carried out by the British Tourist Authority give an overall picture of the relative strength of Britain's principal attractions.[1] Interviews carried out in Belgium, for example, showed that what Belgians wanted on holiday, in order of importance, were attractive scenery, plenty of sunshine, reasonable prices, friendly people and peace and quiet. Spaniards and Italians, too, rated our countryside highly. Brazilians, asked their opinion on the most attractive features of Britain, replied landscape (20 per cent), London (20 per cent) and the people (19 per cent), followed by historic buildings (16 per cent) and shopping (12 per cent). Canadians and Americans are among the highest-spending tourists, and for over a decade Britain has been the most popular destination in Europe for visitors from both these countries. Britain is also a major destination for the growing numbers of Middle Eastern tourists. All these groups come partly to see our peculiarly distinctive countryside.

It is of course just not possible to predict the effects on tourism of a far-reaching deterioration in the quality of our countryside. But it seems reasonable to anticipate some fall-off of interest if visitors were to find not the English countryside they had seen in picture books, but something more like the Kansas-type prairies or Dutch-style polders with which they might well be all too familiar.

On top of the £3,131 million overseas visitors to Britain spent in 1978, British people spent £3,100 million holidaying in their own country. Of the 61 per cent of Britain's adult population who took a holiday of at least four nights away in 1978, 64 per cent took it in England. There is less opinion-poll evidence about British holiday-makers' tastes than there is of foreigners. But there is reason to believe that British people are deeply attached to their traditional landscape forms. During the 1960s two scholars, David Lowenthal and Hugh Prince, examined English landscape tastes as reflected in literature and painting. They concluded that

> the countryside beloved by the great majority is tamed and inhabited, warm, comfortable, humanised .... The favoured landscape is what Turner denoted 'elegant pastoral' .... What is considered 'essentially English' is a calm and peaceful deer park, with slow moving streams and wide expanses of meadowland studded with fine trees. The scene should include free-ranging domestic animals .... When it is arable land, hedgerows and small fields are usually obligatory.[2]

So if the evidence from literature is anything to go by, prairie-style barley fields, tower silos, canalised rivers and ryegrass lots are not what the British people like to see in their country-side. The indications of popular landscape taste that we can get from the assumptions of advertisers and the pictures people buy to decorate their homes also suggest that it is the traditional England landscape that still holds pride of place in the national imagination as the embodiment of the pastoral dream.

At present, the £6 billion-a-year tourist industry employs directly 800,000 people in the United Kingdom. At a time when technological change is destroying employment in most areas of the economy, tourism is one field which remains obstinately labour-intensive, and holds out a real prospect of more jobs for our expanding work force. Agriculture, by way of comparison, directly employs 643,000 as farmers and farm-workers, or one per cent of the population of the UK. At present those in charge of our tourist industry are among the few industrialists confident about their prospects for expan-sion. Michael Montague, the chairman of the English Tourist Board, predicted in 1980 that the number of people employed in tourism in England could easily rise to two million in the following couple of years. As he pointed out in a speech directed at parents anxious about job prospects for their children,

Leisure-time is advancing at the expense of industrial time. But let us look at this another way. One man's leisure is increasingly another man's work, for with five and six week holidays a prospect for the eighties, people are not merely going to stay at home. They will want to occupy this time in an interesting and satisfying way. I therefore commend to parents the leisure-time industries, the growth that is inevitable and the job opportunities that go with it.[3]

Mr Montague made the point that, unlike less fortunate countries with which Britain is competing, we need do little to develop our tourist attractions:

> While other countries are forced to spend hundreds of millions of pounds creating tourist attractions from scratch, our job in England is to promote and develop what our ancestors and benign nature have given us – and to provide the facilities and amenities needed by tourists to be able to enjoy it to the full.

What one set of industrialists – farmers – see as profitable technological changes amounts to the destruction of the basic resources of another industry – tourism – which happens to be a bigger employer. Tourism is also an important creator of wealth for the nation rather than a drain on the economy like agriculture.

In many parts of our countryside, tourism has already become the lynch-pin of the economy. Take Devon. Tourism provided jobs for 38,000 Devonians in 1973[4]; farming, on the other hand, employed 2,250[5]. Employment in tourism is of course seasonal, but even so, an industry that employs seventeen times as many people as farming cannot be dismissed. Income derived from tourism constituted about 5 per cent of total income in Devon in 1973, agriculture provided 8 per cent of Devon's total income in the same year[6]. But if both industries were stripped of the support they get from the national exchequer, tourism would certainly turn out to generate more of Devon's income than farming. (In 1979 the tourist industry in Britain managed to get by with no more than £25 million of public support. The figure for agriculture runs into billions.)

Of course, not all visitors to Devon come to enjoy the beautiful countryside. But it is clearly the main reason for a good many people and an important second reason for many more. Yet if we allow agricultural change to continue to transform the Devon countryside at anything like the rate it has been altering it over the last twenty years, then by the end of the century, the type of countryside tourists enjoy now will have completely disappeared.

We have already seen that Devon's small woods are rapidly disappearing to the plough or the conifer plantation. But it is not only woods which are going. Even outside Dartmoor and Exmoor, 69,000 acres of rough grass and heath in Devon have been turned into intensive farmland since the turn of the century, as odd patches of hillside covered only in gorse and bracken or scattered damp orchid meadows are converted to barley field or ryegrass paddock.[7] Yet another victim is the peculiar Devonian form of meadowland found on the Culm Measures, which give rise to heavy, damp, clay soils over 700,000 acres of central Devon and north-east Cornwall. Although this land used to be considered impossible to drain, it was used for stock-rearing, which enabled its natural vegetation of rough grasses, rushes and sedges studded with butterfly orchids and yellow flags, meadow thistles and bog pimpernel, to flourish. Now these little meadows, hidden behind thick hedgerows, are becoming memories. The Ministry of Agriculture has developed techniques that will enable virtually all this land to be drained, so that it can be worked like the farmland further east. A thirty-one page guide describes techniques whereby these meadows can be converted to ryegrass lots (*Guide to Culm Land Improvement*, 1978). The guide does manage to note that 'conservation of the natural beauty and amenity of the countryside should be considered in your improvement plan', but fails to make any positive suggestion as to how this consideration can be squared with the destruction of the meadows. Larger and larger areas of this typical Devonian scenery are being stripped of hedges and trees, drained and turned over to large, regular ryegrass squares.

Conclusion to Part Four

If a cool look at the economics of the countryside suggest pretty conclusively that public policy towards agriculture is not in the public interest, it may seem strange that the policy involved can be pursued unquestioned for so long. Yet there is nothing unusual about this. Policies do not normally reflect immediately the ever-changing requirements of society. Instead they are shaped laboriously by arbitrary pressures, and once established acquire a momentum through the support of vested interests which will often enable them to outlive their usefulness.

But there comes a moment when the obsolescence of a policy can become so overwhelming that it can no longer be covered up. Suddenly the media notice it and suddenly the public know it. Once that moment has arrived the dinosaur can roll over and die overnight.

There are several areas of public policy in which the approaches laid down in a burst of post-war enthusiasm have collapsed in recent years, as it has come to be recognised that the world for which they were created has changed out of recognition. In the environmental field itself, an outcry against the destruction of the inner areas of our cities in the 1960s led to the abandonment of 'redevelopment' in favour of the 're-habilitation' of old buildings. In the 1970s, the new towns programme was curtailed because it was seen to be killing the cities it was supposed to be helping. Outside the environmental field, the collapse of policy juggernauts has been even more dramatic. The greatest glory of post-war policy, the management of demand in the economy to maintain employment, was unceremoniously dumped in the mid-1970s by virtually the whole of our political establishment. So far, the approach to British agriculture worked out in 1947 survives unscathed, though the conditions for which it was created no longer exist. But because it threatens to destroy one of our few remaining national treasures – the countryside – it is vulnerable. It is hard to believe that if sufficient pressure is applied to the hollow edifice, it, too, will not crumble.

PART FIVE

Future Landscapes and Future Lives

If it is possible to draw up some idea of the amount of money wasted by our present policies towards agriculture, it is not possible to quantify the costs it imposes of a non-financial kind. And yet it is hard to avoid the feeling that they are infinitely greater. Cost-benefit analysis has been bedevilled by the problem that many of the most important costs and benefits human beings incur are not readily translatable into cash terms. As a result, these factors tend to be devalued in favour of those to which a cash value can most easily be assigned. Clearly the cash value of extra agricultural produce is measurable. A cash value could be placed on the loss of enjoyment of the countryside caused by agricultural change, but the facilities for measuring such a thing are so nugatory that any estimate would have to be so subjective as to be open to continual objection. It remains my belief, however, that most citizens, faced with the evidence, would conclude as I do that the costs of the present level of agricultural intensification outweigh the benefits. The ability to take a walk through a wood in spring or wander over a rough downland cliff-top is genuinely worth a lot to some people. Visiting the countryside is the most popular recreation activity among English people after gardening. Even those who do not ramble or picnic, bird-watch or botanise, often value the idea that a place exists where they could do these things, and there are few people whose lives would not be diminished by the destruction of our countryside.

Because of the difficulty of measurement, I do not propose to try to assess the value of the countryside through an exhaustive calculation, though I believe such an exercise, however subjective, might serve some purpose in reminding us all that non-material things do have value. Instead I propose to try to give some inkling of the value of the traditional English countryside by singling out a couple of particular benefits and the experience of two particular groups of beneficiaries. I have chosen to look at the archaeology and the wildlife to be found in the countryside. And I have examined the way in which children and townspeople relate to it. Each of these facets of the relationship between man and landscape could have been replaced by a score of others. But they will probably serve as well as any alternative examples to communicate the flavour of a deep attachment.

16

A Threatened Record

England's landscape enshrines the secrets of our past. It embodies the only record we have of pre-Roman England. For until Julius Caesar wrote down a history of his Gallic wars, no written records of man's activities in England had ever been kept. Archaeological remains provide the only information we have about the previous 50,000 years of human life.

Other landscape features can also tell us much about more recent activities. Hedgerows, shaws, parklands, medieval fish ponds, old coppiced woods and the remains of ridge and furrow can all reveal much about life during recorded historical time to those with eyes to see.

Of course, if there were no change, there would be no archaeology. If societies did not cast out the old for the new, there would be no sequence of artefacts in the soil and on the landscape to tell the story. What's more, it is often change which unearths buried archaeological treasure. In 1869 a farmer in the Lake District drained a tarn at Ehenside near Egremont. To his amazement, he found he had uncovered the remains of a Neolithic village: the moisture had even preserved wooden fishing spears.[1] Today change need not destroy our heritage. But it is doing just that.

The post-war agricultural revolution has brought with it a process of transformation which in almost every case now obliterates archaeological features rather than revealing them. Now agricultural change dwarfs all other threats to our archaeological heritage. The enclosure and ploughing of land that has lain uncultivated for a very long time and through lack of disturbance has provided safe harbourage for archaeological remains for centuries is by far the most damaging of any agricultural activity to our archaeological heritage. The bulldozing of farm roads through roughlands and the erection of farm buildings on top of ancient monuments are also highly destructive, although their impact is less extensive. But even routine activities can be enormously harmful, like the installation of underground drainage pipes through fields or the more recently developed technique of 'pan-busting', that is breaking up soil and sub-soil that has become compacted (often through the use of big new heavy machinery) with a gadget which bursts the bottom of each furrow to a depth of up to 36 inches.[2]

How the law is supposed to protect archaeological remains

About 8,000 or an estimated one per cent of the archaeological remains in our countryside designated as scheduled ancient monuments enjoy better legal protection than any other type of designated landscape – in theory. The Ancient Monuments and Archaeological Areas Act 1979 will[3] require farmers wishing to change the use of the soil on top of an ancient monument to seek permission from the Department of the Environment before going ahead.

This is an improvement on previous practice, which merely required that notice of such action be given to the Secretary of State for the Environment, so that the Department could, if it wished, seek to dissuade the landowner from going ahead. Compensation has been and will under the new Act be payable, however, and in these cost-conscious times, this is likely to mean that consent for ploughing will not be held back all that often.

The rest of our archaeological remains have no protection at all. Once again, the contrast between the fate of landscape features and that of the built environment is striking. The historic thatched and timber-framed buildings of our villages are well protected through the law, and rightly so; but the remains of prehistoric life in the open countryside behind them are being ploughed away.

Any building put up before 1700 is automatically 'listed', that is, it is placed in a central register compiled by the Department of the Environment; if its owner wishes to alter it in such a way that its special historical or architectural interest would be impaired – for instance, by altering a staircase or a window or, of course, by demolishing it altogether – he has to apply to his local planning authority for special permission to do so, in addition to any planning permission that may be needed. If permission is refused, no compensation if payable. These controls are backed up by tough enforcement powers. If somebody damages a listed building without consent, he is deemed to have committed an offence and can be fined heavily.

And if a planning authority considers that an owner is not maintaining his listed building properly it can serve a repairs notice on him requiring him to carry out specified works. If he fails to do so, it can do the work itself and send the owner the bill; or, failing this, it can acquire the building through compulsory purchase. In Great Britain 200,000 buildings have been listed either because they were built before 1700 or because the Department of the Environment considers them to be of special historic or architectural interest. The Cotswolds, to take one example of an area in which the difference in protection afforded to old buildings in villages and prehistoric remains in the open countryside is as stark as it is anywhere, contains 3,865 listed buildings which are energetically protected by local planning authorities. Since 1967, local authorities have also been able to give special protection to whole areas deemed to be of special historical or architectural interest. There are 10,000 'conservation areas' in England and Wales, including 38 in the Cotswolds. In these areas, special permission is needed for the demolition of all buildings, whether or not they have been listed. These two safeguards, superimposed on the requirement for planning permission for major changes to the built environment, have served to conserve both the historical information embodied in the villages, churches, manor-houses and barns of the Cotswolds and also their value as features giving special character to built-up England.

For our prehistoric remains, like our other landscape features, things are very different. A survey in 1979 by Alan Saville of the Committee for Rescue Archaeology of Avon, Gloucestershire and Somerset revealed that 44 per cent of the 906 main visible archaeological sites in the Cotswolds were being destroyed through ploughing – Iron Age hillforts, Romano-British sites, the sites of villages deserted in medieval times and Neolithic long and round barrows.[4] Most of the sites now being destroyed have never been and never will be excavated and the information about our history they embody both in their structure and in their relation to other archaeological and geographical features is unique. Said Alan Saville in his report: 'The chief threat . . . concerns archaeological sites which fall within the date range 4000 BC–AD 400. In this period the threat to sites is so widespread that the actual destruction of individual sites diminishes in importance, because what is at stake is the erosion of whole categories of archaeological evidence.' One such category is the Neolithic long barrows of the Cotswolds, 54 per cent of which are being ploughed up. Our evidence for the way of life of the Neolithic people who came to settle in the Cotswolds around 4000 BC comes chiefly from these great mausoleums of which it is estimated that the stone used to raise one of them would be more than enough to build a parish church. These barrows are unique to their area and of European significance; their destruction is an international scandal.

If it were nearly 50 per cent of the historic cottages of the Cotswold villages that were being dismantled rather than the antiquities that happen to lie in the open countryside, there would be a national outcry. The difference is simply that the threat to landscape features is not generally appreciated.

The fate of one particular relic, the 'thing' in the Lake District, illustrates graphically how irreplaceable are the archaeological remains that are being bulldozed away by farmers. The 'thing' stands at the head of Little Langdale in the heart of the Lake District. It is a square mound whose steep sides have been shaped into a short flight of grassy steps – a truly strange sight viewed from the fellside above after a light fall of snow or in late evening when the sun is low on the horizon. 'The site today conveys a strange feeling of antiquity, a feeling that is enhanced by the solemn line of dark, gnarled yew trees planted along one side of the platform,' wrote landscape historians Drs Roy Millward and Adrian Robinson in 1970.[5] Before a farm building was cut into the side of it in 1976, the 'thing' had not been scheduled because, like the vast majority of our archaeological remains, it had never been excavated so nobody was absolutely sure what it was. But although nobody had ever excavated the 'thing', most archaeologists who had seen it thought they knew what it was – the only remaining 'thing-mount', or Viking meeting-place, surviving in England.

Although the map of central Lakeland bristles with Norse names, the Vikings who invaded the Lake District in the ninth century left few remains that were to survive the following eleven centuries – just a few stone crosses. And as few contemporary documents survived either, this period in the history of north-west England, arguably the most fascinating, is something of an enigma. We do, however, know that the Vikings introduced their crafts, skills and language to the Lake District;

All kinds of people depend on the countryside. Children, for example, nearly always consider the countryside their favourite playground if they get the chance to visit it (Chapter 18). Now, however, one group – farmers – are dismantling the landscape which so many other groups cherish.

The English landscape is known all over the world as
varied, irregular and intimate – a tapestry of field,

wood, hedge, down and stream. This scene by the
River Wye at Symond's Yat is characteristic.

In a new agricultural revolution, the English countryside is now being stripped of its traditional character
by changed farming methods. This monotonous

landscape is near Batcombe, in Dorset, once among
the most charming of England's counties. (Chapters
5, 7, 9 and 22)

Earth-moving equipment (above) is ridding farmland of 'obstructions' – hedges and ditches, woods and copses, ponds and streams. Once this process is complete, the way is clear for other machines like this sugar beet harvester (below) to plough and harvest on the scale of mass production. (Chapter 1)

Mechanisation requires new farm roads and new buildings to house
machinery, as here on the Somerset Levels (above). Farmers can build
roads and erect buildings up to a considerable size without planning
permission. (Chapter 10) Another effect of agricultural rationalisation
(below) may be new curbs on public access to the countryside.
(Chapters 6, 7, 8 and 12)

Graffham Down, in West Sussex, in July 1979 (above) and in January 1980 (below) – before and after agricultural intensification began there. Local people anxious to save what was one of the few remaining areas of traditional downland in the county found there was virtually nothing they could do (Chapters 12 and 22).

and the existence of the 'thing', considers Dr William Rollinson, an expert on the history of the Lake District, suggests they may also have brought something else – their system of assemblies or 'things' where men gathered to elect a 'law speaker' and where the new laws were proclaimed before the assembled people. This tradition has been followed for centuries on a terraced mound, known as Tynwald, in the Isle of Man that closely resembles the Langdale 'thing'. In the 1930s the eminent Anglo-Norse scholar, Professor W.G.Collingwood, concluded that 'this thingmount in Little Langdale may be regarded as the Lakeland Tynwald'.[6] Nobody since then has seriously disputed his conclusion.

When the man who farmed the land on which the 'thing' stands decided to cut out one side of it to make way for a concrete-floored silage store, there was nothing to stop him. A silage store is an agricultural building and therefore does not need planning permission. The line of yews alongside the 'thing' was felled too, because stock had eaten the bark. Since 1976 tractors have been run along the side of the mound, grinding it down and crushing the steps. The 'thing' is no longer anything like the enigmatic landmark it was. We may never know the extent of the damage to archaeological evidence embodied in the structure itself or in any remains that lie or may have lain within it.

What is left of the 'thing' at Little Langdale has now been scheduled as an ancient monument, for what that is worth. But thousands of archaeological remains in our countryside are still unscheduled and therefore without any protection against agricultural intensification whatsoever. Then again, there is no national system at all for listing whole categories of landscape features of more recent historical interest. They are unprotected unless they happen to be threatened with 'development' as defined in the 1947 Town and Country Planning Act. Thus, a 2,000-year-old hedgerow, originally constructed as the boundary of a Celtic estate and comprising a unique record of part of our history, may be bulldozed away without the rest of the community knowing this is going to happen, let alone being able to prevent it. The few remaining tracts of ancient chalk downland turf in the Dorset Downs could be ploughed up at a moment's notice without anybody being able to do anything about it.

So at present we protect only the tip of the iceberg of the

historical record the landscape embodies. What man has built in the last 300 years is usually secure. But the evidence of his past embraced in ancient hedgerows, lanes, shaws, parks, trackways, the wide range of archaeological features our countryside contains and the shape of the landscape itself stands defenceless in the face of an accelerating process of destruction.

Why archaeological remains should be protected

There are four main reasons why the loss of ancient remains matters to us all.

Firstly, things Man has created in the countryside from Iron Age hillforts and Anglo-Saxon hedgebanks to fourteenth-century deer parks are a vital raw material of history. Archaeological remains provide a complete set of information about our past which is not matched by written records. The recent rate of destruction of archaeological remains has been likened by Dr Peter Fowler, the Secretary to the Royal Commission on Historical Monuments, to the burning of ten books from the British Library every day. Only a fraction of the information about our past that is inscribed on our landscape has so far been extracted. Dr Fowler believes this means that the amount of information that we don't know we don't know almost certainly far exceeds the amount of information that we simply don't know. It was not until the early 1970s, for example, that aerial photography, fieldwork and excavation revealed that our countryside, and therefore presumably society, was organised on a much more rational system from 2000 BC onwards than had ever been imagined before. Historians used to think that prehistoric Britain was a jumble of fields thrown higgledy-piggledy on the landscape and that society was organised over large areas only when the Romans came. But recent excavations of prehistoric fields on Dartmoor and the Berkshire Downs have disclosed a network of fields that suggest large-scale organisation and land allotment.[7] Other archaeological remains that still lie waiting to be discovered or unearthed could alter radically the history we think we know from written records. If we are concerned about truth and wish to teach history as it really was, then we must conserve the raw data.

Secondly, the destruction of archaeological remains deprives thousands of people of what could be a source of life enrichment. Urban dislocation has been accompanied by growing enthusiasm for local history as people seek to understand their roots. Over the last decade, archaeology and local history have become more and more popular choices of subject for evening classes. In 1975–76, more adult education students studied archaeology than studied music, and more studied local history than studied English language and literature.[8] Taken together, archaeology and local history attract as much support in adult education as politics, economics and sociology together. The two television series presented by Professor W.G.Hoskins in 1976 and 1978 on the history of England's landscape attracted a million viewers on average for each programme. And every year, thousands of people give up large amounts of free time to work in uncomfortable conditions as volunteers on archaeological digs.

The third reason why archaeological remains matter is that they provide a tool of enormous if as yet largely untapped potential for the education of our children. Many educationists now believe that the opportunity, for example, to piece together, Sherlock-Holmes style, the way in which an Iron Age settlement functioned could be of enormous value in the learning process. The discovery of an earlier form of social organisation through an examination of post-holes, the layout of the buildings and their relation one to another, the position of the settlement in relation to soil, topography, water supply and so on would be as rich an educational experience as many teachers can imagine. And then, on top of this, there are the opportunities to trace the way in which the location of the settlement has influenced more recent geography (the location of long barrows is often responsible for the line of parish boundaries laid down in the eighth century, for example). If we destroy the country's stock of archaeological raw material we condemn not only our children but generations yet unborn to a second-hand view of their past. History (and geography) will have to be understood from books or television alone.

But the destruction of relics also strips our countryside of much of its interest and character.

The landscape of the Land's End peninsula is perhaps thicker with remains of prehistoric man than any other corner of England. They provide the area with a pervasive sense of the past that permeates the life and literature of the area. West Cornwall's megalithic tombs, round barrows and circles of standing stones, Iron Age forts, and prehistoric subterranean refuges or fogous litter the rough grass and gorse fields, half-hidden by massive granite-based hedges, or stand naked on the open, rugged moors. Three things have preserved Cornwall's relics: a pasture-biased rural economy, a large amount of uncultivated moorland, and the apparent immovability of the boulders and stones with which the prehistoric structures were built.

The imprint of prehistoric man can still be detected in Cornwall's settlement pattern. Villages of the traditional English form, clustered around a village green, are rare in Cornwall. Until 1950, when the first wave of second-home owners, retired people and flat-dwelling holiday-makers started to swamp all her communities, Cornwall's typical settlement unit had been a hamlet consisting of a farm and four or five farmworkers' cottages. Nicholas Johnson, the Secretary to the Cornwall Committee for Rescue Archaeology, believes that this settlement pattern is derived from Cornwall's 'rounds'. These are the remains of standard settlements found in Cornwall in Iron Age and Romano-British times (from about 300 BC to 22 AD). A defensible site was encircled by a bank and ditch enclosing just a single main farmstead and four or five probably wooden houses and farm buildings clustered round a cobbled farmyard. Nothing like the Cornish 'round' exists anywhere else in England. And the style of life of which they form virtually the only surviving relic is only now just beginning to be pieced together. At the moment, 94 per cent of the rounds of Cornwall are being destroyed by agricultural change, according to a survey carried out in 1979 by the Cornwall Committee for Rescue Archaeology.[9]

Moorland reclamation and hedge removal are the two types of agricultural 'improvement' that are doing most to strip away Cornwall's antiquities. Moorland reclamation is carried out mainly to intensify sheep production. Normally, rocks, stones and gorse bushes are bulldozed away. The land is deep ploughed, drainage ditches are dug, fences are put down and the moor is reseeded with ryegrass. The result of this process in the St Breock Downs which rise to 200 feet inland from Padstow, for example, has been the removal through agricultural intensification of about as much rough moorland and Bronze Age barrows in the 13 years up to 1976 as occurred during the whole of the 75-year period up to 1963. Now, just three square miles of moorland harbouring 19 barrows remain intact, compared to seven square miles of moor and 40 barrows in 1963. At this rate of ploughing, this distinctive landscape will itself have been consigned to history by the end of the present century. The wealth of archaeological treasures Cornwall possesses at the moment could attract enormous interest if they were exploited a little more energetically. Here, perhaps more than in any other part of England, the opportunity exists for archaeological tours – trips around areas of say 50 square miles in which visitors could alight at different points to examine sites and whole landscapes illustrating particular periods of history and pre-history. Such tours could give the visitor an understanding of the way in which whole landscapes have evolved and shaped the lives of different peoples. They would have much more to offer than the inspection of isolated sites. Yet even relatively unspectacular historical and archaeological sites attract tens of thousands of visitors each year – like the remains of an Iron Age village at Chysauster in West Penwith (28,000 visitors in 1978) or, on the other side of the country, the remains of an Iron Age settlement on Butser Hill in Hampshire (24,000 visitors in 1979). In Cornwall, however, the raw material for archaeological tours taking in, say, clifftop forts, villages, farmed areas, temples, circles of standing stones, rounds and so on will have disappeared – unless something is done to halt the destruction wrought by agricultural change. What has happened in the Cotswolds shows what could happen in Cornwall. Thirty years ago, the Cotswold countryside was almost as rich in archaeological treasures as Cornwall. Now, historical interest in the Cotswolds is virtually confined to the meticulously preserved villages: the countryside, much of it now consisting of featureless ploughland, has been stripped of most of its treasures.

In spite of the destruction which continues to take place, however, there are still corners of our countryside in which upstanding archaeological remains that are still relatively intact add much to the interest and enjoyment people derive from visiting these places. In 1977 a 23-year-old girl described to me the feelings aroused in her by Dartmoor's ancient remains:

> Often when I'm walking alone I think of ancient man and I stand on the hillside, perhaps near a settlement, and I think

he looked out from here and he loved this view. I do feel that our ancestors appreciated their surroundings and built their homes in certain places because they liked them. I often stand and look across to other settlements on other hills and think of our forefathers signalling to each other. You do feel a real link with them, and you know that you're feeling the same feelings as they did here.

The loss of physical evidence of our past would not only rob us of information. It would impoverish our lives.

17

Disappearing Wildlife

For many people (perhaps our poets in particular) the creatures and plants of our countryside have provided the key to its charms. The irregularity and intimacy of lowland England ensure that a degree of cover exists which is unparalleled in any other form of agricultural landscape. As a result, it has been blessed with an extraordinarily rich wildlife community. The plants and animals of England have been a source of pleasure for her people for hundreds of years, though they have taken on a new significance since the Industrial Revolution. Alienated urban man and, in particular, his children, have found contact with nature in the countryside, from bird-watching to dipping for tadpoles, an important means of restoring a relationship with their natural environment.

The mix of species that make up England's wildlife has developed over centuries. To tear it apart is an act of vandalism that may astound future generations. But that is what we are doing. While some groups of plants and animals, such as perennial ryegrass and wasps, have not been adversely affected by agricultural change, many other species have seen their populations decimated by the post-war agricultural revolution. It is not only rare animals and plants which have been hit. The effect on the everyday creatures central to everyone's idea of rural England has been far more alarming. These creatures include butterflies and spiders, crickets and grasshoppers, many species of bird, frogs, toads and newts, badgers and deer, moles, voles, shrews and harvest mice, slugs and snails, lichens and mosses, countless species of flowering plant, reptiles, moths and dragonflies.[1] To this list many more species, like earthworms, could probably be added if survey information existed for them. The conservation of our wild creatures is inseparable from our agricultural policy, since agriculture is the main activity over 70 per cent of England's surface. If we want to save our wildlife we must contain agricultural change.

What has been happening to our wild birds is mirrored throughout our wildlife.

Some species have been able to adapt to the changed circumstances of agricultural Britain, like the kestrel, the starling
and the wood pigeon. But others have suffered as the conditions on which they depended ceased to exist. They include
some of our most attractive and characteristic birds. The
stone curlew, a bird of the chalk downlands, and the woodlark,
which depends on sandy heathland, have virtually disappeared
already. Wetland birds like redshank, lapwing and snipe have
been decimated. And one bird whose existence was totally
bound up with agriculture, the corncrake, seems to have
become completely extinct in England. It is a large, brown,
secretive crane-like bird, whose weird cry stamped its name
into our literature.

The corncrake is a relative of the moorhen. Its mistake was
to adapt its life-cycle too closely to the traditional pattern of
haymaking. After winging its way to England from Africa
each May, the corncrake would find a mate and then lay its
speckled yellow eggs under the cover of the tall plants of the
rough pasture and damp meadows, like yellow iris, nettles,
docks or sedges. By the time the hay was cut in July or August,
the chicks would have hatched and could move with their
parents away from the nest site. Once it was a relatively
common bird in Britain. But over the last half-century its
numbers have shot down and its range contracted dramatically.
A survey in 1978 by the Royal Society for the Protection of
Birds found corncrakes in only 23 per cent of the 10km
squares in which they had been recorded apparently breeding
in 1968–72.[2] The RSPB believes the main cause of the
corncrake's disappearance from much of our countryside is
agricultural change. Some birds simply could not find fields
with long grass. Some nested in ryegrass leys which were
being grown as a crop for silage; when this was harvested,
usually earlier in the year than traditional hay-cutting, the
chicks were killed. If you want to see (or hear) a corncrake in
Britain now, your best bet is to head for the Hebrides where
traditional hay-cutting, and the corncrake, survive.

The corncrake is, however, a loss that will be mourned
mainly by bird-watchers. Some people may never have heard
of it. The danger is now, however, that the ordinary, much-
loved birds of the English countryside may be following the
corncrake to extinction.

Flycatchers, thrushes, tits, warblers, woodpeckers, the

nightingale, and perhaps most of our characteristic bird species, belong ecologically to the woodland edge. The clumps of trees, woods and hedgerows of lowland England have multiplied the equivalent of woodland edge habitat and this is the reason for the richness of England's bird life. Now, of course, this kind of habitat is being destroyed and big reductions in the populations of our typical British birds are resulting. Over 70 per cent of bird species on British farms depend on trees and bushes to feed or nest in, according to the Nature Conservancy Council. When trees disappear these birds disappear; only ground-nesting species can survive in a treeless and bushless landscape. Says the Conservancy:

> If all farms were totally modernised so that they consisted solely of arable crops, grass leys, chemically treated ditches, farm buildings and a few trees and bushes grown for visual amenity, they would support far less wildlife than does the average farm today; about 80 per cent of the birds and about 95 per cent of the butterfly species would be lost from the farmed landscapes.[3]

This devastation is taking place at a time when people are interested in birds as never before. The Royal Society for the Protection of Birds has more than 300,000 members; between 1969 and 1979 its membership numbers multiplied nearly sevenfold. The Society's Youth Section alone, the Young Ornithologists' Club, boasts 30,000 members. But for all these people the countryside is becoming a more and more disappointing place. A bird-watcher in Sussex, for example, now stands something like a quarter of the chance of seeing a yellow wagtail that he would have had in 1947. Between 1947 and 1956, the Sussex breeding population of this delightful bird was cut in half, according to a survey by Michael Shrubb of the Sussex Ornithological Society.[4] Mr Shrubb attributes the decline during this nine-year period to the widespread drainage of marshlands for more intensive agriculture and building over coastal wetlands.

But birds far less fragile than the yellow wagtail are suffering. In Huntingdonshire, the use of large amounts of pesticides on crops has rendered the sturdy-looking magpie virtually extinct.[5]

The plight of our mammals, like the badger and the otter, is well known. But less well appreciated is what's happening to our tiny group of reptile species. These small, prehistoric-looking beasts have always been under-represented in Britain, though the few species that exist have nonetheless played a vital role in country life. The British Isles have only six indigenous species of reptile: three lizards and three snakes. They are all found together only on the broken ribbon of heathland stretching across southern England from Surrey to Dorset, the remnant of a once continuous swathe of heather-dominated vegetation growing on poor sandy soils. Thomas Hardy was almost certainly thinking of the heaths of east Dorset when he introduced the central character of *The Return of the Native*, Egdon Heath, in chapter one of his novel:

> To recline on a stump of thorn in the central valley of Egdon, between afternoon and night, as now, where the eye could reach nothing of the world outside the summits and shoulders of heathland which filled the whole circumference of its glance, and to know that everything around and underneath had been from prehistoric times as unaltered as the stars overhead, gave ballast to the mind adrift on change, and harassed by the irrepressible New. The great inviolate place had an ancient permanence which the sea cannot claim. . . . The sea changed, the fields changed, the rivers, the villages, and the people changed, yet Egdon remained.

Since Hardy wrote, these heaths have been reduced in area by 80 per cent, mainly as a result of agricultural intensification and conifer afforestation but also, to a lesser extent, through building development and mineral working.[6] This process of erosion has left two of our six native British reptiles on the verge of extinction. Millions of years of evolution have left the beautifully patterned smooth snake and the sand lizard (like a miniature dinosaur) highly adapted to life in one of England's oldest and most distinctive landscapes – the Dorset heaths. Hampered by their need for big territories and unable to travel easily, the lizards have simply been unable to adapt quickly enough to the loss of their habitat. For our remaining four native reptiles – the adder, common lizard, slow worm and grass snake – national data do not exist. Local surveys of the position of the last two have been made, and they indicate a decline.[7] These surveys do not show the reasons for this decline, but the grass snake is restricted to marshes and to

woods and hedgerows near water, so it does not seem unreasonable to suppose that agricultural change is at least in
part responsible for the apparent decline of this species in
Buckinghamshire, Cheshire, Suffolk, Nottinghamshire and
Shropshire.
Agricultural change is hitting Britain's reservoir of wild
plant species as hard as it is hitting our animals. Between 1930
and 1960, the numbers of Britain's 278 rarest plant species
were cut by 30 per cent, according to Dr F.H.Perring, formerly
of the Institute of Terrestrial Ecology's Biological Records
Centre, who has compared the number of 10km grid squares
occupied by these species at different dates. Dr Perring
suggests:

> It is reasonable to assume that the present number of
> localities of our 278 rarest species is only about one third of
> what it once was [in 1600, the first date for which figures
> are available]. . . . It is dangerous I know to use these slender
> figures to project forwards, but if the present apparent loss
> continued (about 15 10km squares per annum) the majority
> of these species would be extinct or nearly so by the year
> 2050.[8]

Nature reserves: our desperate remedy?

In the face of the relentless erosion of natural habitats,
naturalists have sometimes felt obliged to reach for what has
seemed the only possible way of clinging to some shreds of
our botanical and zoological heritage: they have urged the
creation of nature reserves, devoted exclusively to the preservation of wildlife. This approach has of course been welcomed
by the NFU and the Ministry of Agriculture who have seen it
as a way of getting naturalists off their backs. After early
experiences, however, naturalists have come to believe that
the idea of preserving samples of the nation's wildlife in neat
ghettoes is just not going to work. Most notably of all, the
Royal Society for the Protection of Birds, which once put
virtually all of its efforts into buying up land for reserves, has
now changed tack and become keenly interested in agricultural methods.
The fate of the large blue butterfly demonstrates the dangers of reliance on special nature reserves to preserve en-
dangered species. The two sanctuaries devoted to the species

just didn't provide a big enough area to guarantee its survival, and by 1979 it appeared to have become extinct.[9] The Nature Conservancy Council considers that if we were to rely on nature reserves as our only means of conserving our existing flora and fauna we would have to devote a great deal more land to this purpose than the 4 per cent of land in Britain which in theory (though not in practice) is safeguarded for nature conservation at present. But, says the Conservancy, if we are *not* going to increase this land area substantially, then we are forced to rely on plant and animal populations in farmland to ensure that the small populations protected in nature reserves remain viable. Since there are now relatively few pieces of marginal land on farmland left, virtually all of them are now crucially important for the conservation of our wildlife species.

Of course, even if it were possible to maintain museum-like collections of English wildlife in special sanctuaries, the achievement would be of limited value. A world in which people living in the big cities had to travel many miles to see a primrose or a wren would be of doubtful appeal. The charm of our wildlife has always been inseparable from the country-side of which it is a part. If our plants and animals are to be relegated to reserves, they might as well be relegated to the zoo, some at least may think. Of course, the elimination of traditional wildlife from much of our countryside is already under way.

Twenty years ago, on station platforms throughout the length and breadth of England, clusters of children could be seen on spring mornings armed with fishing nets and jam-jars, all set for a day's tadpoling in the country. At the end of the day they would be there again, comparing catches and antici-pating the thrill of transferring their wriggling catch to a new home – an old sink, perhaps, or a glass tank, into which stones had been dropped in strategic sites – and then watching their tiny guests gradually sprout legs, lose their tails and meta-morphose into frogs. The tadpole's high-speed demonstration of the miracle of growth was taken for granted as a basic experience of childhood. Today, however, for many children, it is a thing of the past.

The reason is not that contemporary children prefer drier pursuits to the slimy pleasures of the pond. They no longer have the opportunity to taste the joys of dipping for tadpoles, newts, sticklebacks, pond-skaters, water-boatmen, caddis-flies and all the other tiny creatures that used to abound in England's ponds, dykes and streams. For modern agriculture has been steadily eliminating the habitat of all these creatures. Water was the cradle of life: all plant and animal life, leading up to man himself, is supposed to have originated in water, and many plants and animals still depend on spending at least one stage of their life cycle in water – like our amphibians, for example: frogs, toads and newts. Frogs take two years to develop sexual maturity, and through an instinctive faculty as yet not understood, they return to the very pond or stream from which they hatched as tadpoles from frog spawn two years earlier. One of the saddest spring-time sights in the English countryside now is that of thousands of frogs, toads and newts sitting hopelessly round the spot where the pond of their birth, now destroyed, should have been.

Frog populations have declined by more than 99 per cent in some parts of England, according to a study in 1974.[10] Three scientists found that an estimated average density for adult common frogs of five to the acre in the 1940s had become 0.08 in the Isle of Wight, 0.02 in West Yorkshire and 0.01 in Huntingdonshire. In some areas, they believe the decline may have exceeded 99 per cent; and they blame loss of breeding sites as the main reason through sites being filled in or drained. The post-war decline in numbers of the common toad were probably spatially and temporally similar to those of the frog. Newts too have suffered. Of eleven colonies known within six miles of Brighton in the mid-50s, for example, only one now survives.[11]

Land drainage has made once common marshland plants rare in many areas. Between 1950 and 1976 fifteen plants of marsh and water meadow in Bedfordshire, or 23 per cent of the county's wetland plant species, became extinct, according to Luton naturalist Dr J. G. Dony. The plants that are now no longer found in Bedfordshire, mainly because of drainage to increase agricultural output, include grass of parnassus, sundew, marsh orchid, heath spotted orchid and snake's head fritillary. What this means is that if, like Dr Dony, you live in Luton and want to feast your eyes on the nodding, mottled, maroon heads of a fritillary ('snakes'-heads like drops of blood' in the eyes of Gerard Manley Hopkins), a plant that used to be common near Luton, you now have to travel to a nature reserve in Suffolk. A characteristic flower of damp hay meadows, the fritillary is known today in England as a whole from only twenty-four localities in twelve 10km squares. Before 1930 there were records from a hundred such squares.[13] Important habitats like fritillary meadows lost through agricultural intensification are most unlikely to be replaced by any other habitat elsewhere of comparable individuality and scientific interest.

Fifty years ago, the cowslip, the bluebell, the comon frog and the common toad were ubiquitous and plentiful in the English countryside. In *Lark Rise to Candleford*, Flora Thompson describes the way in which children in north Oxfordshire a hundred years ago used to play ball with handfuls of cowslips, the stalks tied tightly together and the blooms pulled down to cover the stems, so plentiful were these flowers. But playing ball with cowslips or gathering armfuls of bluebells are joys known to few English children today. The cowslip and the bluebell have become rare plants in large stretches of rural England, just as the common frog and common toad have become rare animals. In other areas, gathering primroses and bluebells, blackberrying, or looking for the first snowdrops are still delights to be enjoyed in the countryside. But for how much longer?

If wild creatures and plants were to be confined to nature reserves, our children would be deprived of one of the greatest pleasures the English countryside has always offered: the joy of discovering wild creatures by chance. The thrill of unexpected discovery is the main theme in W.H.Hudson's book *Afoot in England* (1909), in which he says:

> If I have a purpose in this book . . . it is only this – the charm of the unknown, and the infinitely greater pleasure in discovering the interesting things for ourselves than in informing ourselves of them by reading. It is like the difference in flavour in wild fruits and all wild meats found and gathered by our own hands in wild places and that of the same prepared and put on the table before us.

That is what the countryside is all about; and there is no short cut to protecting it.

18

Impoverished Lives

Contact with wildlife and our own past are just two of the opportunities which our countryside has offered us up till now. There are plenty of others. The countryside has provided the direct inspiration for a great swathe of our nation's art: painting, sculpture, poetry, literature and music. It is no accident that England has produced great landscape painters like Constable, Turner and Gainsborough; Italy, for example, has no comparable school of landscape painting. Even within our present century, and the demise of representational art, the natural world continues to inspire our artists. A top ten of our own century's painters, sculptors, musicians, poets and novelists might include Paul Nash and Graham Sutherland; Barbara Hepworth and Henry Moore; Edward Elgar and Ralph Vaughan Williams; Robert Graves and W.H.Auden; D.H.Lawrence and Virginia Woolf – all influenced to a greater or lesser extent by the natural world. At the age of sixty-four Elgar wrote: 'I am still at heart the dreamy child who used to be found in the reeds by Severn side with a sheet of paper trying to fix the sounds.' The titles of a few of Paul Nash's paintings bear witness to the importance of the everyday countryside to our nation's greatest artists: 'The Pond', 'Study of Trees', 'Pond in the Field', 'The Wood on the Hill', 'Event on the Downs', 'Landscapes of the Red Fungus' and 'Chilterns under Snow'.

More important than any particular activity for which England's countryside provides opportunities, however, is its overall role as a reservoir of joy and spiritual refreshment for the community at large. Throughout the ages, the countryside has offered urban man the chance to relax and enjoy himself in beautiful and interesting surroundings. To try to get an idea of how the current agricultural revolution threatens recreation opportunities, I have looked at its impact on just two groups: children and townspeople.

Children and the countryside

Play, the means by which children gain most of their understanding of the world, remains a mystery. Adults who can never be in on the secret do their best to help by setting up traditional playgrounds, adventure playgrounds and parks and a welter of seaside amenities. Yet the evidence suggests that the really important opportunities for play are those that are not structured by adults, but which instead offer children the chance to create their own experience. Iona and Peter Opie, the authors of *The Lore and Language of Schoolchildren*, 1959, explain it like this: 'The literature of childhood abounds with evidence that the peaks of a child's experience are not visits to the cinema, or even family outings to the sea, but occasions when he escapes into places that are disused and overgrown and silent. To a child there is more joy in a rubbish tip than a flowering rockery, in a fallen tree than a piece of statuary, in a muddy track than a gravel path.'

The countryside is of course a boundless treasure-house of opportunities for creative play, and one for which no real substitute has ever been found. George Eliot captured the impact of rural sights and sounds on the youthful consciousness in *The Mill on the Floss* (1860). She wrote: 'We could never have loved the earth so well if we had had no childhood in it. . . . These familiar flowers, these well-remembered bird-notes, this sky with its fitful brightness, these furrowed and grassy fields, each with a sort of personality given to it by the capricious hedgerows – such things as these are the mother tongue of our imagination.'

When I spent a day in 1978 with primary school-children from Minster, a village in east Kent, I found them adamant that the country was a much better place to play in than the street, the playground, the recreation ground with its grass, swings and slide, or even the seaside. Minster, a village of about three thousand people, is bounded by intensively culti-vated farmland. A major land drainage scheme in the 1960s removed marshes on the southern side to which villagers had traditionally enjoyed *de facto* access and on which children from Minster and Ramsgate had fished for tadpoles, newts and sticklebacks. Nonetheless, several scraps of rough, marginal land still remain – a rough meadow used for clay pigeon shooting, a few remaining dykes that support tadpoles, small fields used as rough grazing for horses, odd hedgerows and clumps of trees. Minster children prefer this country to the playground or the seaside for five reasons.[1] First, it provides a much greater variety of 'props', from bullrushes to spiders, long grasses (musical instruments as well as craft materials) to snails. Second, the countryside provides for much greater freedom of movement: not only does long grass make possible games like 'Soldiers': it also enables children to feel safe. They believe they can take a tumble while playing leapfrog, for instance, without hurting themselves. Third, the countryside provides a separate place to which they can retreat from their homes, or rather their parents' homes, in the village. The construction of little dens or miniature houses is a much favoured activity. Fourth, the animals of the countryside provide a rich source of enjoyment – watching birds, catching tadpoles, collecting spiders to frighten parents with, racing snails, letting grass snakes slither through the fingers, letting frogs bounce up and down in the hand. Finally, the countryside is a source of the unknown: it provides endless surprises and makes possible unexpected scrapes. Because there is so much to discover in the country, many of the children I spoke to were happy to spend time simply looking around, finding new places, stumbling across exciting, unusual things, getting into scrapes, skipping from one pursuit to another. Whereas woods, for example, are ideal for anything from playing hide-and-seek to chasing animals or playing stunts on bicycles, 'at the seaside all there is to do is swim and walk along the beach and make sandcastles'.

Yet the Minster children were all too well aware that their favourite playground was being eroded. They cited one form or another of agricultural change as the most usual reason for the destruction or alteration of their favoured play areas. Across the countryside, this kind of devastation must already have changed the experience of childhood in England substantially.

Scraps of rough land are not being created afresh to replace those that are eliminated. Local councils provide recreation grounds, but these may not meet the needs of children for reasons grown-ups may not appreciate. In Minster, for instance, eight-year-old Georgina told me of a buttercup meadow opposite her house which has now been ploughed up: 'We used always to go and play there. Because there was lots of grass we used to make daisy chains. Sometimes when it rained there was a big ditch and all the water overran like a pond. We used to run about and hide because there was an old stable filled with straw.' Georgina explained that no substitute for her buttercup meadow exists in Acol, the little offshoot of Minster in which she lives: there are no other similar meadows in which farmers allow children to play, and the village green has few flowers and lots of nettles.

Or take the felling of some trees in Minster, which were of no value to the farmer but were very important in the life of one nine-year-old boy:

> Up the top of our road there's these big green trees, short trees. My friend and I cut through them and got inside and made a tunnel from one end to the other and sat in it and it was comfortable inside and then beside it we made a path through the trees. Inside you can see outside and it's a bit cold. We covered it over with leaves and grass outside so that the rain couldn't get in at the top because it did. Now it's been cut down, we can't use it. The farmer cut it down because it looked untidy. There's no other places to play like that. We liked it there and when it was chopped down we were disappointed because we had quite a bit of fun up there.

It is not, of course, only country children who suffer from the obliteration of the rural playground. Their parents, too, regard the odd scraps of uncultivated marginal land supporting hedgerows, spinneys, rough meadows and heaths, streams and woods on the edges of the small towns and villages in which they live as essential to their experience of country life. These little lungs close to people's homes enable them to live hand in glove with nature – which is what many of them came to the countryside to do. They use these pieces of land for anything from an early morning stroll or jog to exercising the dog, botanising, bird-watching or picnicking. It is on these patches of rough ground that most country pursuits from clay pigeon shooting to courting depend. It is almost impossible to categorise the uses to which these pieces of rough countryside are put, so deeply are they bound up with people's lives, as Francis Kilvert's diary or Flora Thompson's *A Country Calendar*, for example, make clear.

Townspeople and the countryside

The rest of us are compensated no more adequately than our country cousins for the loss of the great outdoors. The main extensions in the amount of rural land to which the public have a right of access in our countryside have come through the acquisition of new sites by the National Trust, the reclamation for recreation of disused gravel workings, and the creation of local authority 'country parks' – although there was already *de facto* or even *de jure* access to many of these places before they became country parks. But the gain in the number of rural playgrounds has been far outweighed by the loss to the plough of areas like Graffham Down to which *de facto* public access existed in addition to the loss of the attractions of large stretches of countryside that formed a beautiful and interesting backcloth to a wide range of rural pursuits.

By a bitter stroke of fate, the recreation policies followed since 1960 have increased the disadvantage of townspeople wishing to visit the countryside. For policies have been designed to keep them out of the countryside that has managed to escape the plough and still retains much of its beauty – shooting estates for example – and to confine them to artificial playgrounds in far less attractive countryside near to towns. Though the conservation of fragile landscapes and wildlife communities has usually been cited as the reason for this policy, the agricultural lobby has had a lot to do with it. Farmers have vigorously supported the 'protection' of the countryside from visitors, as visitors (and the problems or supposed problems they bring) would be kept away from farmland at the same time.

Hereford and Worcester County Council is one local authority that makes its concern to keep visitors from bothering farmers explicit. The Herefordshire Structure Plan, proposes that agriculture shall be protected from 'the unnecessary interference and disruption arising from the large and increasing number of visitors to the countryside by a positive policy of discouragement'.[2] The areas to which people will be steered for recreation, then, will not necessarily include the countryside from which they might be expected to derive the most enjoyment. The council points to disused mineral workings as an example of the type of countryside on which it intends to develop recreation facilities. Another county

council, Buckinghamshire, intends to minimise 'conflict with
the interests of agriculture, forestry, local residents, landscape,
archaeology and wildlife conservation', by encouraging 'the
concentration of countryside recreation in the Colne Valley
Regional Park [on the north-west fringe of London] and centres
around Milton Keynes and other urban areas'.[3] The idea in
this case is to provide 'honeypots' near the main towns so people
will not get into the heart of the countryside where they might
interfere with agriculture or other activities like pheasant
shooting. Thus the Buckinghamshire plan contains no mention
of plans to secure public access to the forbidden territory of
mid and north Buckinghamshire's thousands of acres of
glorious private parkland and woodland – areas that have
been protected from the ravages of the agricultural revolution
because of their importance for pheasants. Pheasant shooting
is a rural activity that could quite easily be combined with
recreation provision for the general public. But the assumption that it is not the local authority's job to challenge the
existing bias against public recreation in the use of rural land
goes unchallenged not only in Buckinghamshire but by the
vast majority of county councils.

The idea that councils should try to protect the countryside
from people rather than open it up to them grew out of panic
fed by forecasts of population and economic growth in the
early 1960s. The post-war baby boom led demographers of
the early 60s to predict a population explosion. And people
were expected to become much more prosperous as well as
more numerous: economic growth would give ordinary
working people wealth which would enable them to buy
luxuries like cars and holidays which had hitherto been the
prerogative of the rich. Recreation planners responded energetically to the projected population and economic expansion.
Planner Michael Dower captured their mood in an influential
treatise called 'The Fourth Wave'.[4] He warned that the
expected growth in demand for somewhere for people to
spend their leisure time would put enormous pressure on the
face of Britain. Dower advised planners to 'see people like
ants, scurrying from coast to coast, on holiday, swarming out
of cities in July and August by car, coach, train and aeroplane
to a multitude of resorts and hidden places throughout the
isles of Britain.' 'Can we enhance the lives of our people
without ruining the island they live upon?' he asked.

So great was the pressure of people and cars that was expected that Dower rejected the idea of meeting countryside recreation needs by spreading 'a thin layer of gambolling humanity across the whole island'. Instead he proposed that visitors be concentrated into what have now become known as 'honeypots', so leaving the mountains and moors for the wilderness seeker.

As a matter of fact, the projections on which Dower and many others based their assessment of future recreation pressures on England's countryside have proved wildly wrong. Dower thought the population of England and Wales would zoom from 52 million in 1965 to 70 million by the year 2000. Now at an estimated 49 million, it will almost certainly not go over 51 million by the end of the century. Similarly with car ownership, Dower assumed that by the year 2000 almost every other person in England and Wales (including children and elderly people) would have his own car, and that the number of cars in Britain would quadruple from 1965's mere 7 million to 30 million. In fact, however, the number is now only 14 million; the Department of Transport's current guess for 2000 is only 24 million. But in the early 60s only a tiny handful of people doubted the projections on which planners and policy-makers were working. And as the decade wore on, more and more people and organisations joined Dower in warning of the enormous damage the teeming 'fourth wave' of leisure seekers could wreak on Britain's fragile countryside.

During this period little reference was made to people's recreation needs, let alone the ways in which the countryside could best meet them. Instead, people were seen as a threat from which the countryside had to be urgently protected. Gradually the new orthodoxy emerged complete: there has been and will continue to be a dramatic increase in the already large numbers of car-borne visitors forging their way from towns and cities into the countryside; as a result, many areas of mountain, downland and clifftop will be eroded to bare rock; the seashore can absorb millions of visitors with less damage and possesses an infrastructure of facilities so people should be steered towards it. In the countryside, country parks and picnic sites should be established as buffers between town and farmland; these will be near the built-up areas and will decoy people into places where they cannot do much harm.

It is now apparent that the fears that created the existing policy are pretty well groundless. Taking wildlife, for instance, it is certainly true that countryside recreation affects eco-systems – indeed, it would be surprising if it did not.[5] Walking and picnicking on grassland, for instance, can cause species more resistant to trampling or to nutrient enrichment to replace those less resistant over a period of time. In very heavily used spots, like Box Hill and Kynance Cove, the bare ground which is exposed may be eroded by wind and rain. This, however, seems to be the *only* significant identifiable ill-effect of any form of recreation on wildlife or natural landscape features. And it is a very small problem indeed. Very, very little countryside is actually trampled away. Damage to land-scape or wildlife caused by recreation pressure pales into in-significance when compared to that resulting from, say, herbi-cides, building or pollution.

The story is not very different where farming itself is concerned. What the surveys so far carried out suggest is that serious problems are few and far between. Townspeople visiting the countryside seem to pose no more general problems for agriculture than they do for wildlife or landscape. Empirical, rather than anecdotal evidence, suggests that farmers as a whole do not incur serious financial losses as a result of trespass, vandalism, sheep worrying and so on: such losses as have occurred are never estimated to reach more than a few per cent of a farmer's income.[6] What is more, farmers can make quite a lot of money out of townspeople who take an interest in the countryside, through anything from farm-gate sales and 'pick-your-own' to bed and breakfast accommodation and caravan sites. This contribution to farmers' income far outweighs any losses which visitors seem to be inflicting on them. Indeed, the townsman in the country-side is a very different kind of creature from the rampaging brute of farmers' legends. The evidence (see pp. 235-36) suggests that he is most of the time a rather timid person, far too afraid of the mysterious world around him to start trying to damage it.

The 154 country parks and 193 picnic sites that have been set up since the 1968 Countryside Act empowered local authorities to provide them do of course fulfil a valuable function in reducing the risk of visitor damage to fragile landscapes and farmland and in providing recreation facilities near to towns. But the approach they reflect, coupled with the steady erosion of the attractions of the wider countryside through agricultural intensification, presents a bleak picture for those English people who would enjoy their landscape. If we are to begin to use out countryside to its best advantage, honeypots need to be complemented by a host of other measures. Local authorities must attempt to open up countryside of the highest quality as well as providing playgrounds in drabber, if more convenient, places. Efforts to curb damage wrought by agricultural change, the opening up of tracts of attractive but inaccessible countryside and the provision of public transport to the country for people without cars are the kind of steps which would at least suggest an appreciation of the real issues on the part of the authorities responsible for recreation.

At present, central government and the vast majority of local authorities treat countryside recreation as if it were merely an optional extra in the lives of a few people. But, in fact, visiting the countryside is an activity to which a very substantial proportion of our people choose to devote a very substantial slice of their spare time. In 1978 the Countryside Commission carried out in-depth interviews with a sample of 5,000 people to try to pinpoint the leisure preferences of the English.[7] Fifty-four per cent of their sample had visited the countryside at least once in the previous month. Making trips to the country was more popular than any of the other activities, apart from gardening, that could be considered as comparable activities – watching or taking part in outdoor sports, visiting the seaside, do-it-yourself, or visiting urban parks. For some people, visiting the countryside is simply a pleasant pastime. But for others the countryside or some aspect of it meets a deeply-felt need. For a significant proportion of our population, the spiritual refreshment which the countryside can offer is a vital psychological lifeline that, quite literally, helps them stay sane, or at least free from depression, anxiety or any of the thousand other minor psychological ills which contemporary flesh is heir to. 'In this country, . . . the significance of recreational provision has not been appreciated', wrote the Select Committee of the House of Lords on Sport and Leisure in 1973: 'Society ought to regard sport and leisure not as a slightly eccentric form of indulgence but as one of the community's everyday needs.'

Conclusion to Part Five

There is no getting away from the fact that post-war technological change has rendered many features of the traditional
English landscape obsolescent. Farmers do not really have
much interest in maintaining a colourful patchwork of small
fields divided by hedgerows and stone walls, scattered with
woods, copses and solitary trees and drained by streams and
dykes. The demands that shaped this landscape have disappeared and new farming practices do not require many of
the old features.

But of course the rural landscape as it has evolved over the
last six thousand years satisfies many needs other than those
of farmers: it is the environment for those who live and work
in the countryside, it is the home of countless wild plants and
animals, and it meets a profusion of recreational needs for
many people who live in towns and cities. Just as the second
agricultural revolution dispossessed the peasants, with the
enclosure hedges described as their 'economic gravestones',
so the current agricultural revolution threatens to dispossess
those people who value the countryside as more than a food
factory. Hard as their fate was, the peasants of the eighteenth
century possessed rights over the common fields and had to
be compensated for their loss. But now, the interest of the
general public in what is to farmers marginal land goes unrecog-
nised, even though it may embrace anything from wildlife,
history, archaeology, landscape painting or picnicking to the
impact of a decline in tourism on the national economy. No
legal rights protect the use of ponds for tadpoling or the use
of meadows for picking flowers. It is popularly supposed that
the power of the landowning classes was eradicated in the
eighteenth and nineteenth centuries. But in fact, the 0.5 per
cent of our population who own our farms are finding it easier
to dispossess the rest of us of what we value in the countryside
than their eighteenth-century predecessors found the task of
evicting the peasants.

PART SIX

Stop, Thief!

If the people of England knew what was happening to their countryside, they would not stand for it. They would quickly recognise that the advantages of the new agricultural techniques for society at large – as opposed to the farmers themselves – are vastly outweighed by the price they exact: the loss of a priceless national resource, the landscape.

Up till now, an urban nation's ignorance about the working of the countryside has saved farmers from the wrath of the people. But, of course, organisations directly concerned with countryside matters are well aware of what is going on. And some of them have proposed measures designed to reduce the damage agricultural intensification is inflicting. Extra tax concessions and grants from the taxpayer to reward farmers who agree to retain valuable landscape features are the basis of one approach. The other side of this coin would be the imposition of tougher controls on the provision of the farm capital grants: such controls could be used to weed out proposals involving unacceptable environmental damage. The Ministry of Agriculture itself has floated one such idea. It has even suggested that farmers applying for grant might be required to produce a certificate from their local authority stating that the authority did not object to the scheme on environmental grounds. Education programmes designed to persuade farmers to mend their ways are suggested by those looking for the least contentious course. The reform of the Common Agricultural Policy, a measure much sought after for other reasons, might, if it could be achieved, reduce existing incentives to exploit uncultivated land to the full. Controls on land buyers unlikely to rate conservation interests highly, like absentee foreigners and financial institutions, are being demanded in some quarters.

My view, however, is that though some of these indirect approaches might help, none of them, taken singly, or indeed together, would begin to measure up to the scale of the problem. They are being discussed, rather than more direct measures, mainly because they are thought to be relatively acceptable to the interest groups involved. It is undoubtedly true that if the tax and grant system, for example, had from the beginning been carefully constructed to maintain the optimum balance between agriculture and conservation, the present difficulties would not now be so acute. But now a mentality has been bred in our agriculture industry which would not disappear if a few of the factors which have stimulated it were lessened. Intensification is now the name of the game for the people now running our farms, and at present financial conditions are such that most forms of intensification would still be profitable even if marginal disincentives were introduced. If farm capital grants were abolished tomorrow, for example, a great many schemes would go ahead anyway, now that so much momentum has been allowed to build up behind intensification.

I believe the only real hope of stemming the tide of destruction lies in the introduction of direct, surgical measures to control the fate of the landscape, coupled with a shift in the distribution of power over the countryside. The tiny group who control the shape of the landscape at present must start to share their power with the nation as a whole. The process that is called for seems to me parallel to the process whereby control over the built environment passed into the hands of the community under the 1947 Town and Country Planning Act. But there will have to be one important difference. The planning of towns is almost entirely a matter for local authorities. But in the country, the local authorities are dominated by the major rural interest groups. If the countryside is to be saved, some voice must be given to the mass of the people who live in towns and cities. I believe that the way to do this is to ensure that certain key decisions are made at regional level, as regional authorities would reflect urban as well as rural interests. So I propose the following arrangements.

1. The town and country planning system should be extended to cover farmland. Farmers should have to seek the consent of the community for major changes to the countryside, just as industrialists and householders have to seek consent for changes to the built environment.

2. Nine regional countryside planning authorities should be set up to cover England and Wales. Their members would be nominated by the county authorities and metropolitan county authorities within their borders. These new regional authorities would draw up plans for the countryside of their regions just as county councils now draw up structure plans, and these plans would set out the priority to be given to agriculture, conservation and recreation in different parts of the region. Local authorities in each region would administer development control in the countryside within the parameters set by the regional countryside plan.

3. Organisations and individuals should campaign for better access to and greater understanding of the countryside, in a drive to involve the people of our towns and cities so that they will insist on imposing their view of the shape the landscape should take.

4. As an immediate crisis measure, six new national parks should be created immediately in lowland England. These areas, selected for their outstanding quality and the magnitude of the threat they face from agricultural change, would serve as a test-bed for new techniques for reconciling agriculture and conservation. In these parks, the nation, through the Secretary of State's nominees, would be able to exert a direct influence on the fate of key landscapes.

Let's look at these proposals one by one.

19

The Planning Weapon

The planning system is the means our society has chosen for reconciling the private pursuit of gain through land-use change with the public interest. In Britain, planning procedures, which are the envy of much of the world, require industrialists seeking to enhance their operations by even the most minor changes in land use to satisfy their local authorities that their proposals will not seriously disadvantage the rest of the community. If they fail, they must drop their proposals.

Where the system has been criticised, it has usually been because unwelcome development has been permitted rather than because planners have been too restrictive. On the whole, the history of development control in the built environment does demonstrate that it is possible for arbitration to enable potentially conflicting activities (like industry and residence) to be carried on side by side without either the developers or those whom they have affected suffering unduly. Obviously the planning system has imposed a burden on certain sections of the economy. But even where the interests involved have been far weaker than agriculture (like hard-pressed manufacturing industry, for example) it has remained generally accepted that they must carry that burden. For even those people who benefit most from industrial change generally accept that the planning system provides necessary protection for the built environment at an acceptable cost to the would-be developers.

But the nature of the threats to the environment can change. And not all the things that concerned people in the 1930s and 40s still concern people today. An advantage of our planning system is that it can be fairly responsive to such changes since it is administered through elected bodies representing directly the communities affected by development. For instance, one of the planners' main preoccupations in the early 1950s was the desire to separate people's homes from the noisy, smelly industries alongside which their forefathers had been forced to live. They achieved this both by refusing planning permission for factory extensions in town centres and by providing industrial estates outside them. Now, however, a growing number of people want to live in areas where they are not completely cut off from their own or other people's places of work, and planners are responding to this change by relaxing development control.

It was always anomalous that most activity in the countryside should have been beyond the reach of the town *and country* planning system. Agriculture was exempted only because its impact on the countryside was relatively small at the time when the planning system was crystallising and because home food production was considered sacrosanct in the aftermath of the war. Now that agriculture has become a major threat to our environment, however, the most logical way to deal with it within our existing system would be to extend the definition of 'development' to include agricultural activity. The destruction of an ancient wood, a stretch of down or the remains of an Iron Age village matter at least as much to the community as the erection of a new porch on a house.

Many (but not all) farmers would undoubtedly resent any such encroachment on their existing freedom to do whatever they like with their land. In fact, however, nobody has absolute ownership of land in England: all land belongs to the Crown, and the ownership of freehold merely provides entitlement to certain rights. In towns, freeholders' freedom to do what they want with their property is circumscribed by planning controls. There would be nothing peculiar in imposing a similar constraint on rural freeholders.

Interference with our most important types of landscape feature could be brought within the definition of 'rural development' by a new Act of Parliament. Any person or organisation could be required to seek planning permission from his local planning authority before carrying out any of the following activities:

I taking out hedgerows or drystone walls;

II chopping down trees or woods or coniferising deciduous woodland;

III draining marshes or destroying or damaging the character of ponds, streams, dykes or stretches of river whether through filling-in, drainage, piping underground or straightening;

IV destroying or damaging the character of tracts of moor, heath, hay meadow, down, coastal marshland, cliff roughland, or any other pieces of roughland designated by regional countryside planning authorities or local planning authorities as specially important for recreation or other uses, whether through ploughing or through the application of large quantities of fertiliser or herbicide;
    V constructing farm roads;
    VI erecting farm buildings of any size.

Permission need not be required for activities which do not involve the destruction of a landscape feature. There would be no need to interfere with farmers' freedom to change their farming methods and their crops as they have always done, where these changes did not interfere with the features specified. At present, almost all development control is carried out by district councils (rather than the county councils which used to be responsible for much more development control than they are at present). It would be entirely logical for district councils to administer the control of 'rural development'. The requirement that local planning authorities must issue a decision on any planning application within two months of receiving it should of course apply to rural development too, as should the right of any applicant aggrieved by a planning decision to appeal against it to the Secretary of State for the Environment.

The new system would benefit from the retention of the earmarking of sites of special scientific interest by the Nature Conservancy Council and scheduled ancient monuments by the Department of the Environment. Once identified, the safeguards these special sites would enjoy under the new system of planning control would be far greater than those they enjoy at present. The Nature Conservancy Council's power under the Countryside Act 1968 to pay farmers to carry out particular conservation activities could of course be retained. The clause in the Ancient Monuments and Archaeological Areas Act 1979 entitling farmers to compensation if they are required to desist from making fundamental changes to scheduled ancient monuments would need to be restricted to activities (such as deep ploughing) which would not already be covered by the new definition of rural development.

Clearly, once the new system of rural development control was in force, the existing clumsy machinery through which national park authorities now try to inhibit the large-scale ploughing of open moorland could be forgotten: far greater protection would at last be available not just for heather moorland in national parks but for all the main types of roughland throughout our countryside. There would be little point in repealing the tree preservation order legislation, however, since the vast majority of these orders are used to protect trees in towns; what the new system would mean would be that planning authorities wishing to resist the clearance of woods and trees for agricultural use, whether by farmers themselves or by water authorities or internal drainage boards, would no longer have to rely on the highly restricted, politically unpopular, expensive and administratively cumbersome tree preservation order machinery: instead they could simply refuse planning consent for tree or woodland felling.

Water authority drainage schemes

Long before any moves to extend planning control in the countryside can come into effect, the government ought to impose an immediate embargo on water authority and internal drainage board pump drainage and river canalisation schemes intended for agricultural improvement. Every year water authority and drainage board canalisation and pump drainage schemes are destroying valuable stretches of English countryside. The North West Water Authority's five-year programme 1981/82–1985/86, for example, lists 24 schemes for the protection or improvement of agricultural land at a total cost of £13.5 million, like the elimination of 100 acres of wild, marshy woodland and grassland at Hale Moss in the Arnside and Silverdale Area of Outstanding Natural Beauty or the straightening and deepening of the little river Lyth on the southeastern edge of the Lake District. All our water authorities are carrying out surveys aimed at identifying tracts of countryside where there is scope for increasing agricultural output by changing the water through-put. Their objective is to eliminate any regional variations in water quantity: they hope in this way thay can make every piece of country able to grow as wide a range of crops as possible. These plans, if implemented –and the authorities' five-year programmes simply take a batch of schemes from these surveys – threaten to eliminate such character as is still imparted to our countryside by undrained areas, from wet, rushy meadows in the Kent and Sussex Weald

to peat carrs in Northumberland and peat mosses in Shropshire, Cheshire and Lancashire, as well as to transform countless little brooks and rivers up and down our countryside into
deep, faceless, canal-like drainage channels. The report of the
Avon and Dorset Land Drainage Committee of the Wessex
Water Authority is not untypical. It lists in detail 58 schemes
designed to ensure that water conditions are ideal for agricultural production. These schemes include proposals to
convert marshes alongside the Rivers Frome and Piddle
around Poole Harbour and Wareham to intensive cropland at
a cost of £5 million and to carry out major works including
much canalisation to 21 miles of the River Piddle between
Puddletown, Tolpuddle and Wareham and more than 16
miles of the River Stour and its tributaries mainly in north
Dorset.

Eventually I would like to see the land drainage activities of
water authorities brought under the control of regional
countryside planning authorities; such authorities would
doubtless find the water authority plans now being drawn up
useful but would not feel obliged to treat them as prescriptive.
In any case, drainage schemes would be subject to planning
control if planning was extended to include 'rural development'. But such is the pace at which such schemes are being
implemented that it is essential now that new schemes should
not be allowed to go ahead without public scrutiny of the kind
applied in the Amberley Wildbrooks case.

Enforcement

The sanctions available to local planning authorities for the
enforcement of the new system of rural development control
need be no different from those operated in our existing
system. If an authority found that a farmer had cleared away a
wood, for instance, or piped a stream underground without
first securing planning permission, and considered that
permission would have been refused if sought, it could serve
an enforcement notice on the owner requiring him to remedy
the loss – that is, to replant the wood or reinstate the stream,
in the same way that a man who builds a house without
planning permission may be obliged to pull it down. A right of
appeal to the Secretary of State and, failing satisfaction there,
to the High Court, is an integral feature of the existing enforcement procedure. However, the detection of breaches of

the law would require different methods from those used by urban planners. To enforce the new system, every local planning authority would need precise information on the location of all those landscape features in its area which would be covered by the new controls. This would be a big task but it need not be an impossible or expensive one. All the types of roughland that would be brought under planning control if my proposals were enacted have already been mapped in detail at some time during the last twenty years. During the 1950s, for instance, most county councils surveyed their areas to identify tracts of rough moor, heath, down and cliff roughland; and during the 1970s the Nature Conservancy Council carried out surveys to identify herb-rich meadows in several regions. The use of volunteers, favoured now for many purposes by cost-conscious politicians, would enable most local authorities to build up a map of landscape features quickly and easily. In just three years (between 1960 and 1963) three thousand volunteers mapped the land-use of the whole of England and Wales. Under the supervision of Miss Alice Coleman, the Director of the Second Land Utilisation Survey, they went so far as to record details like the kind of crop grown in individual fields (distinguishing between wheat, barley and oats, for instance) and the type of industry within factories. For a separate study, one student on a moped mapped the location of a total of thirty thousand acres of unimproved chalk downland scattered over 400 square miles in Dorset in seven weeks in the summer of 1972.[1]

There is every reason to believe that the problem for many local authorities would be in handling a surplus of enthusiasts. My travels through the English countryside over the last six years have convinced me that there are a very large number of people who would gladly give up part of their spare time to help operate a system designed to protect the countryside they love. I am not thinking only of the potential among the estimated three million people who are members of environmental pressure groups,[2] like the 34,000 members of the Ramblers' Association or the 250 local and national societies affiliated to the Council for British Archaeology. I am also thinking of the thousands of at present uncommitted people in our big cities who would jump at the chance of doing something positive for the countryside.

Any authorities which found volunteer effort insufficient

would find aerial photography, which has already covered much of the countryside, an enormous benefit. Aerial photographs, when looked at through a stereoscope, present a three-dimensional picture of the land surface which makes it instantly possible to tell whether a hedgerow or a tree is present and even to distinguish a tract of pure heather moorland from one consisting of grass and heather.

Clearly each landscape feature would need to be carefully defined in the new legislation to avoid confusion or abuse. Hedgerows, for example, would need to be defined in terms of minimum length and minimum height. Roughlands coming within the scope of the new Act could be areas of grass or bushes that had not been ploughed or substantially 'improved' by some other means for agriculture for at least twenty years. Coastal marshland and cliff roughland would be defined mainly in terms of location. Moor, heath, meadow and chalk downland could all be defined by species description. No new problems would be involved.

Maintenance

Hedges, woods, streams and meadows can all be managed in certain ways that enhance their conservation value and often their scenic interest too. For instance, if a part of woodland is coppiced each year, a new variant habitat is created as the wood is colonised by a succession of plant species quite different from those that grow under a close leaf canopy. And if some hedgerows are trimmed to one height and some to another (provided they are all over about four feet) or if some are laid one year and some another, the result is a far greater variety of wildlife than if they are all trimmed every year to an identical level. Some features, like chalk downland or lowland heathland, *need* interference by Man if they are not to change their character completely: for these two features, annual mowing or grazing is necessary to prevent the hawthorn and birch saplings from turning the rough grass into scrub woodland. At present, the traditional arts of managing our farmed countryside are disappearing along with the features to be managed. Arts like hedging and ditching, stone-walling, woodland coppice management and traditional skills of shepherding and stock management are dying out, along with the one hundred and one other crafts that depend on centuries-old methods of exploiting the natural resources of the countryside, from harvesting gorse for fuel to making rushlights from reeds and tallow – for the growing uniformity of purposes to which our countryside is put is bringing with it a uniformity in the way in which the land is worked: more convenient forms of land management are replacing older, more idiosyncratic practices which varied from one region to another.

If we are to conserve traditional features of our farmed countryside in any significant quantity, low-cost maintenance procedures will have to be devised. One possible approach would be to rely on volunteers to exercise the old skills now being discarded by farmers and farmworkers. Volunteers have already shown themselves able and anxious to take up specialised crafts. The British Trust for Conservation Volunteers, for example, has run successful courses on hedging-and-ditching and stone-walling, and has now published detailed manuals on them. More simple tasks, like the clearance of footpaths or the clearance of scrub from grassland, are already easily accomplished by volunteers with a little organisation. The Chiltern Society, for example, surveyed 2,000 miles of public path in the Chiltern Hills in 1968–69, and has since then waymarked 700 miles of path and cleared vegetation from another 200 miles. The Society has taken it upon itself to ensure that all public rights of way throughout the 300 square miles of the Chiltern Hills are usable. Typical of its approach was the coordination of volunteers from the Youth Hostels' Association to clear away 20 acres of hawthorn bushes on chalk downland at Pitstone Hill over six weekends in 1979.

If local authorities chose to use their own labour to maintain landscape features for farmers, the cost would not necessarily be astronomical. Surrey County Council, for instance, employs a team of fourteen men to maintain the council's 9,000 acres of public open space. Amongst other things, these men plant trees and maintain plantations, carry out hedging and ditching, make wooden picnic furniture and footpath signs and cut back scrub and grass. The cost to the council in the financial year 1980–81 is £84,000 which includes the cost of machinery, the running of a depot and a sawmill and the men's wages.

Cost

In the present political climate, the costs of new curbs on agricultural change are bound to be one of the main causes

for concern about them. The costs would be attributable to
two different things: the administration of the system and the
loss of profitable activity. It would be up to Parliament to
decide who should bear what proportion of these costs. It is
clearly out of the question at present that the public purse
should bear either of these costs. But neither is likely to be
large in practice and both could be borne quite easily without
any call on the taxpayer or ratepayer. Industrialists denied
planning permission for new factories have to put up with the
loss of potential profit entailed. There seems no reason why
farmers should not do likewise. Up till now they have had to
pay no betterment levy of any kind on land 'improvements'
even though they usually make their improvements with the
aid of grant from the community at large. The evidence suggests
that the farming community could bear any loss of profit
associated with the planning controls without too much
trouble. And as we shall see, there is plenty of public money
that could be reallocated from subsidies that further the destruction of the countryside to cover the relatively small costs
of extending the planning system.

Let's look first at the farmers' loss of profit. The costs
involved in retaining hedgerows, hedgerow trees or trees
standing singly in fields need not be great. However, there are
other areas in which substantial potential profit will have to
be foregone if important features are to be saved. If a farmer is
prevented from draining a marsh, clearing a wood or ploughing
an area of roughland, significant losses may be involved.

But while farmers would be foregoing profit in some cases,
they would still be reaping the full benefit from improvement
in profit and land value when they succeeded in securing
planning permission. There are those who would argue that
these benefits should be shared with the rest of the community,
through a betterment levy. Certainly the extra burden which
farmers would be asked to bear would leave them in far more
favourable circumstances than many other producers in the
economy.

The National Farmers' Union gives two main reasons why
farmers should be exempt from anything like planning control
or compensated if required to forego potential gain – unlike
the rest of the community.

First, it argues that whereas a manufacturer refused permission to build or expand a factory can move somewhere

else, a farmer is not so mobile. Second, it says that farmers, unlike other industrialists, cannot pass on cost increases to the consumer by putting up their prices.

Neither of these arguments, however, does much to establish the farmer's claim to be considered a special case. A farmer, particularly in view of his small labour force, is likely to find it easier to move than the average industrialist, not harder.

Equally, farmers are often freer than industrialists to raise their prices; competition often removes this option from manufacturers, who, unlike farmers, lack the reassurance of a guaranteed minimum price for their goods.

In fact, planning controls are most unlikely to force many farmers into bankruptcy, for the truth is, much as the farming lobby seek to disguise it, that farmers are among the most comfortably off people in our society. The *Annual Review of Agriculture*, 1980, estimated that the average full-time post-tax farming income in England for 1978–79 was £9,000. This figure is derived from a 10 per cent survey of farm incomes carried out each year by the Ministry of Agriculture.[3] However, it does not include other sources of income, which can be considerable – such as income from other employment, holiday lettings, the letting of shooting and fishing rights or farm-gate cash sales. Twenty-five per cent of Essex farmers, for instance, sell produce direct to the consumer at the farm gate; and a survey of these farmers by Alasdair Blair of University College, London, in 1973[4] found that the average percentage contribution to total farm sales by value from all kinds of sale direct to the consumer, like 'pick your own', special deliveries and farm-gate sales, was 20 per cent for the whole of Essex. So farmers whose net farming income was the average £9,000 a year on the Farm Management Survey would also be getting an extra £1,800 from this other source. And of course we also have to bear in mind that, unlike other industrialists, farmers do not have to pay rates on their farmland or buildings.

Unlike many other groups, farmers are also assured of a regular increase in their incomes, irrespective of demand for their products, through the annual price review, whether negotiations with the Common Market as it is now or the British Government as it was before 1973. When the Government is particularly sympathetic to their cause, they may get even more frequent increases: during the eight months of 1979 when Peter Walker was Minister of Agriculture, the extra financial benefits awarded to farmers included three Green Pound devaluations, two increases in milk prices and a rise in subsidies for hill farmers. During the 1970s the net farm income of the average full-time farm, as recorded by the Farm Management Survey, increased by a factor of 4.8. Retail prices rose by 2.9, average earnings by 3.5 and company profits by 3.2.

Farmers do of course deserve to earn a good wage for what is a skilled job. But it would be hard to argue that completely uninhibited land 'improvement' is vital to their economic survival.

The colossal increases in land values over the last decade have also represented big increases in potential income for our farmers. There is, of course, no annual tax related to increases in the value of farmland, since farmers are exempt from payment of rates. And although a farmer who decided to sell a piece of land would be liable for capital gains tax, this would not be too crippling, as Alistair Sutherland showed in a paper he prepared in 1979 for the Northfield Committee.[5]

Taking the years between 1969 and 1978, Mr Sutherland showed that the capital gain on farmland averaged about £934 per acre. On the average 229-acre farm considered in the Farm Management Survey in 1976–77, that would amount to £24,000 a year. If a farmer wished to realise this capital gain, capital gains tax would of course be payable. Assuming that the whole of the gain were taxed at a flat rate of 30 per cent, then a farmer with 229 acres would receive £150,000 in capital gain for the 1969–78 period after tax. A man who sold 1,500 acres (maybe only a part of his holding) would, according to Mr Sutherland's calculations, be left with nearly £1 million simply in capital gain after capital gains tax had been paid. The National Farmers' Union argues that farmers should be granted more concessions on capital transfer tax because at the moment they are having to sell off pieces of land and pay CTT bills with the revenue from sale. In fact, neither Mr Sutherland nor the Northfield Committee could find any evidence to show that this was happening to any great extent. Even if it were, both studies show that agriculture would not necessarily be less efficient if holdings were smaller.

In any case, an owner of land will have seen the value of his asset increase much faster than the owner of ordinary industrial shares, for instance. Land prices have increased relative both to retail prices and to ordinary share prices. The NFU points out that CTT can cause the fragmentation of farms. But as Mr Sutherland points out,

> if land prices continue to increase relative to the retail price index, then a desire on the part of the farmer to hand on the *same* acreage becomes a desire to hand on an asset which has become much larger in real terms. Handing on the same real value in purchasing power still would leave the heirs with a much *physically* smaller farm. . . . Farmers do feel strongly that they should both have the cake (the ability to hand on the physical farm, with its greatly increased real net advantages per acre), and also to eat the cake (to enjoy in the meantime the increased annual profit until they decide to hand on the farm). No proposal has been made to us that farmers should pay higher taxes on *income* in exchange for lower taxes on *capital*.[6]

To be fair to them, many farmers accept the idea that planning controls should be introduced into the countryside without compensation. There is evidence to believe that at least some farmers would readily accept the new system, so long as they could see that it was fair. The authors of the Countryside Commission study 'New Agricultural Landscapes' (1974) found that the farmers they interviewed were not so wholeheartedly opposed to planning controls over their activities as the consultants had imagined they would be. What is more, several farmers

> questioned the desirability of any form of compensation for conservation measures since they felt these were the responsibility of the farming community . . . . The principle of paying farmers for conservation measures which may not be in their best interests (agriculturally) is certainly not accepted by all, even in the farming community.[7]

In their Dorset and Herefordshire study areas, for instance, the consultants found that most of the farmers considered that farmers should themselves bear the costs of the imposition of planning conditions on farm buildings provided these did not exceed 5 per cent of the total cost of the building.

But if farmers can stand the cost of planning controls, can the local authority which would administer them? It is certainly true that, compared with other local authority functions, planning costs relatively little. Our existing development control system, covering such activities as industry, housing, quarrying, shopping, transport and office building and location, costs a little less than £50 million a year to administer throughout England and Wales, according to the Department of the Environment. (This estimate, made late in 1979, includes work by Whitehall – in hearing appeals, for instance – as well as work by local authorities.) The operation of rural development control might be expected to add somewhere between a quarter and a third to the cost of the existing system – perhaps £16 million, so long as volunteers helped provide the policing. In terms of the nation's public spending, this is a tiny sum. But being tiny, it could easily be raised without the taxpayer or ratepayer being troubled at all.

In 1980 the Thatcher Government was considering introducing charges for the handling of planning applications to try and recoup 30 of the £50 million annual cost of administering development control. If such charges were also made in the new system of rural development control I have put forward and a similar proportion of the costs recovered, only a little over £6 million a year would need to be found elsewhere.

Another possible source of funds is the introduction of rating to farmland and farm buildings. The Layfield Committee on Local Government Finance, reporting in 1976, could see no good reason for the continuing discrimination in favour of agriculture where rates are concerned and recommended that agricultural land and buildings should be rated, as had the 1966–69 Royal Commission on Local Government in England and various groups including the National Union of Agricultural and Allied Workers. The Layfield Committee calculated that full rating of agriculture would have brought in £120 million in 1974/5 (see page 29). The sum of £150 million a year or so that the rating of farmland and farm buildings would now bring in could itself pay for a new rural planning system many times over.

Perhaps, however, the most obvious source of finance for the administration of a new system of rural development control would be the reallocation of some of the taxpayers' money paid to farmers through farm capital grants to finance the destruction of the countryside. So large is this potential source of funds that it could easily pay not just for the administration and enforcement of the new control system but also for all the other main proposals I have put forward. In the financial year 1979/80 the British taxpayer paid farmers an estimated £171 million for farm capital improvements; the water authorities received an extra £21 million for capital improvements. At least two-thirds of this money (£126 million) financed environmentally damaging activities. It would be possible to take all this £126 million and spend it on new measures to safeguard the countryside. This money could for example provide the regional countryside planning authorities I am proposing with considerable funds to conserve landscapes, reconstitute ravaged areas and increase public access to the countryside. It could also provide district planning authorities with more than enough money to administer rural development control without any recourse to the rates and whether or not charges were imposed for applications for rural development. Even without any changes to the planning system, some of this money could be spent immediately on a variety of measures to conserve England's countryside from agricultural intensification, for example the new national parks I have suggested. A little redeployment of unnecessary and destructive farm capital grants in directions such as these would not do any harm.

Radical though the idea of planning controls on agriculture may seem, there is no real reason why they should not be imposed. They are the response to the problem of agricultural intensification which would fit most naturally into the machine of land-use management operating in the rest of our society. In 1976, Professor Gerald Wibberley asked this question at a conference:

> Why do we not accept that in modern agriculture as for most other industries that whereas the community in general is prepared to help in the maintenance and improvement of the incomes of the people engaged in modern agriculture, in return for this the community wishes to have some say in the location of that industry, the way in which its waste products are distributed and the effects which it has on the landscape, on nature conservation and on other amenities of the area?

A convincing answer has not been forthcoming.

20

Regions to the Rescue

Any attempt to curb undesirable landscape changes through the town and country planning system has to come to terms with an obvious problem. The system is administered by local authorities, and despite local government reorganisation, farmers and landowners still dominate many of our district councils. So they would not be ideally suited to the exercise of sole responsibility for a task that comes down to resolving disputes between farmers and the rest of the community. There has to be some means of representing the will of the millions of people who live in metropolitan areas but are interested in the countryside, as well as those people who live in rural areas.

The most obvious forum for resolving conflicts between interest groups is Parliament. And it would clearly be possible for the Government to hammer out a national strategy for the countryside, which would allocate broad areas for agriculture or for conservation and even pick out particular spots for special treatment. In fact, however, the centralisation of decision-making in this way would be neither popular nor efficient. The struggle that would take place between the Department of the Environment and the Ministry of Agriculture would benefit nobody. Land-use decision-making is the kind of area of government that cries out for devolution. It is best dealt with by the smallest local government unit which is practicable, and in this case I believe that unit to be the region, as this is the smallest unit in which town and country would be evenly represented. Regional planning would not be an unheard-of novelty. Ten regional sport and recreation councils already exist. Until recently there were regional economic planning councils too. These were set up in 1965, to advise the Secretary of State for Economic Affairs on regional economic matters. They soon came to draw up and publish economic plans for their areas and eventually what were essentially strategic land-use maps. County structure planning authorities were required to work within the frame-

Map 2. Regional Countryside Planning
Authorities : Proposed Boundaries

NORTH

YORKSHIRE AND HUMBERSIDE

NORTH WEST

EAST MIDLANDS

WEST MIDLANDS

EAST ANGLIA

WALES

SOUTH EAST

SOUTH WEST

0   80km

Based on an Ordance Survey map

work laid down in these maps when drawing up their structure plans. These councils were abolished in 1979 after incurring various criticisms. It was argued, quite rightly, by bodies such as the Council for the Protection of Rural England that the system as constituted was undemocratic. Elected local authority representatives made up only half of the membership of the economic planning councils at most (the other members were industrialists and trade union officials). Yet these councils were preparing the framework within which the county councils had to work when preparing their county structure plans. A more telling criticism in the end was that the regional economic planning councils had no real function. Neither objection would apply to a network of regional countryside planning authorities charged with preparing regional countryside plans.

The areas of the nine economic planning councils would provide reasonably suitable areas for regional countryside planning authorities to administer. These areas are shown in Map 2: each region contains several major towns or conurbations encircled by large stretches of countryside.

Regional countryside planning authorities should contain representatives of every county and metropolitan county in their areas. The Maud Committee on Local Government Reform, which reported in 1967,[1] proposed that provincial or regional councils should be created as an essential complement to the city-region authorities which they saw as replacing both counties and districts. The Maud Committee's plan for representation on their provincial councils would be quite appropriate for countryside authorities. This plan would give each county or metropolitan county council two members on the regional authority for each 250,000 of its total population and one further member for each additional 250,000 or part of 250,000. However, every county and metropolitan county would be guaranteed a minimum of two representatives, even if its population were less than 250,000, so that every area, however sparsely populated, would have a voice. In the West Midlands region, for instance, this plan would give Shropshire and Warwickshire three representatives each, Hereford and Worcester four, Staffordshire five and the West Midlands conurbation (including Birmingham, Wolverhampton, Coventry and Dudley) twelve. In the South-East, Greater London would hold nearly one-third of the total number of seats.

The main function of each RCPA would be to prepare and continually up-date a strategic plan, showing the priorities to be allocated to agriculture, conservation and recreation in the different parts of the region. The district councils administering rural development control would be required to work within the confines of the regional countryside plan. In the event of disputes between regional and district authorities, the Secretary of State for the Environment could arbitrate.

It would make sense for the procedure for the preparation of regional countryside plans, including arrangements for public consultation, to follow closely the present procedure for the preparation of county structure plans. If this happened, the RCPA would first of all set broad goals and objectives for the future of its region's countryside. Then the authority would carry out surveys of the countryside: it would not just look at the existing situation but would also plot trends and express views on the implications of these trends. The authority would consider the Ministry of Agriculture and Forestry Commission views on present and future needs of food and timber. The views of such other bodies as the regional tourist board, the regional council for sport and recreation, the Countryside Commission and Nature Conservancy Council would also be sought at this stage. The regional authority would then prepare a number of alternative strategies for the countryside. Finally, one of these would be selected.

Ample opportunity for the public and pressure groups to make their views known would be vital. The most important provision for public participation in the existing structure planning process is the requirement that the Secretary of State for the Environment should hold a public examination into each draft structure plan at which opposing views can be thrashed out over a period of about three weeks. These examinations do of course have to cover a much wider range of issues than would be thrown up by a regional countryside plan, but three weeks would nonetheless be a reasonable period for inquiries into regional countryside plans, for the arguments surrounding rural activities are less well understood than those surrounding urban development, and any extra time would be put to good use.

Public participation during the early stages of the plan-making process would also be very important. Structure plan authorities are required to publish a report of the surveys they have carried out and then to ensure that those people and organisations that might be expected to wish to express their views are informed of their right to do so and given adequate opportunity. In practice, most structure planning authorities actually try to bring in the public at an even earlier stage, by consulting them before deciding what surveys to carry out. Such arrangements would be ideal for regional countryside planning – so long as the views of the public were sought as actively in each region's towns and cities as they are in the countryside.

I am confident that, over most of the country, the approach I have outlined would lead to a slow-down in destructive landscape change. However, farmers would have the opportunity to persuade the people of their regions that such changes as they wished to make were justifiable. If they won the complete support of the RCPAs for the activities they are currently pursuing, we would at least know that the people support what is happening to the landscape rather than being both ignorant and ineffective in this sphere, as they are at present. I do not imagine that the new planning arrangements would lead to the freezing of the countryside in its present form. That would be absurd. In the West Country, for instance, there are still hedgerows enclosing fields of only half an acre that were used in the past for sorting sheep when lambing was practised out of doors. Now that very few stock are lambed outside, a ban on the removal of these hedgerows would, I imagine, be considered unreasonable by any regional countryside planning authority or district council. On the other hand, attempts to remove hedgerows enclosing arable fields of, say, twenty or thirty acres merely to add a few extra furrows to an already profitable enterprise and facilitate the operation of machines would, I hope, be resisted.

The regional countryside plans that emerged would probably embody four main strands. First, each plan would advance a firm framework for the future of each of the main types of landscape feature in the region. Taking chalk downland as an example, the plan would point out the importance of such rough downland as survives in the region for nature conservation, archaeology, landscape, tourism and recreation, from hang-gliding and botanising to pigeon-racing and picnicking. It would assess the weight of these demands in comparison with such benefits as would accrue to the community from land reclamation. It would then provide district councils whose areas included downland with some idea of how much they should allow to go over a given period. And in areas like Cambridgeshire and Humberside where virtually all the downland has been ploughed up, it would provide targets for reconstitution.

The regional countryside plan will need to indicate how areas of country like chalk downland, which are to be conserved, should be managed. Chalk downland rapidly changes to scrub and then woodland if it is not mown or grazed regularly; it would be up to each individual district council to make any particular arrangements that might be necessary, but the regional plan could usefully indicate some of the agencies and methods by which management could be achieved. As we have seen,, there are several sources from which regional countryside planning authorities could acquire quite considerable income. They should be in a position to provide district councils with funds for the management of sites, whether or not the district council were to seek the help of volunteers.

Regional countryside plans should go on to indicate in detail what they considered the future should be for particularly significant areas facing intensive change. I am thinking of areas now being transformed, like Exmoor, central Northamptonshire, the Yorkshire Wolds and the Weald.

The regional plans should also include some proposals for landscape reconstitution in areas like Lincolnshire and Worcestershire, for example, where very few landscape features remain. Although what has gone can never be completely recovered, a considerable amount can be achieved in this direction. The authors of the Countryside Commission's study 'New Agricultural Landscapes' reported that attractive new landscapes could be created in areas from which all natural cover had been removed through planting on unproductive land, like steep banks and ownership boundaries. But in the areas most intensively farmed, such unproductive land covers only about one per cent of total land. A sense of the traditional English landscape cannot be created on one per cent of the land surface, so the main problem in the path of landscape reconstitution would be securing the release of the necessary land. Farmers who value game tend to keep about 3 per cent of their arable land devoted to cover, on top of any woodland they may maintain.

If this figure were to be matched in efforts to reconstitute landscape, landowners and farmers would have to be required to take some land out of cultivation. But this need not be too forbidding a prospect. Farmers need not give back all that they have taken, and land made available for reconstitution need not be in the same place as the features that were originally destroyed. If a regional countryside plan has marked out an area for extensive reconstitution, it could be the local planning authority's job to prepare a detailed reconstitution plan. As in the case of the protection of existing features, much of the groundwork could be done by volunteers. Once the plans were prepared, local authorities could invite landowners to release whatever proportion of land was considered appropriate. And powers could be provided to force reluctant landowners to turn farmland over to other uses where necessary. Landowners who felt they could not afford to take the required amount of land out of cultivation could appeal to an independent assessment panel, just as people who have been refused planning permission can now appeal to the Secretary of State for the Environment.

The final function of the regional countryside plan could be to propose ways in which the region as a whole could best serve the recreation needs of the region's people. As we have seen, many of the county authorities around London and Birmingham, for example, adopt a purely defensive approach to recreation at present. They establish 'honeypots' near the conurbations without also opening up more attractive but inaccessible areas beyond. At the moment there is almost nothing that the people of our metropolitan areas can do about this. Ten regional councils for sport and recreation have existed since 1976. But these are advisory bodies with no power to take executive action: they provide a forum for consultation only. Their huge membership, and, in several cases, illogical boundaries, make them completely unsuited to the task of cutting through what is at present a negative approach to recreation provision. The Greater London and South East Council, for example, has 172 members but covers only Kent, Sussex, Surrey and Greater London: the other south-eastern counties are split between two other regions.

On the other hand, the resources of and membership of the regional countryside planning authorities I have proposed would enable them to combine the honeypot approach to the protection of fragile areas with other, complementary measures designed to widen people's enjoyment of the countryside. They could be expected to want to secure access to attractive areas from which the public are at present barred, and to provide public transport services from towns and conurbations into the heart of the country. The regional authorities should have funds available to promote bus services, for which local authorities of the region could compete. The regional authority could also have reserve powers to make access agreements itself, which it could threaten to use if a local authority dragged its feet in this area.

21

Opening up the Countryside

The proposals I have put forward to protect the countryside through reform of the planning system are unlikely to get very far without backing of real political weight. Unfortunately, the conservation movement is not at present a force with which politicians have to reckon, as they know it represents no interests strong enough to threaten them. I suspect that the conservation of the countryside will become a real political issue only when it arouses the passions of townspeople as well as those people who already know and love the countryside. The vast majority of our people live in urban areas. To many of them the countryside is a closed book. But if they had wider opportunities to enjoy the countryside they might grow as concerned about its future as those who have the good fortune to dwell in it. If this happened, the conservation movement might acquire the wider political base that would make it a force to be reckoned with. And it is for this reason that I believe conservationists have an interest in stimulating public interest in the countryside, instead of the reverse being the case, as some conservationists seem to have thought in the past.

As we have seen, public bodies have tended to dissuade people from making trips into the most beautiful areas of our countryside: thay have sought to protect the countryside and rural interests from townspeople rather than open it up to them for their enjoyment. If the support and influence of more of our town-dwellers is to be enlisted in defence of the landscape, then current recreation orthodoxy will need to be overturned. Not, of course, that helping people to enjoy the countryside is not a valuable end in itself. The great majority of people have up till now received relatively little from the countryside in return for the burdens it has imposed on them. These go beyond agricultural support: green belts, for instance, can be partly blamed for excessive housing densities in the inner cities. The countryside is a great treasure-house of potential enjoyment. It is time more people were able to take advantage of it.

There are three simple and inexpensive steps that could be taken without legislation that would make it easier for city-dwellers to benefit from the countryside.

The plight of those without cars

Whole sections of our community at the moment have no opportunity of visiting attractive countryside. If they can get out of the town, they can reach only countryside along bus routes. These are people who do not have their own car. And they are much more numerous than most people think. In 1978, twenty million households in Great Britain – 43 per cent – were without a car.[1] Since by no means all members of car-owning households have unlimited use of a car, a more realistic indication of mobility is perhaps given by the number of *people* who have their own cars. In 1976, the most recent year for which figures are available, only 26 per cent of the people of Great Britain had their own cars.[2] Nor is there any prospect of universal car ownership. Department of Transport projections carried out in 1976 indicate that, even in the year 2000, 60 per cent of our population will *not* own a car.[3]

Since the mid-60s, public transport services from town to countryside have been savagely cut. Sixty-three per cent of the railway track in Somerset was axed between 1938 and 1978. This track had provided Bristol people with access to Exmoor, Cheddar Gorge and the Quantock Hills, as well as such lovely country towns as Glastonbury, Wells, Wellington, Chard, Wookey and Dulverton. On the other side of the country, Sunday bus route mileage in the square of country in east Kent with the towns of Whitstable, Ramsgate, Sandwich and Canterbury at the corners of the square was cut by 40 per cent – from 134 miles to 80 miles – between 1965 and 1978. Virtually the only services left run along the main roads between towns. What this means is that the 56 per cent of Thanet households who do not have a car and the holidaymakers who tend to come by train and coach have a much narrower choice of accessible venues for a rural trip than was available to their counterparts in 1965.[4]

Elderly people are just one group of non-car-owners for whom the axeing of bus and train services into the countryside has greatly narrowed opportunities for enjoyment. Eighty-four per cent of households in Greater London and the Outer

Metropolitan Area in which the head of the household was aged seventy or over had no car, according to a survey in 1970.[5] Public transport services from London to the surrounding countryside are poor: it is almost impossible to reach the countryside from London in less than one hour's travelling time by public transport, and large areas beyond fifteen miles out can be reached only after more than one and a half hours' travel, if at all, according to a survey carried out by the GLC in 1970.[6] There is reason to believe that elderly people without cars would jump at the chance to visit the countryside if they were given it. An indication of attitudes to the country lies in the finding by K.K.Sillitoe in 1969 that people aged between sixty-one and seventy who are fortunate enough to possess cars go on excursions to the country and seaside more often than any other age group.[7]

Although those parts of our countryside which have been ravaged by agricultural change cannot easily be restored to their former glory, it is a relatively easy matter to put back bus services. And a little-known service launched by Surrey County Council in conjunction with London Country Buses in the summer of 1977 shows that Sunday buses into the country need sometimes cost the taxpayer and ratepayer nothing at all.

Surrey County Council launched the 'Ramblers' Bus', as it is called (London Country Service 417), with the specific intention of opening up one of the most beautiful parts of Surrey to people without cars. The bus makes four 1½-hour trips from Dorking Station deep into the countryside of the Surrey Hills and North Weald every summer Sunday and Bank Holiday. It travels through woods and commons, through little villages and farmed countryside well served with clearly-signposted public footpaths. One of the service's special attractions is that walkers are allowed to get on or off the bus at any point. The trip is not expensive: 85p (43p for children and old people) buys unlimited travel on the bus for one day. And as there are frequent rail connections between Dorking and London, the bus attracts families from London as well as Dorking people. It also attracts overseas visitors staying in London who find when they arrive here that sampling the pleasures of the English countryside is surprisingly difficult.

A handful of bus services introduced in 1978 and 1979 have followed where the Surrey Rambler has led; and in most of our existing national parks there is some kind of a bus service specifically intended for visitors without cars. But much more could be done. None of these new services runs outside the summer period and the Easter weekend. And there are many more towns which look as capable as Dorking of supporting viable Sunday bus services into the country, but which do not yet do so. There are at least thirty-five such towns just in south-east England, for example.[8] These towns all have sizeable populations, are linked to London by British Rail or underground train service, and lie on the doorstep of attractive countryside.

In ways such as these, people without cars would be enabled to enjoy some of our beautiful countryside from which they find themselves at present barred. The Surrey Rambler shows that bus services for recreation can break even, and there seems no reason why the Rambler should not make a profit in future. But even if some of the services that may be developed do lose money – and there is an argument for keeping fares down so that low-income groups are able to use these buses – the price would be low compared with what little money has been spent each year since the war on countryside recreation provision of use only to the car-owning members of the community who need least help.

People versus fish and pheasants

Landscape reconstitution coupled with the creation of country parks and the 'reclamation' for recreation of disused gravel pits – the two main sources of new rural recreation opportunities of which local authorities have so far made use – will never contribute more than a little to replacing the country playgrounds which have been lost. The only real hope of replacing what has gone lies in opening up what attractive countryside remains. There are possibilities all over our existing countryside to widen the range of people's countryside recreation opportunities. The target areas fall into two main categories: woods and parks used for the rearing and shooting of pheasants, and rivers, streams and lakes used at present only for angling.

While grouse shooting has helped conserve the Pennine moors against intensive agriculture and afforestation, it is to pheasant shooting that we owe the preservation of thousands of woods, parklands, hedgerows and marshy meadows. But for pheasants, we should have even fewer landscape features left in lowland England than we have at present: even more of the landscape would be dominated by vast fields of wheat and grass punctuated only by pylons or the stumps of grubbed-out hedgerows, stretching as far as land incapable of producing significant quantities of food, like the mountains of Snowdonia. Landscape conservationists and sportsmen have a common interest in the preservation of the roughland. Up till now, however, sportsmen have insisted on excluding others from the benefits of the countryside they have rescued. Hunting, shooting and fishing landowners have tended to bar public access to their woods, rivers and lakes for fear that visitors would interfere with their sport. So much of our most attractive countryside has been reserved for sportsmen while the rest of us have had to make do with the remainder.

Oxfordshire is one county in which the access apartheid can be seen clearly – although similar portraits could be painted in Cheshire and Staffordshire, Northamptonshire and Nottinghamshire, Norfolk and Suffolk, Bedfordshire and Buckinghamshire, Wiltshire and Gloucestershire, Dorset and even parts of Cornwall. Oxfordshire's countryside has changed radically in recent years. Thousands of hedgerows, small woods, wetlands and tracts of rough downland in the county have been swept aside to accommodate big new farm machines or to create more ploughland. Those woods and parks that remain provide oases for wildlife. In Oxfordshire, for instance, there are 27,000 acres of woodland scattered through the county which appear ideally suited for recreation. However, a survey in 1974 by the Countryside Commission disclosed that only 111 acres of these woodlands are open to the public.[9] Oxfordshire also has thirty-nine areas of parkland – a landscape type which surveys have also shown to be popular with the general public. But only ten acres of these are freely open to the public. A handful of parks are open on payment of a fee or on particular occasions. But public access to the vast majority of Oxfordshire's thousands of acres of woodland and parkland is confined to any public footpaths that happen to pass through them. By way of example, the Cornbury estate, about ten miles north-west of Oxford, outside the village of Charlbury, consists of Cornbury Park, about 600 acres of lovely parkland dotted with lakes and small woods, and the ancient forest of Wychwood, some 2,150 acres. One of the favourite hunting forests of the medieval kings, after centuries of evolution Wychwood now teems with wildlife of all kinds. The only public access to this exceptionally appealing estate is by a short public footpath that crosses one corner of the park and a path in Wychwood Forest which is open to the public one day a year. 'On that day, the Forest is alive with visitors. Scores pour in, rejoicing at this one meagre opportunity to wander in this glorious historic woodland.'[10]

Local planning authorities have powers under the 1949 National Parks and Access to the Countryside Act to secure public access to 'open country', as defined in the statute, by agreement, order or acquisition. This Act defined 'open country' as land consisting wholly or predominantly of mountain, moor, heath, down, cliff or foreshore; the 1968 Countryside Act widened the definition to embrace woodland, lakeside and riverbank. Very little use of the access powers has been made in lowland England. However, they are a tool ideally suited to the securing of public access over pheasant woods and parks.

Only forty years ago, thousands of acres of moorland on the doorstep of Sheffield and Manchester were the jealous preserve of gamekeepers who banned walkers on the grounds that they would damage grouse bags. Now, access agreements cover seventy-six square miles of moors in the Peak Park on which the rearing and shooting of grouse coexist happily with general public access. Ramblers are prohibited on specified days each year, when the moors are handed back to the sportsmen; byelaws control activities which could damage the moors, like the lighting of fires. Landowners can claim compensation from the Peak Park Planning Board for any financial loss they incur through the presence of the public, although recent research has shown that grouse bags are usually quite unaffected by the removal of constraints on access. The woods and parks of south-east England have considerably more potential than the moors of the north as playgrounds for city-dwellers, who are finding less and less countryside suitable for a decent walk available to them. There seems to be no real reason why the principle of multiple land-use so successfully applied over the northern moors should not now be applied to the woods and parks of the English lowlands.

Sportsmen argue that if the public were permitted to walk

through pheasant woods they would frighten the birds away to other woods. This would mean a financial loss to the land-owner, which could be substantial, especially near towns, where shooting rents can be high. (Sportsmen do not seem to think that ramblers would try their hand at poaching.) But just what evidence is there that disturbance by ramblers, picnickers or children playing would damage a pheasant shoot?

As it happens, there is none. But there is, on the other hand, some evidence that pheasants are not easily rattled. It comes from sportsmen themselves. A few years ago, the British Field Sports Society was faced with conflicts within its own ranks. Shooting folk claimed that hunting posed a threat to their sport. They said a pack of fox hounds tearing through a pheasant covert frightened the birds away to fresh woods, if not to pastures new. The society ran packs of hounds through pheasant woods in an experiment designed to determine just how flighty pheasants are. They discovered that, although the hounds startled the pheasants so that they flew up in the air, the birds did not leave the wood or, if they did, they soon came back. In fact, the disturbance caused by the dogs seems to have helped the shoot by making the pheasants, by nature reluctant to take to the air, more jumpy and ready to take to the wing. Several landowners are now taking advantage of this discovery to increase their pheasant bags. Lord Dulverton, for example, who owns a 5,300-acre estate on the border between Gloucestershire and Worcestershire, regularly runs hounds through coverts in which reared pheasants have been turned down only a few days before a shoot is to be held there.[11] On one occasion, hounds drew a covert on one day and accounted for four foxes; two days later, 400 pheasants were shot in the same wood.

The second main problem which would go with public access to pheasant woods is disturbance by dogs allowed to run loose. Hen birds frightened off their nests by dogs can leave, never to return; young birds put out into coverts after being raised indoors can also be frightened away. But these difficulties could be overcome fairly easily. For one thing, members of the public visiting pheasant woods could be re-quired to keep their dogs on the lead. And general public access could be restricted at specific times of the year and in specific places where hens are incubating eggs or young birds have just been turned down. The problem, anyway, is a small one:

few estates now rear more than a small proportion of pheasant eggs in the wild: most are incubated indoors. And it is hard to believe that any losses caused by visitor disturbance would be significant when compared with the inevitable, huge losses caused by foxes, cold weather and the rain. Certainly, the more woods and parklands that are opened up, the smaller the problem would be. The numbers of birds flying from one wood to another could be expected to cancel each other out. What happens in Blenheim Park shows that there need be no real conflict between rambling and shooting. The public are allowed to wander anywhere in this 2,500-acre park in which some of the thousands of pheasants reared on the Duke of Marlborough's estate every year are turned down. In addition, public footpaths penetrate other parts of the estate frequented by pheasants like woodland and farmland. Conflict is minimised by a requirement that visitors to the park must keep their dogs on a lead. Only when shooting is actually taking place are some of the private roads running through the park shut, but any one road never stays shut for more than an hour.

No access agreements appear to have been made over land used for pheasant shooting, so it is not easy to estimate what, if anything, would be considered an appropriate amount to pay a landowner in return for access to pheasant woods. The only guideline is the amount currently paid when access agreements are made over land used for sheep grazing or grouse shooting. In 1973/74, payments to the landowners granting access in upland areas averaged 25p per acre per year as compensation for loss of income from sheep grazing and grouse shooting, and in lowland areas £1.88 per acre, mainly in respect of loss from intensive sheep grazing.[12] Access agreements would clearly cost much less than the acquisition of freehold, the course councils normally adopt when they establish country parks.

Regional countryside planning authorities would have much to do in surveying the extent of 'open country' in their areas and drawing up plans to secure public access to the most beautiful or interesting areas from which the public are at present barred. It would then be up to district (or county) councils to implement these plans mainly through the negotiation of access agreements or, if landowners prove reluctant to enter into agreements, through access orders.

Two minor changes to legislation would help. Regional countryside planning authorities could themselves be empowered to secure access agreements and orders and to own land for access or for conservation. Secondly, a widening of the definition of 'open country' to embrace parkland would enable access agreements to open up some of the tens of thousands of acres of extremely beautiful yet completely inaccessible country parklands dotted throughout England.

Opportunities for widening townspeople's enjoyment of the countryside are also to be found in those stretches of attractive lake and riverside that are out of bounds at present because they are used for angling.

The natural game rivers of Hampshire like the Test and the Itchen provide some of the loveliest scenery the South-East has to offer. Their banks make ideal long-distance walking routes. But access to most of their length is barred except to those who hold fishing rights. Similarly, some of the beautiful hammer ponds of the High Weald, like Hawkins Pond and Hammer Pond in the St Leonard's Forest outside Horsham, are inaccessible: walkers may only gaze at their limpid beauty from the road since in both fishing rights have been let to a local angling club and, as usual, the general public are barred. Anglers argue that ramblers would damage catches by casting shadows over the water which would disturb the fish. As far as coarse fishing is concerned, however, there is no evidence that passing shadows disturb fish at all: what could frighten them away and damage the catch are dogs swimming in the water, or stones being thrown in. And for game fishing, salmon and trout seem to be disturbed by passing shadows only in narrow, shallow streams. But of course there are times when coarse and game fishing are out of season, when there is no reason whatsoever why these rivers and lakes should not be opened up for general public access.

Daventry District Council, in Northamptonshire, has recently secured public access for walkers, canoeists, underwater swimmers and anglers to a beautiful reservoir on the edge of the town which was until 1978 the exclusive reserve reserve of a private fishing club. What it has done could point the way to more general enjoyment of many more stretches of water throughout our countryside which are at present inaccessible.

The issue is not trivial. Lewis Silkin, the Minister of Town and Country Planning in 1949, declared to Parliament when introducing the access powers: 'If the Bill fails the people will be fettered, deprived of their powers of access and facilities needed to make holidays enjoyable. With it the countryside is theirs to preserve, to cherish, to enjoy and to make their own.'

Understanding the countryside

In 1977 the Countryside Commission interviewed 5,000 people about the use they made of the countryside.[13] A quarter of the people they talked to had made no trips to the countryside at all from August 1976 to August 1977. The people who never or only rarely visited the countryside were not scattered evenly through the sample population, as they might be expected to be if they reflected the unpopularity of the coutryside. Those least likely to visit the countryside were low-income manual workers, who worked long hours, left school early and did not own a car. Apart from what must be millions of people who never visit the countryside at all, if the Commission's survey is anything to go on, many people who do visit the country hardly venture from places they know well. Sixty-five per cent of the trips made by the remaining 3,750 people whom the Countryside Commission interviewed involved sites the respondents had visited before, usually on several occasions. The Commission describe what they call a 'conservatism' in countryside visits which, they say, 'inclines people to stick with the familiar and is reinforced by an uncertainty about where they can and cannot go in the countryside'.

If we want to help all our people to make as much use of the countryside as the might wish, then the easiest way in which we can widen access opportunities for the sort of people the Commission's survey picked out as being less likely to visit the countryside is through the provision of public transport. Helping townspeople to understand the ways of the countryside would also break down some of the barriers.

To try and find out what the countryside means to people who might be expected to visit it infrequently, if at all, I spent a day in 1978 talking to boys at a comprehensive school in inner London. Although many of them said they would like to visit the countryside, virtually none of them ever did. In spite of this lack of contact, however, they were very well versed in what they should *not* do, if they ever went there. The Country Code was extremely familiar. But this group of rural prohibitions was matched by striking ignorance about what is *permitted* in the countryside. These boys who knew they must not leave gates open or start fires had no idea whatsoever about where, if anywhere, they might be allowed to walk: the concept of a public right of way, for example, meant nothing to most of them. This did not seem to mean, however, that they would treat the countryside recklessly. On the contrary, it seemed that they would be constantly wary of doing something wrong. They seemed nervous about the idea of venturing far into an alien world.

Since the Country Code does seem to be well known, a simple extension of it, to explain to people where they *can* walk in the countryside and what their rights are, would be an obvious first step in helping those people to make use of the countryside. At present the Country Code restricts itself to telling people what they should *not* do in the countryside; it does not tell them what they can do. The evidence suggests that the philosophy of 'Trespassers will be Prosecuted' and 'Beware of Adders' (spurious admonitions both) has sunk deep into the attitudes of our townspeople. They are too afraid of the countryside to pose a threat to it. Most people need to be led by the hand into the countryside and shown what it can offer them, rather than bolted out of it. Public rights of way in the countryside are part of the heritage of the boys I talked to, even if they do not realise it. Public footpaths are one of the few concessions made by landowners to the rest of us. As these public rights of way can be lost through lack of use, it is doubly important that ordinary people, and in particular young people, should understand their function.

Although the Countryside Commission set up a study group in 1978 to review the Country Code (first devised in 1957), they have declined to widen it to include help for people seeking to visit the countryside as well as prohibitions. They have also declined to remind landowners and farmers of their responsibilities. In 1980 the Commission put forward three extra prohibitive clauses as its only proposed changes to the Code. Christopher Hall, the Director of the Council for the Protection of Rural England, commented:

The Code will now enjoin us to 'Keep to public paths

across farmland': the word 'public' is an addition. It will not remind farmers and landowners that they should restore such paths after ploughing. We are told to cross fences and hedges by stiles and gates but the owners are not warned against festooning them with barbed wire. You and I must take our litter home. Farmers and landowners are not told to remove the detritus of old fertiliser bags draped on those hedges which happen to have survived the bulldozer. You and I must (quite rightly) help to keep water clean, but the man who pours fertiliser on riverside land and so pollutes a watercourse goes unrebuked. It seems to be a clear case of one code for the country and another for the town.[14]

If more townspeople do visit the countryside, some of them will undoubtedly uproot wild flowers, steal birds' eggs, and otherwise damage what they have come to see. They will also leave gates open and pose other real problems for farmers. But there are plenty of ways in which the damage done by the new visitors can be minimised, of which the most important is education.

Education will not, of course, remove all evil motivation, but there is evidence that as people begin to have at their disposal a more sophisticated understanding of their surroundings the desire to destroy them may give way to other activities that exploit their understanding. Sylvia Law, who heads the GLC's recreation department, has suggested that a countryside interpretation centre should be built in Hyde Park to tell Londoners how to get to the country and where to go in it once they are there. Centres such as these would be invaluable in towns and cities everywhere in helping people who wish to venture into the countryside but who are unfamiliar with it. And in London in particular, they could also prove of great benefit to tourists.

Holidays are often full of opportunities to benefit from the countryside of which many holiday-makers are quite unaware. At many of our resorts, apart from Ordnance Survey maps, the literature available on how to get out to the countryside and where the interesting walks are to be found is at best sketchy and hard to understand, at worst non-existent. What is needed is straightforward information on how to get into the countryside and suggestions for walks, together with a Country Code that includes basic information on where people are allowed to walk in the country and how they can recognise a public right of way. If all this can be combined with a special bus service into the country on the Surrey Rambler model from resorts such as Ilfracombe, Swanage, Cromer, Scarborough, Blackpool, Eastbourne and Ramsgate, so much the better. There is also scope for guided walks from points accessible from population centres – ideally, all year round. Northamptonshire County Council already organises weekly guided walks into the country that go on through the winter. There is scope for many more.

Finally we need to give our children a much clearer idea of how to enjoy the countryside. Most people who love the countryside can point to a particular person or trip which first introduced them to the delights of the countryside. Regional countryside planning authorities could organise education campaigns in their areas and encourage the provision of many more trips to the countryside and holidays there for city children than are available at present.

22

National Parks for the Nation

The creation of a new system of countryside planning would inevitably take time. But the countryside cannot wait. And alongside a complete re-examination of the role of planning in the countryside, some form of instant action is called for. Such action would not only do something to stem the tide of destruction until long-term arrangements arrive, but would also demonstrate that the will to solve the problem exists – something that would doubtless help the long-term process along. Instant action will depend on existing procedures, so I should like to see the existing system of landscape designation mobilised in support of landscape threatened by agriculture. At present no form of landscape designation is effectively deployed in the struggle against agricultural change. The majority of the thirty-three areas designated AONB are heavily threatened by agricultural intensification. But in fact, this designation (as we have seen in Chapter 12) is of little help. The more significant form of designation is national park status, and this form of protection has been denied to the areas threatened by agricultural change and reserved instead for upland areas in the North and West which are relatively unthreatened. I should like to see the immediate designation of a set of new national parks in those lowland areas most urgently in need of protection from agricultural change. The Countryside Commission should immediately set about selecting half a dozen of our most attractive and unspoilt lowland areas for designation as national parks. At least as much money as is currently spent on our existing ten upland parks, if not much more, should be devoted to the conservation of these lowland areas.

Six areas of lowland England suggest themselves to me as suitable candidates for national park status. Throughout these areas I would like to see the landscape take immediate priority over agricultural change. The areas I have in mind are:

The Lower Wye Valley and the Vale of Herefordshire;

the Somerset Levels;
the Dorset Downs;
the Chilterns;
the Norfolk Broads;
the Downs of West Sussex and East Hampshire (the
Western Downs).

These areas all seem to me to contain large stretches of
relatively unspoilt lowland countryside offering substantial
opportunities for recreation. At the same time, the shadow of
agricultural change hangs threateningly over all six.

In fact, the six areas I have mentioned meet the statutory
requirements for national park status better than most of our
existing parks (mainly because they offer better opportunities
for recreation since they are nearer population centres). The
objection most commonly made to the designation of lowland
landscapes – that they do not contain a high proportion of
roughland open to free wandering – is based on a complete
misreading of Parliament's original intentions for national
parks. So the creation of a new string of lowland parks would
remedy a long-standing bias in the location and character of
our existing national parks which was not intended by Parliament.

At present, national parks cover about 9 per cent of the
land surface of England and Wales; AONBs cover 9.6 per
cent. If the six tracts of country listed above became national
parks, national parks would cover altogether 12.6 per cent of
our land surface and AONBs 7.2 per cent (since some of the
areas I have suggested for national park designation are already
AONBs). Land earmarked for conservation on account of its
national landscape importance would then total 12,920 square
miles, or nearly 20 per cent of our land area. This figure would
be very high by international standards and perhaps so high
that there would be a constant risk of devaluation of the
system in the face of competing pressures for land use.

However, as we have seen, AONB designation means very
little in practice. I suggest it should be abolished. If this
happened, the creation of the six new national parks I have
proposed would leave us with a smaller total land area covered
by a national landscape designation than we have at present.

What national park designation offers, in essence, is the
representation of the national interest (through one-third

representation on national park authorities) in land-use decision-making. Once regional countryside planning authorities had been established, there would be no further need for this. And both national parks and AONBs would wither away in the face of the new, more subtle gradations imposed right across each region by the RCPAs. In the meantime, however, the immediate designation of national parks in the lowlands offers an immediate curb on the uninhibited expression of the will of those who own the countryside.

And the creation of new national parks in lowland England would not only safeguard the areas themselves: it would also enhance prospects for conservation elsewhere in the countryside. Firstly, the designation of these areas would provide a signal that the gravity of the threat posed by agricultural change was being recognised: it would be an invaluable step towards raising the consciousness of the whole nation. Then, the extra money, staff and interest these areas would attract as national parks would enable them to be used as test-beds for new methods of resolving the difficulties that are bound to arise in any real attempt to meet the problems posed by agricultural change head-on. Lessons learned within the new parks could be extended to the countryside at large.

Some idea of what national park status might contribute can be gleaned from another look at the case of Graffham Down, whose unhappy fate was outlined on pages 129-35. Had Graffham Down lain within a national park, it might never have been despoiled.

Graffham Down: A suitable case for treatment

It is of course the case that planning permission is not at present required for the ploughing of rough land even in national parks. And the cost of acquiring Graffham Down to stop it being ploughed would probably have been beyond a national park authority even if one had existed. Nonetheless, there are several reasons why at least part of the site would have stood a much better chance of survival in a Western Downs National Park.

A national park authority would have had to prepare a national park plan in which it would have had to set out precisely how it intended to carry out its main function: conservation of the beauty of the area. National park plans normally set out conservation measures in far more detail

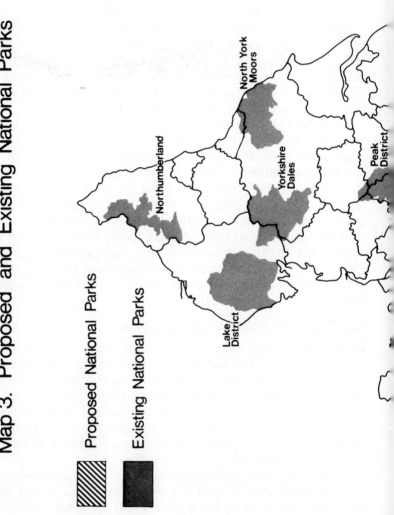

Map 3. Proposed and Existing National Parks

Proposed National Parks

Existing National Parks

Northumberland

Lake
District

Yorkshire
Dales

North York
Moors

Peak
District

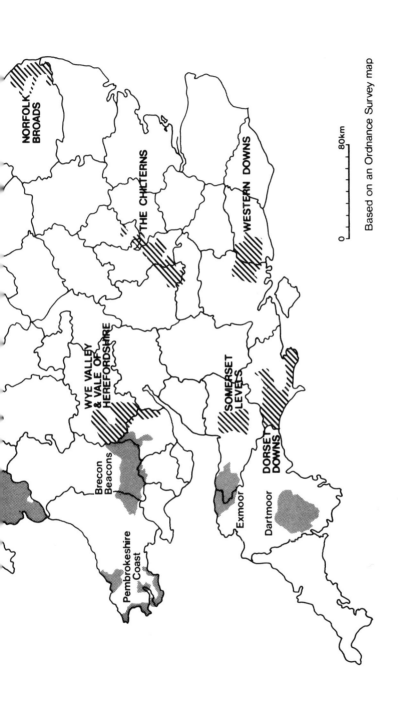

NORFOLK
BROADS

THE CHILTERNS

WESTERN DOWNS

WYE VALLEY
& VALE OF
HEREFORDSHIRE

SOMERSET
LEVELS

DORSET
DOWNS

Brecon
Beacons

Exmoor

Dartmoor

Pembrokeshire
Coast

Based on an Ordnance Survey map

0

80km

than structure plans, and the existence of these plans in themselves puts pressure on the authorities to live up to the com-
mitment contained in them. In explaining how it intends to
'oppose land use changes which are ecologically harmful' in its
structure plan, West Sussex County Council says no more than
that it will liaise with other organisations with the same objective
and implement the policy through 'a combination of development control measures, direct action and co-operation with
others'. In contrast, the Exmoor National Park Committee's
National Park Plan devotes 91 pages to a description of threats
to the attractions of the park and the measures with which it
plans to tackle them.

National park authorities have little enough money to protect threatened landscape features. But they do have more
money available for this purpose than local authorities, and
this is the second reason why Graffham Down's chances would
have been greater in a national park. The woods that clothe
Exmoor's steep-sided coombes have much in common with
the woods on the steep slopes of the Western Downs (the
main difference being that Exmoor's woods are much less
threatened by clearance for agriculture or conversion to conifers). To conserve them, the Exmoor National Park Authority
has acquired 1,000 acres of deciduous woodland and imposed
tree preservation orders on 25 other woods.

Things like these are only some of the measures that are
more likely to be put into effect in a national park than
outside. Safeguarding a national recreation resource is the
primary function of a national park authority. A third of its
members are exclusively concerned with the national interest
in landscape and recreation in the area. So a national park
authority is bound to try harder to ensure that conservation
and recreation get a fair crack of the whip in competition with
other forms of land use. In the Graffham Down case there
were many things a planning authority might have done if it
had been required to give landscape conservation a higher
priority. For a start, it could have made much more of a fuss
about the whole thing. If it had, that in itself might have made
Mr van der Vegte feel himself under greater pressure to retain
at least a part of the gallops. The planning authorities could
have urged the Ministry of Agriculture to withhold its grant
for the ploughing of the gallops or the clearance of bushes
and trees. They could have sought a public inquiry into the

application for a grant. This, after all, is what West Sussex County Council and several other organisations did – successfully – when the Southern Water Authority applied for a grant in 1977 to drain Amberley Wildbrooks, just six miles from Graffham Down. Either the county or the district council could at least have threatened to make a tree preservation order. Even if orders had not been imposed over the whole area of woodland, there were several very attractive groups of trees over which orders could have been made. At the very least, the district authority could have safeguarded the features, other than the gallops, which it wanted retained. In particular the district council could have made tree preservation orders on the relatively small numbers of trees in the triangular area and, even more important from the recreation point of view, on the trees in the strip of vegetation along the southern edge of the South Downs Way. It could also have regulated the erection of fences on the site. District councillors expressed considerable concern lest Mr van de Vegte or a subsequent owner impose a lattice of wire fences all over the area on either side of the many public rights of way that criss-cross Graffham Down. It is possible to bring fencing within planning control through an Article 4 Direction and in this case the compensation would not be great.

A national park authority might have been expected to put up more of a fight not only for conservation interests but also for recreation interests. Graffham Down was not of outstanding scientific importance (though it was clearly of considerable wildlife interest): its real value lay in the joy its wealth of beautiful flowers, trees and bushes and wild creatures offered to walkers. Thousands of people enjoyed its charms every year, for the South Downs Way, running along its longest edge, is joined on Graffham Down by a series of well-trodden paths leading up to it through the beech hangers from Graffham and other points down in the Weald. The Society of Sussex Downsmen made the value of Graffham Down clear in a letter it sent to both the county and district councils:

> The Society urges that at least part of the scrub and the gallops should be left . . . in view of their value to wildlife and the pleasure given to the public using the various rights of way here. . . . The songs and sight of the considerable bird population supported by this habitat add considerably

to the pleasure of those walking the South Downs Way and the network of paths connecting it with here. In spring and early summer the numbers of singing willow warblers are unforgettable, together with others including whitethroat, blackcap and chiff-chaff. All the year round there are five or six kinds of titmice, crowds of finches including bull-finches, and the usual 'back-up' of blackbirds, thrushes, robins and dunnocks. These would not inhabit ploughland.

The part of the South Downs Way that runs along the edge of Graffham Down was one of the few remaining wild, secluded stretches. Now, in common with most of the rest of the path, the Graffham Down stretch runs beside a stark food factory. Any pleasure to be had from stretches like that at Graffham Down now consists almost entirely of the views of the Weald that are available. Yet the long-distance footpaths are one of the greatest triumphs of post-war rural recreation planning. A walk along the Graffham Down stretch of the South Downs Way should convince anybody that the time has come for new priorities.

Six new national parks

Below I spell out the claims of the six areas I have put forward for national park status. Their location is shown on Map 3.

The Lower Wye Valley and the Vale of Herefordshire

A horseshoe of country covering about 300 square miles in southern and western Herefordshire has been preserved from agricultural change almost miraculously by three main factors. Until recently most of the land here was either in the hands of large private estates which managed it for shooting as well as agriculture or was farmed in smallholdings by families content to forego maximum profit for the enjoyment of an un-blemished landscape. There has been a tradition of sheep farming, and the sheep is the one animal that until recently had managed to resist factory-farming techniques. And the local Ministry of Agriculture official has happened to be a man much more sympathetic to conservation than most of his colleagues elsewhere. As a result, this area, two arcs curving out from the Golden Valley in the far west of the county overlooked by the glowering Black Mountains of Wales, con-tains some of the most unspoilt and beautiful farmed land-scape in England. And more than in any other of the national parks I am proposing, this one would severely test plans for reconciling agricultural change with other demands on our countryside. Here, virtually all of the main forms of reclamation are beginning to get under way. Hay meadows are just one of the area's specialities. They can still be found all over the horseshoe, thick with butterfly orchids and wild liquorice, marsh marigold, cowslips and wild daffodil, and haunted by snipe and redshank. But eight of the sixty meadows the Nature Conservancy Council identified in 1973 as of special natural history importance had been destroyed by agriculture by 1979.

The area of woodland, fields, villages and river at present covered by the Lower Wye Valley Area of Outstanding Natural Beauty (250 square miles) would form a southern extension to this proposed park. This dramatic stretch of river was the birthplace of the Picturesque Movement in art. Here, the river swirls through narrow limestone gorges clothed in oak, ash and lime Wildwood, overlooked by the ruins of Tintern Abbey, Chepstow Castle and Goodrich Castle. And it was here that William Gilpin formulated the principles of picturesque beauty which have remained the basis of popular appreciation of landscape to this day.

The Somerset Levels

The Somerset Levels are one of the most ecologically important, as well as the most attractive, stretches of wetland left in England. They offer scope for a wide variety of recreation activities: landscape painting and fishing, cycling and birdwatching, botanising and the study of history. The patterns of field boundary, road and rhyne tell a 5,000-year story of man's endless battle against water. The villages, set on little islands of higher ground above the Levels, are tiny, their cottages built square of yellow or grey limestone. The churches are superb, with stately perpendicular towers of red sandstone. Wherever you are in the Levels you can hear church bells over the willows and pastures, for few towers contain less than six bells and this is the county of ringers.

A national park in the Somerset Levels would be centred on those Levels that have not yet been drastically improved. The authority would aim to conserve them in their existing state, and this would involve not only ensuring that no further pump drainage takes place, but also influencing the management of the rhynes and rivers within the park by the Wessex Water Authority and by internal drainage boards. At present waterways are cleared of vegetation which might impede water flow mainly through herbicides, which are sprayed from a machine. These kill plants on contact and remain active in the water for up to about a fortnight. Scientists have shown that herbicides are far more damaging to natural life than mechanical methods of cutting back weeds.[1] This is but one example of the areas in which a national park authority might take steps to ensure that the natural assets of the Levels could flourish rather than, as at present, being regarded largely as an impediment to intensive agriculture which must be removed.

The Dorset Downs

Variety is the essence of Dorset. Within the 400 square miles covered by the Dorset Area of Outstanding Natural Beauty virtually all the main landscape features characteristic of our lowland countryside can be found – chalk downland hills, lush green vales, great brooding, furzy heaths, thatch and stone villages, wide acres of parkland, beautifully sited towns and rivers bordered with gentle watery meadows ablaze in March with marsh marigolds. I should like to see all of the AONB designated a national park.

All these landscape features are threatened by agricultural reclamation. If the Wessex Water Authority's plans for fifty-eight major schemes in Dorset go ahead, the river valleys, for instance, will be completely transformed. At the same time, deciduous woodlands are being rapidly turned into conifer plantations, while thickly hedged vales and rough downland turf are both disappearing under the plough.

Far from enjoying the benefits of the kind of planning I am advocating, Dorset (with the exception of the Bournemouth and Poole conurbation) lacks even a structure plan setting out a broad outline of the county's future of the kind that almost all England's other counties now possess.

A national park authority in Dorset would have much to do: it would need to draw up general planning policies and proposals covering such activities as are currently within the scope of planning. It would need to take what action it could to maintain the essence of a landscape that relies heavily on a combination of uncultivated and cultivated land. It could usefully create a string of country parks to relieve recreation pressure on the cliff-tops; but at the same time some of the woods, parks and lakesides of the country house estates could be opened up for less intensive forms of recreation, and more public transport services into the countryside could be provided.

The Chilterns

Perhaps more than any other area, the Chiltern Hills are a treasure-house of unexploited opportunities for public enjoyment. The Chilterns' 300 square miles of rolling, thickly wooded chalk upland crowned by cathedral-like beech woods and remote hilltop commons, and studded with charming, historic villages, stately parklands, Saxon churches and secluded stretches of rough heath and down, became an AONB in 1965. But although this stretch of valuable countryside lies on the doorstep of some of the biggest towns and cities in south-east England and although it boasts a dense lattice of public footpaths, it is remarkably inaccessible, at least to people who do not have a car. Nearly half of Britain's households have no car, and that includes those in the many towns close to the Chilterns, like Luton, Reading, High Wycombe, Watford, Slough, Henley, Hemel Hempstead and St Albans. The Chilterns sit astride some of England's most important communication routes, and bus services still run along the main roads linking big towns. But the bus services that used to run up into the heart of Chiltern countryside have been cut back severely. My own calculations indicate that the route mileage along which Sunday bus sevices ran within the Chilterns declined by over 50 per cent between 1955 and 1976. In the 1950s, a Londoner could take an underground train from Baker Street to Amersham or Chesham and then transfer to a bus that took him into the very heart of the Chilterns. In the 1920s, all the main railway companies ran their own fleets of buses, whose routes were coordinated with train services and included Sunday services for recreation. In the Chilterns, for example, this meant frequent bus services from Slough station into the south Buckinghamshire countryside, including Burnham Beeches. Now, this countryside is more or less a closed book to people without cars.

If the area covered by the Chilterns AONB became a national park, I should like to see a national park authority promoting new Sunday bus services immediately. Four routes suggest themselves to me:

1. A service could make a roundabout trip between Luton, Tring and Berkhamsted main-line train stations, providing access to the National Trust's Ashridge estate, Pitstone reservoirs, Ivinghoe Beacon and the Ridgeway and attractive old villages like Whipsnade, Studham and Aldbury.

2. A service could make a round trip from Amersham underground station, concentrating on the woods and downland around Chequers, Great Kimble, Ellesborough, Halton Wood and Coombe Hill and also taking in Ivinghoe and Aldbury.

3. A service could link High Wycombe and Henley (both of which have main-line train services), running through the Fingest, Turville and Hambledon, and Watlington Hill, Beacon Hill and Christmas Common areas and passing the following country houses open to the public: Stonor, West Wycombe (which also has a farm trail), and Greys' Court.

4. A service could cut through the Oxfordshire Chilterns from Reading, go down to the Thames at Mapledurham House, Goring and Wallingford and run into the heart of the wild, remote country around Ipsden Heath, Nuffield and Shepherds' Green.

Services along these routes could operate just like the Surrey Rambler. If they did, there would be four or five services every Sunday running along each route; passengers would be able to get on or off wherever it was safe; and one ticket would entitle a passenger to make as many trips as he liked on that particular route for the whole day. Leaflets putting forward particularly interesting walks that linked in with the bus routes could be provided as an encouragement to people living in urban areas around the Chilterns who have till now had little opportunity to venture into them.

The Chilterns are, of course, already familiar to motorists. And at some spots the fabric of the countryside has been eroded. A national park authority would be able to spread the visitor load in the Chilterns as well as providing better public transport access into it. This could be achieved through the opening up for public access of areas from which walkers are at present barred and the creation of motorless zones around the most heavily used areas. Within these zones – the most obvious candidates are the Ashridge area and the Hambledon Valley – cars could be banned on summer weekends. As in the similarly heavily used Goyt Valley in the Peak Park, motorists would have to park outside and travel into these areas on foot or on specially provided buses. If these buses connected with the longer bus routes I have proposed, motorists too would have the choice of leaving their cars at home or quite outside the Chiltern countryside if they wished to.

The Norfolk Broads

National park status offers the only real hope of stemming Broadland's ecological decline. On top of direct action to rescue damaged areas, new recreation facilities need to be created to draw visitors away from environmentally damaging activities to which there are at present no alternatives offered. In 1969 the entire fish population of two broads died; in 1976 more than a thousand water birds were killed by pollution. The Broads have been described as the most polluted lakes in Europe. What seems to have happened is that the water in the broads and rivers has become over-enriched by nutrients. These have stimulated excess growth of unicellular algae which have stopped sunlight penetrating the water, making it impossible for aquatic plants to grow. Apart from an ever-rising volume of sewer discharge, the main cause of this nutrient enrichment is drainage from farmland to which large quantities of fertiliser have been applied. The effects of nutrient enrichment are thought to be accentuated by the impact of the 12,000 power boats that ply up and down the rivers and broads each year. The threshing of boat propellers destroys any remaining aquatic vegetation, stirs up muddy deposits and accelerates bank erosion, thus increasing the muddiness of the water and making it yet more difficult for sunlight to penetrate the water.

In 1978 the Countryside Commission proposed that the Broads should be designated Britain's eleventh national park, but the plan was abandoned after local interests campaigned against it. As a 'compromise', a new body has been formed to coordinate the administration of the Broads. The 26-member Broads Authority, established in 1979, has representatives from Norfolk and Suffolk County Councils, the six district councils involved, the Anglian Water Authority and the Great Yarmouth Port and Haven Commissioners (the navigation authority). It also has three independent members. But the Authority has only such power as these local organisations have been prepared to give up, and these powers could never secure the conservation of Broadland. The Authority's territory is virtually restricted to the open waters, and the activities of two bodies represented on it are in direct conflict with the needs of conservation: the Water Authority is promoting widespread drainage of the grazing marshlands, and the Port and Haven Commissioners are continuing to licence more and more boats to use the Broads.

A national park here would cover about 200 square miles of shallow lakes, reed beds, alder-wood carrs, dyke-seamed grazing pastures, little villages, lonely churches and derelict windmills.

A Norfolk Broads National Park Authority would almost certainly be empowered by existing legislation to control the number and type of craft using the Broads and also to ban or at least restrict boats on selected broads for limited periods. There is some debate on this point. It turns on whether or not national park authorities' powers over lakes would also apply to broads. But if they were found not to, a very minor legislative change could block the loophole. Off the waterways themselves, the real task, as elsewhere, would be to tackle farming operations. Land drainage, which is currently affecting several hundred acres a year, threatens to transform the landscape of the marshes completely. Pollution has driven the wild creatures that used to live in the broads into dykes running through grazing pastures. If these dykes disappear, so will the prospects of bringing back to the broads themselves the wealth of wildlife for which they were once famous.[2] A national park authority could also do much to extend facilities for enjoying the broads on foot. It is partly because there are no public footpaths passing through the vast majority of the broads and surrounding marshes that so many people take to the water to explore the area, causing still more pollution of the waterways. A national park authority could secure and publicise widely a comprehensive land access system to Broadland so that visitors had the choice of different ways of enjoying Broadland. And it could stimulate the creation of country parks to relieve pressure on the waterways still further.

The Western Downs

As well as embracing some of our most classic lowland country-side, the South Downs west of the river Arun are a living museum of Britain's history. The Downs here are littered with Neolithic flint mines and great causeway camps, Bronze Age bell barrows (burial chambers), Iron Age field systems and hillforts, Roman villas, bath-houses and roads. But as well as these relics of prehistoric life, there is also a high concentration of more recent yet historically valuable features: old hedgerows, woodland commons, historic gardens and parks, the remains of deserted villages, old churches, farmsteads and attractive old domestic buildings. The Western Downs' links with the past help to conjure up an unexpected sense of remoteness. Yet these Downs are certainly close to population centres: a new national park here would lie on the doorstep of the Southampton–Portsmouth conurbation and the built-up coastal strip to the east from Littlehampton to Brighton as well as lying within easy reach of London.

The special claims of the South Downs have been recognised before, when the Hobhouse Committee proposed that they should have national park status in 1947. The National Parks Commission rejected this proposal in 1956 on the grounds that so much of the downland coast east of the Arun had then been ploughed up that the area was no longer worth designating. But this is not true of the Downs of the West Sussex and East Hampshire section of the AONBs. And the western stretch of the Downs happens to be bordered by other stretches of peculiarly valuable country which, if included in a national park, would more than make up for the lack of the eastern downs.

The Wealden scenery on the north-east border of the Downs is among the most distinctive of England's landscapes. Dense, often ancient oak woods hiding little fields bordered by shaws alternate with heaths, rivers, lakes, parks and villages, their churches and cottages hewn from the warm, honey-coloured sandstone that is the main underlying rock. The Western Downs Park would include a triangular area of the western part of the Weald: about 70 square miles of the gault clay and lower greensand at the foot of the South Downs' northern escarpment lying between Petersfield, Haslemere and Pet-worth. This park would also include two stretches of river

valley. The valley of the Arun between Pulborough and
Arundel, including Amberley Wildbrooks and the wooded
estate of Parham Park, would form the eastern boundary of
the national park, and the valley of the Rother cuts east–west
across the Wealden area. The area of the whole park would be
almost 400 square miles.

A new national park authority could ensure greater access
to the banks of the Rother, much of which is barred to walkers
by angling clubs which have rented banks. Access on foot to
the rest of the park is generally good, although there are many
small areas in which access agreements could enormously
increase people's enjoyment. The biggest need to enhance
recreation opportunities is for bus services. The eastern part
of the proposed park is one of the few areas of countryside
already served by a special ramblers' bus: from the summer of
1979 the Southdown Bus Company, with the help of West
Sussex County Council, has run a bus service on Sundays
from Arundel station up into the Downs. But there is scope
for many more. People without cars are completely unable to
reach on Sunday the famous little village of Selborne, that
nestles in the northern outlier of chalk. This area's hills are
smaller and more intimate than those of the main stretch of
Downs. They are carved up into irregular fields with thick
hedgerows and little thickets and bounded on the eastern side
by a steep, beech-clad escarpment.

Throughout the new park the main task for a national park
authority would be to try to prevent the sort of destruction
that has already threatened Amberley Wildbrooks and destroyed Graffham Down – agricultural change. The greater
part of the Downs is still in the hands of private landowners
and, at least partly because of their interest in pheasant
shooting, there are still large areas here of traditional and
extremely beautiful English countryside. The case of Graffham
Down shows what can so easily happen at the moment when
somebody with a different approach arrives to take over.

Regaining Paradise: What You Can Do

Although the threat confronting the English countryside has remained largely undiscussed, it is not true that it is not understood at all outside the small world of those people whose lives revolve round the countryside. Michael Heseltine, the Secretary of State for the Environment, for instance, told a conference in 1979:

> We have . . . to preserve the habitats of wildlife, and reconcile conservation of the countryside with the demands of modern agriculture and forestry, and of leisure activities. Particularly harmful are the effects of draining wetlands; enlargement of fields by hedge removal and clearance of small woodlands; ploughing up of permanent pastures; infilling of ponds and ditches; and the injudicious use of fertilisers and pesticides. Then there is the abandonment of traditional management of established woodlands, and their replacement with fast-growing conifers which support poorer communities of flora and fauna. . . . There are an important range of policies here for the conservation of our countryside and wildlife to which I attach the highest importance.

No enthusiast for the countryside can quarrel with a Minister who seeks to attach 'the highest importance' to conservation. But if a problem is important, action to solve it is called for.

I have made an attempt to translate Mr Heseltine's sentiments into action. Property speculators, mining companies, those who would pull down historic buildings, retailers, industrialists and householders have all been required to operate within the requirements of the rest of the community. I ask no more from farmers. And they can deliver if they have to. Food production can be reconciled with the other activities to which the countryside is home, just as the infinitely more complex activities of our cities have settled down alongside each other.

The task of rescuing the countryside from the forces intent

on its destruction may seem intimidating. What hope can there be that a movement as yet unborn can prevail against interests firmly entrenched in the institutions that count? The answer to this question is that the enemy's appearance of strength masks an underlying weakness – a weakness that will certainly prove fatal if it is successfully exploited. The weakness lies in the fact that there is no public support for the agricultural 'reclamation' which is destroying the countryside, and there never will be, however vociferous the farming lobby becomes. It is only because people do not know what is going on that the process continues. The most that the apologists for reclamation can hope for is that the argument over it will never begin. If it does, they will lose it.

All that is now required is for those who care about the countryside to alert their fellow countrymen to what is going on and to ask them to make a choice. If that happens, the apparently unstoppable movement for the industrialisation of the countryside will collapse overnight.

Small committed groups have been a civilising force on our society throughout our history. Many major reforms can be attributed to the early efforts of bands of amateur enthusiasts. Even in the environmental field itself, change has usually been engineered through campaigns waged at first by small minorities. The introduction of the first effective controls over air pollution in the Clean Air Act of 1956 was very largely the result of campaigning by the National Smoke Abatement Society. At the end of the last century, it was the efforts of a few individuals working together as the Commons, Open Spaces and Footpaths Preservation Society that preserved the London commons – from Hampstead Heath to Wimbledon and Putney Commons – against what then seemed inevitable enclosure by landowners. The efforts of one local society, the Warwickshire branch of the Conservation Society, were largely responsible for the introduction to Parliament of what was to become the Deposit of Poisonous Wastes Act 1972. And a decade's hard campaigning by the Council for the Protection of Rural England, encompassing farmers and landowners as well as others anxious to prevent haphazard, unplanned building and quarrying in the countryside, did much to secure the passage of the 1947 Town and Country Planning Act. The Protection of Birds Act, the ban on dangerous pesticides, the conservation of our historic buildings against a range of forces for change – all these things seemed remote prospects when those campaigning for them began work. Up till now we have been content to leave the countryside in the hands of those who happen to own our farms. To protect our birthright we need only claim it. But political change requires organisation. There are, of course, many existing bodies dealing with countryside conservation. Many do excellent work and deserve as much support as we can give them. But no existing body is equipped for the task of mobilising the mass of the people, most of whom live in towns, for the struggle that lies ahead. Organisation must start from scratch.

The springboard for action, if there is to be any, will be public pressure. For that pressure to be effective it must be organised. It will be organised most successfully at grass-roots level: pressure groups are at their healthiest when their roots are strongest.

Countryside Action Groups

If you want to help our countryside, place an advertisement in your local paper inviting like-minded people to contact you. If anybody does, you have the makings of a Countryside Action Group. What your group does will be up to its members. But the waters you sail will not be uncharted. In recent years plenty of other movements have changed the world from the same starting-point. Wisdom acquired through experience gained in these campaigns has been distilled in books. I recommend *Campaigning for the Environment* and *Pressure Groups in Britain*, both by R. Kimber and J. Richardson and published by J.M. Dent. Christopher Hall's *How to Run a Pressure Group* (Dent, 1972) is a handy guide to organisation and tactics.

Below are a few ideas for the kind of steps Countryside Action Groups may take. But any suggestions are no more than guidelines. If a new movement springs up, no one can predict where it will go or how it will get there.

Consciousness-raising

Forming a group will help the cause of the countryside by spreading the message in your community, even if it only organises meetings with speakers and discussions. And once you have a group you will be able to use its corporate status to push the message further. The local media will be interested in what you have to say to them and the events you organise. Do not forget that the NFU is a long way ahead of the pack in impressing its view on the media as far as countryside matters are concerned. The diligence and energy of the NFU, coupled with the lack of conflicting voices, have enabled the principles of the farmers' case to permeate even the most 'objective' news reporting. Take on the NFU on their own terms. Learn to see how the 'news' has originated, and whose interests disclosures aid. Don't let editorials, features, stories or even cartoons giving an incomplete picture pass without reply. In a fair fight it is your cause which will win the hearts and minds of readers, viewers and listeners.

Action

Nothing will impress the media and raise the morale of your members more than a little action at the battlefront. Impose your Countryside Action Group's presence on a stretch of countryside. If your group is based in a city, pick an area that most of your members can agree to take an interest in, and adopt it. Remember that the smaller the area you choose, the more impact you can have in it. Once you have chosen it, find out what is going on in it. Survey agricultural operations within it and publish your findings as widely as you can, outside the area as well as within it. Get to know the local authorities, water authorities, landowners. Pester all of them. Hold meetings, demonstrations, marches and bring-and-buy sales to acquaint local people with your thinking. Ammunition to back up calls for change will be thick on the ground. Try to find out about cases involving the transformation of the countryside as they happen and focus as much attention on them as you can. In the absence of any public register of proposed changes, this will require a certain amount of detective work. The easiest plans to track down will be your water authority's proposals for pump drainage and river canalisations and the applications to clear or coniferise woodlands that come to your Forestry Commission as applications for felling licences. These two areas alone will keep you busy. But when you have got on top of these schemes, you can move on to consider the vast stockpile of information that lies undocumented in the countryside. Work out how many miles of hedgerow or acres of wood have been cleared and turned over to the plough in your area and what the future will hold if the trend is maintained. Take particular towns and villages, study old maps, interview people who can remember how things used to be and then demonstrate to the local community how agricultural change has robbed them.

Don't let the farmers tell you that you can't criticise them because you don't understand farming: study their methods. Read *Farmers' Weekly*, attend farm open days, Ministry of Agriculture demonstrations of new methods (after all, we all pay for them), open days at the Ministry's own experimental farms, and so on. Offer your services to farmers and landowning institutions as a voluntary labour corps, available to maintain hedgerows, to stop scrub encroaching on downland and to clear footpaths. Even if your offer is not taken up, it will make it more difficult for farmers to argue that shortage of labour makes the protection of the countryside impossible. Bombard political parties and trade unions with the group's findings and accounts of its activities. Persuade these bodies to make the defence of the countryside one of their objectives.

Countryside Action Groups would of course be able to exert pressure at national level as well as local level by petitioning their local MPs, by demonstrating, by sending deputations to Ministers, by promoting private members' bills, by seeking adjournment debates and so on. They will find action at national level more effective if they group together for this purpose. Even so, vigorous grass-roots action will aid national effort by providing visible evidence that demands are backed up by public feeling. To channel pressure from the Countryside Action Groups at national level, a federation of groups will eventually be needed. The central officers will then be able to use the public opinion they will represent to press the Government for the legislative changes – in the planning field, for example – which will be needed if the countryside is to be changed. But the amount of pressure that can be expected will bear a close relationship to the level of activity which the Countryside Action Groups are able to achieve.

Of course, if legislation is passed which subjects rural de-velopment to planning control, and regional countryside planning authorities are established to administer the new system, the role of Countryside Action Groups will change radically. Their task would then be to make the system work, largely by offering themselves to their local authorities as a source of free labour, to do anything from mapping important landscape features to helping to clear scrub from chalk downland and generally maintain the wide range of landscape features that would be conserved. Groups would probably also want to help local authorities police the system and at the same time act as watchdogs on the way in which the local authorities were operating it.

Because Countryside Action Groups will have such a wide range of things to do, they will need a broadly based membership. And there are a number of ways in which they ought to be able to attract to their ranks people with the necessary skills and resources. One way of attracting just a few of the millions of teenagers who live in our cities who have time to spare, would be to organise trips into the countryside for them. Some obvious Countryside Action Group activities, like promoting new bus services from towns to the countryside and pressing for public access to beautiful but inaccessible areas, could in themselves bring the groups into contact with outsiders who would have much to offer if recruited.

Think and act. The activities of organised enthusiasm are constrained only by the limits of the imagination of the ethusiasts.

It may be that the struggle now facing those who would like to save the English countryside will be fiercer than any that has yet been waged on the environmental battleground. But that does not mean that the prospects of success are small. They actually look better than prospects must have looked at the outset for many other campaigns that eventually succeeded. Our countryside has not yet been stolen: the thieves can be stopped in the act. Because we live in a democracy, the countryside will be saved, paradise will be regained, if the people will it. And if we fail to save our countryside, we shall have no one to blame but ourselves.

References

CHAPTER 1: TECHNOLOGICAL TRANSFORMATION
1 Agricultural statistics are taken from *Annual Review of Agriculture, 1980*, HMSO, 1980, or *Agricultural Statistics, United Kingdom, 1975*, HMSO, 1978.
2 For a detailed account of the impact of the current agricultural revolution on the social structure of the countryside, see H.Newby, *Green and Pleasant Land?*, Hutchinson,1980.
3 Farmers spent an estimated £687 million in 1979 on plant, machinery and vehicles, according to the *Annual Review of Agriculture,* 1980. If income tax had been payable at 40 per cent on the proportion of this that went on the purchase of new machinery (probably about £500 million), the Exchequer would have netted £200 million in tax revenue.
4 The Game Conservancy, *Annual Review for 1978*, 1979.
5 N.W.Moore, 'Arable Land', in J.Davidson and R.Lloyd (eds), *Conservation and Agriculture*, John Wiley and Sons, 1977.
6 G.Leach, *Energy and Food Production*, IPC Science & Technology Press for the International Institute for Environment and Development, 1975.
7 ibid.

CHAPTER 2: SUBSIDIES FOR DESTRUCTION
1 Food prices rose by 212 per cent whereas inflation, as measured by the retail price index and including food prices, rose by only 195 per cent, according to figures in the Department of Employment Gazette, January 1978.
2 C.N.Morris, 'The Common Agricultural Policy', *Fiscal Studies*, Vol. 1, No. 2, 1980.
3 EEC Draft General Budget, 1980. I have assumed that one European Unit of Account is equal to 60p.
4 R.Bacon, W.Godley and A.McFarquar, 'The Direct Costs to Britain of Belonging to the EEC', *Economic Policy Review*, March 1978.
5 Intervention Board for Agricultural Produce, *Report for the Calendar Year 1978*, Cmnd 7600, HMSO, 1979.
6 C.N.Morris, op. cit.
7 ibid.
8 House of Commons Hansard, Vol. 982, cols. 29-30, 31.3.80.
9 *Annual Review of Agriculture, 1980*, op. cit.
10 For a detailed explanation of the grants available to farmers, see Ministry of Agriculture, Fisheries and Food, *At The Farmer's Service, 1979/80*.
11 Staff were to be released to carry out a survey to map 'marginal land' – an estimated one-and-a-half million acres of England and Wales which the National Farmers' Union considered should attract the same high

rates of capital grant and the livestock compensatory allowances as are available in the 'less-favoured areas' (Ministry of Agriculture press notice, *Marginal Land*, 1.2.80).

12 Ministry of Agriculture press notice, *Changes in Farm and Horticulture Capital Grant Schemes*, 31.1.80.

13 *Local Government Finance: Appendix 9 to the Report of the Committee of Inquiry under the Chairmanship of Frank Layfield Esq QC, Rating: Evidence and Commissioned Work*, HMSO, 1976.

14 *Annual Review of Agriculture, 1980*, op. cit.

15 Board of Inland Revenue, *Inland Revenue Statistics 1979*, HMSO, 1979.

16 ibid.

17 For a detailed explanation of these reliefs see *Report of the Committee of Inquiry into the Acquisition and Occupancy of Agricultural Land*, Chairman: The Rt.Hon.Lord Northfield, Cmnd 7599, HMSO, 1979.

18 A.Sutherland, unpublished report presented in March 1979 to the Northfield Committee of Inquiry into the Acquisition and Occupancy of Agricultural Land, available at the Ministry of Agriculture library, Whitehall Place, London.

19 Board of Inland Revenue, *Inland Revenue Statistics*, op. cit.

20 *Supply Estimates 1979–80*, HMSO, 1979.

21 ibid.

22 I have calculated this figure by dividing the total financial gain UK farmers receive through subsidies from taxpayers and consumers by 293,000 – the estimated number of whole-and part-time farmers in the UK in 1979 (*Annual Review of Agriculture, 1980* figure). I have included in the total the cost to the UK Exchequer of rate and tax reliefs to farmers, capital grants to farmers and to water authorities for agricultural 'improvement' schemes, and the administrative and research costs of the Ministry of Agriculture. I have also included the £1,550 million that the Institute of Fiscal Studies has estimated UK farmers receive by way of price support from the CAP, and the money UK farmers receive direct from Brussels through the livestock compensatory amounts and capital grants under the Farm and Horticulture Development Scheme.

CHAPTER 3: HEDGEROWS

1 E.Pollard, M.D.Hooper and N.W.Moore, *Hedges*, Collins, 1974.

2 For a detailed picture of the extent of the eighteenth-century enclosures, see E.C.K.Gonner, *Common Land and Inclosure*, Macmillan, 1912, and J.A.Yelling, *Common Field and Enclosure in England 1450–1850*, Macmillan, 1977.

3 F.Emery, *The Oxfordshire Landscape*, Hodder and Stoughton, 1974.

4 N.Johnson, *Rural Survey Report – Cornwall*, Cornwall Committee for Rescue Archaeology, 1979.

5 Hereford and Worcester County Council, *New Agricultural Landscapes: Report on the Bishampton and Grafton Trial Sites*, 1976.

6 W.W.Baird and J.R.Tarrant, *Hedgerow Destruction in Norfolk 1946–1970*, Centre of East Anglian Studies, University of East Anglia, 1973.

7 Countryside Commission, *New Agricultural Landscapes: Report of a Study undertaken on behalf of the Countryside Commission by Richard Westmacott, B.Sc.,*

M.L.A., and Tom Worthington, B.Sc., during 1972, 1974.
8 See for instance Ministry of Agriculture, Fisheries and Food, 'Paddock grazing and extensive grazing for lactating cows', *Results of Experiments at the Experimental Husbandry Farms 1976: Dairy Cattle, Pigs and Poultry*, 1976, and Ministry of Agriculture, 'A comparison of set-stocking and 28 day grazing frequencies for dairy cows' and 'A comparison of rotational and continuous grazing for spring calving dairy cows', both in *Results of Experiments at the Experimental Husbandry Farms 1977: Dairy Cattle, Pigs and Poultry*, 1977.
9 British Trust for Conservation Volunteers, *Hedging: A Practical Conservation Handbook*, 1975.
10 Ministry of Agriculture, 'Paddock grazing and extensive grazing for lactating cows', op. cit.
11 P.Brandon, *The Sussex Landscape*, Hodder and Stoughton, 1974.
12 Countryside Commission, 'New Agricultural Landscapes', op. cit.
13 M.D. Hooper, 'The Botanical Importance of our Hedgerows' in F.H.Perring (ed), *The Flora of a Changing Britain*, Report of the Botanical Society of the British Isles, No. 11, 1970.

CHAPTER 4: HEDGEROW TREES

1 A Forestry Commission census of trees outside woods in 1951 recorded 55 million trees in England. No similar census has been taken since then, so it is impossible to know exactly how many trees have been lost. But the Countryside Commission's consultants, Richard Westmacott and Tom Worthington, in their study 'New Agricultural Landscapes', 1974, estimated the annual loss of trees outside woods in England to have been 2 per cent. On this basis, 24 million trees would have been lost between 1951 and 1980.
2 Countryside Commission, 'New Agricultural Landscapes', op. cit.
3 P.Hardy and R.Matthews, *Farmland Tree Survey of Norfolk*, Norfolk County Council, 1977.
4 Forestry Commission, *Report of the Committee on Hedgerow and Farm Timber*, HMSO, 1955.
5 Countryside Commission, 'New Agricultural Landscapes', op. cit.

CHAPTER 5: WOODS

1 G.F.Peterken and P.T.Harding, 'Woodland Conservation in Eastern England: Comparing the Effects of Changes in Three Study Areas Since 1946', *Biological Conservation*, Vol. 8, 1975.
2 *Broadleaved Woodland Survey: Report of the County Planning Officer to the Amenities and Countryside Committee, Devon County Council*, 26.11.75.
3 Nature Conservancy Council, *Nature Conservation and Forestry: A Consultation Paper*, 1979.
4 O.Rackham, 'Historic Woodlands and Hedges', *The Architects' Journal*, 21.1.78.
5 O.Rackham, *Trees and Woods in the British Landscape*, J. M. Dent and Sons, 1976.
6 Countryside Review Committee, 'Report of Working Party on Trees in the Countryside' (1975, unpublished); referred to in M.J.Feist, *A Study of Management Agreements*, Countryside Commission, 1975.

7 *Report of the Committee of Inquiry into the Acquisition and Occupancy of Agricultural Land*, op. cit.
8 M.S.Warren, 'The Dorset Woodlands – Their History and Conservation', unpublished MSc thesis, University of London, 1976.

CHAPTER 6: ROUGHLANDS
1 C.A.Jones, *The Conservation of Chalk Downland in Dorset*, Dorset County Council, 1973.
2 E.Duffey, 'A population study of spiders in limestone grassland', *Journal of Animal Ecology*, Vol. 31, 1962.
3 J.O.Green, *Preliminary Report on a Sample Survey of Grassland in England and Wales, 1970–72*, The Grassland Research Institute, Hurley, Maidenhead, 1973.
4 Nature Conservancy Council, *Nature Conservation and Agriculture*, 1977.
5 D.Ratcliffe, 'The End of the Large Blue Butterfly', *New Scientist*, 6.11.79.
6 'Farming threat to National Park moor', news story in *Yorkshire Evening Press*, 8.11.75.
7 Council for the Protection of Rural England, *Landscape –The Need for a Public Voice*, 1975.
8 For details see for instance F.Beckett, 'Spraying on our Minds', *Landworker*, September 1978 and Royal Commission on Environmental Pollution, *Seventh Report: Agriculture and Pollution*, Cmnd.7644, HMSO, 1979.

CHAPTER 7: DOWNS
1 For a detailed description of the location of rough downland turf in 1970, see J.W.Blackwood and C.R.Tubbs, 'A Quantitative Survey of Chalk Grassland in England', *Biological Conservation*, Vol. 3, No. 1, 1970.
2 W.H.Hudson, *Nature in Downland*, J.M.Dent and Sons, 1951.
3 Ministry of Town and Country Planning, *Report of the National Parks Committee (Chairman: Sir Arthur Hobhouse)*, Cmnd 7121, HMSO, 1947.
4 C.A.Jones, *The Conservation of Chalk Downland in Dorset*, op. cit.
5 C.Gingell, *Archaeology in the Wiltshire Countryside*, Devizes Museum, 1976.
6 H.V.Basford, *A Survey of Isle of Wight Archaeology*, Wessex Archaeological Committee, 1980.
7 A.Bailey, 'Our Far-Flung Correspondent's Island Walk', *The New Yorker*, 8.9.75.
8 W.Marshall, as quoted by J.A.Yelling, op. cit.

CHAPTER 8: MOORS
1 For a detailed account of the appeal of moorland as a wilderness, see my forthcoming chapter entitled 'The Lure of the Moors' in J.Gold and J.Burgess (eds), *Valued Environments*, Allen and Unwin, 1981.
2 J.Hawkes, *A Guide to the Prehistoric Monuments of England*, Chatto and Windus, 1973.
3 W.Dyfri Jones, 'A Review of Some Economic Aspects of Hill and Upland Farming' in R.B.Tranter (ed.), *The Future of Upland Britain*, Vol. 1, Centre for Agricultural Strategy, Reading University, 1978.

4 EEC Council Resolution of 15 May 1973 on Farming in Less-Favoured Areas, Official Journal of the European Communities, No. C33/1.
5 W.Dyfri Jones, op. cit.
6 *A Study of Exmoor: Report by Lord Porchester KBE*, HMSO, 1977.

CHAPTER 9: WETLANDS
1 Wessex Water Authority, *Somerset Local Land Drainage District: Land Drainage Survey Report*, 1979.
2 For details of the precise impact of pump drainage on wildlife see C.N.G.Scotter, P.M.Wade, E.J.P.Marshall and R.W.Edwards, 'The Monmouthshire Levels drainage system: its ecology and relation to agriculture', *Journal of Environmental Management*, Vol. 5, 1977.
3 P.D.Round, *An Ornithological Study of the Somerset Levels 1976–77*, unpublished report by the Royal Society for the Protection of Birds and the Wessex Water Authority, 1978.
4 N.W.Moore, 'Speed the Plough and Waste the Land', *Guardian*, 20.6.77.

CHAPTER 10: FARMING AND FORESTRY – ABOVE THE LAW
1 Vaughan Cornish, *National Parks and the Heritage of Scenery*, Sifton Praed, 1930.
2 Council for the Protection of Rural England, *Landscape – The Need for a Public Voice*, op. cit.
3 J.Davidson and G.Wibberley, *Planning and the Rural Environment*, Pergamon Press, 1977.
4 H.Newby, *Green and Pleasant Land?*, op. cit.
5 F.Beckett, 'How Farmers Hi-Jacked the Airwaves', *Landworker*, October 1979.
6 L.Moss and S.Parker, *The Local Government Councillor*, HMSO, 1967.
7 H.Newby et al., *Property, Paternalism and Power: Class and Control in Rural England*, Hutchinson, 1978.
8 Under Section 165 of the Town and Country Planning Act, 1971.
9 Under Section 52 of the Town and Country Planning Act, 1971.
10 J.Tubbs, *The Concept of Sites of Special Scientific Interest: A Review*, University of Southampton, 1977.

CHAPTER 11: THE EDUCATION EXPERIMENT
1 Countryside Commission, 'New Agricultural Landscapes: Issues, Objectives and Action, 1977; second edition, 1979.
2 P.Drewett, *An Extensive Survey of Plough Damage to Known Archaeological Sites in West and East Sussex*, Institute of Archaeology, University of London, 1976.
3 Department of the Environment, *Wildlife and Countryside Bill: Consultation Paper No. 4: Conservation of Habitats* and *Consultation Paper No. 6: Moorland Conservation in National Parks*, 1979.
4 About two per cent because Consultation Paper No. 4 confines the proposed new SSSI procedures to the thirteen sites under which Britain has an international obligation to conservation and to those sites where a change in management practice could render extinct in Britain a particular species.

5 Countryside Review Committee, *Food Production in the Countryside*, HMSO, 1978.
6 Advisory Council for Agriculture and Horticulture in England and Wales, *Report on Agriculture and the Countryside*, Ministry of Agriculture, 1978.
7 Anglian Water Authority, *Yare Basin Flood Control Study*, 1977.
8 Land Use Consultants Ltd, *A Landscape Assessment of the Yare Basin Flood Control Study Proposals*, 1979.

CHAPTER 13: THE NATIONAL PARKS
1 Ministry of Town and Country Planning, *National Parks in England and Wales: Report by John Dower*, Cmnd 6628, HMSO, 1945.
2 Ministry of Town and Country Planning, *Report of the National Park Committee (Chairman: Sir Arthur Hobhouse)*, op. cit.
3 Department of the Environment, Welsh Office, *Report of the National Parks Policies Review Committee*, HMSO, 1974.
4 M.Blacksell and A.W.Gilg, 'Planning Control in an Area of outstanding Natural Beauty', *Social and Economic Administration*, Vol.11, No.3, 1977.
5 Cornwall County Council, 'Structure Plan Topic Report: The Environment', 1976.
6 J.Tinker, 'Do We Need Wilderness Areas?' *New Scientist*, 4.11.73.
7 Countryside Review Committee, *Conservation and the Countryside Heritage: A Discussion Paper*, HMSO, 1979.

CHAPTER 14: THE FARMERS' CASE
1 *Food From Our Own Resources*, presented to Parliament by the Secretary of State for Northern Ireland, the Secretary of State for Scotland, the Secretary of State for Wales and the Minister of Agriculture, Fisheries and Food, Cmnd 6020, HMSO, 1975.
2 *Farming and the Nation*, presented to Parliament by the Secretary of State for Northern Ireland, the Secretary of State for Scotland, the Secretary of State for Wales and the Minister of Agriculture, Fisheries and Food, Cmnd 7458, HMSO, 1979. The extract is Crown copyright and is reproduced by permission of the Controller, HMSO.
3 S. George, *How the Other Half Dies: The Real Reasons for World Hunger*, Penguin, 1976.
4 K.Mellanby, *Can Britain Feed Itself?*, The Merlin Press, 1975; K.Blaxter, 'Can Britain Feed Herself?, *New Scientist*, 20.3.75.
5 Conservative Party Conference press release, 'Food, Farming and Fishing', No. 1043, 1979.
6 S.George, op. cit.
7 Food and Agriculture Organisation of the United Nations, *The Director-General's Programme of Work and Budget for 1980–81*, 1979.
8 Ministry of Agriculture, Fisheries and Food, *Report on Research and Development, 1974*, HMSO, 1975.
9 R.Roy, *Wastage in the UK Food System*, Earth Resources Research, 1976.
10 Royal Commission on Environmental Pollution, *Seventh Report: Agriculture and Pollution*, op. cit.

CHAPTER 15: THE TOURISM BONANZA: CONSERVATION AS A CASH CROP
1 M.Binney and M.Hanna, *Preservation Pays*, SAVE Britain's Heritage, 1979.
2 D.Lowenthal and H.C.Prince, 'English Landscape Tastes', *The Geographical Review*, Vol.55, No.2, 1965.
3 English Tourist Board News Release, 28.11.79.
4 English Tourist Board, 'West Country Tourism Regional Fact Sheets, 1978', 1979.
5 Office of Population Censuses and Surveys, *Census 1971 England and Wales Economic Activity County Leaflet: Devon*, HMSO, 1976.
6 South West Economic Planning Council, *Economic Survey of the Tourist Industry in the South West*, HMSO, 1976 and South West Economic Planning Council, *A Strategic Settlement Pattern for the South West*, HMSO, 1975.
7 Devon County Council and the Nature Conservancy Council South West Region, *The Changing Face of Devon*, 1979.

CHAPTER 16: A THREATENED RECORD
1 For details see *Archaeologia*, Vol.44 1873, pp 273–92.
2 For details see G.Lambrick, *Archaeology and Agriculture*, Council for British Archaeology, 1977.
3 'Will require' since although the Ancient Monuments and Archaeological Areas Act received the Royal Assent in April 1979, part of it will not come into force until late in 1980 and the rest not until 1981.
4 A.Saville, *Archaeological Sites in the Avon and Gloucestershire Cotswolds*, Committee for Rescue Archaeology of Avon, Gloucestershire and Somerset, 1977.
5 R.Millward and A.Robinson, *The Lake District*, Eyre Methuen, 1970.
6 W.Rollinson, *A History of Cumberland and Westmorland*, Phillimore, 1978.
7 For details see H.C.Bowen and P.J.Fowler (eds), *Early Land Allotment in the British Isles*, British Archaelogical Reports 48, 1978.
8 The National Institute of Adult Education (England and Wales), *Annual Report 1977–78*, 1979.
9 N.Johnson, *Rural Survey Report – Cornwall*, Cornwall Committee for Rescue Archaeology, 1979.

CHAPTER 17: DISAPPEARING WILDLIFE
1 For details of the impact of agricultural change on the populations of all these animals and plants, see D.L.Hawksworth (ed.), *The Changing Flora and Fauna of Britain*, The Academic Press, 1974.
2 J.Cadbury, 'Last Cry from the Corncrake', *Birds*, autumn 1979.
3 Nature Conservancy Council, *Nature Conservation and Agriculture*, 1977.
4 M.Shrubb, 'The Status and Discrimination of Snipe, Redshank and Yellow Wagtail as Breeding Birds in Sussex', *Sussex Bird Report*, Vol. 20, 1968.
5 A.S.Cooke, 'Population Declines of the Magpie *Pica pica* in Huntingdonshire and Other Parts of Eastern England, *Biological Conservation*, Vol.15, No.4, 1979.
6 N.W.Moore, 'The Heaths of Dorset and their Conservation', *Journal of*

Ecology, Vol.50, 1969; B.Rippey, 'The Conservation of the Dorset Heaths', unpublished MSc thesis, University of London, 1973.
7 I.Presst, A.S.Cooke and K.F.Corbett, 'British Amphibia and Reptiles', in Hawksworth, op. cit.
8 F.H.Perring, 'The Last Seventy Years', in F.H.Perring (ed) *The Flora of a Changing Britain*, Botanical Society of the British Isles, 1970.
9 D.Ratcliffe, 'The End of the Large Blue Butterfly', op. cit.
10 I.Presst, A.S.Cooke and K.F.Corbett, op. cit.
11 T.Beebee, 'Habitats of the British Amphibia, (1) Chalk Uplands', *Biological Conservation*, Vol.12, 1977.
12 J.G.Dony, 'Change in the Flora of Bedfordshire, England, from 1798 to 1976', *Biological Conservation*, Vol.11, 1977.
13 D.Wells, 'Changes in the Populations of Flowering Plants', in D.L.Hawksworth, *The Changing Flora and Fauna of Britain*, op. cit.

CHAPTER 18: IMPOVERISHED LIVES

1 For a detailed report on the way in which Minster children use the countryside, see my article 'Children in the Countryside', *The Planner*, May 1979.
2 Hereford and Worcester County Council, 'Herefordshire Structure Plan', 1974 draft, approved by the Secretary of State for the Environment in 1976.
3 Buckinghamshire County Council, 'Draft Structure Plan', 1976, approved in 1980.
4 M.Dower, 'Fourth Wave', *The Architects' Journal*, 20.1.65.
5 For details, see for instance M.C.D.Speight, *Outdoor Recreation and its Ecological Effects*, University College, London, 1973.
6 See for instance Ministry of Agriculture, *Agriculture in the Urban Fringe: A Survey of the Slough/Hillingdon Area*, Agricultural Development and Advisory Service Technical Report 30, 1973 and A.Blair, *Spatial Effects of Urban Influences on Agriculture in Essex*, unpublished PhD thesis, University of London, 1978.
7 Countryside Commission, *National Household Survey*, 1978.

CHAPTER 19: THE PLANNING WEAPON

1 This was C.A.Jones, the author of *The Conservation of Chalk Downland in Dorset*, op. cit.
2 Estimate quoted by P.D.Lowe, J. Clifford, S. Buchanan, 'The Mass Movement of the Decade', *Vole*, January 1980.
3 Ministry of Agriculture, *Farm Incomes in England and Wales, 1977/78*, HMSO, 1979.
4 A.Blair, op. cit.
5 A.Sutherland, report for the Northfield Committee, op. cit. (Ch. 2, note 18).
6 ibid.
7 Countryside Commission, 'New Agricultural Landscapes', 1974.

CHAPTER 20: REGIONS TO THE RESCUE

1 *Report of the Royal Commission on Local Government in England 1966–69* (Chairman: Lord Redcliffe-Maud), Cmnd.4040, HMSO 1969.

CHAPTER 21: OPENING UP THE COUNTRYSIDE
1 Department of Transport, *Transport Statistics 1968–78*, HMSO, 1979.
2 Department of Transport, *Interim Memorandum on National Traffic Forecasts*, 1978.
3 ibid.
4 For a detailed account of what these cuts have meant in reducing access on the ground, see 'Access: Can Present Opportunities be Widened?', a paper written for the Countryside Commission's 1978 conference 'Countryside Recreation for all?', Countryside Commission, 1978.
5 P.Willmott, 'Car Ownership in the London Metropolitan Region', *Greater London Council Intelligence Quarterly*, June 1973.
6 S.Law and N.H.Perry; 'Countryside Recreation for Londoners – a Preliminary Research Approach', *Greater London Council Intelligence Quarterly*, March 1971.
7 K.K.Sillitoe, *Planning for Leisure: Government Social Survey*, HMSO, 1969.
8 For details, see my article 'Metropolitan Escape Routes', *The London Journal*, Vol.5, No.1, 1979.
9 Countryside Commission, 'Study of Informal Recreation in South-East England', 1978.
10 A.Kemp, 'Access to the Forest of Wychwood', *Rucksack*, Summer 1978.
11 According to a report in *The Field*, 31.5.78.
12 R.S.Gibbs and M.C.Whitby, *Local Authority Expenditure on Access Land*, Agricultural Adjustment Unit, University of Newcastle upon Tyne, 1975.
13 Countryside Commission, *National Household Survey*, op. cit.
14 C.Hall, 'Country Matters', *Vole*, February 1980.

CHAPTER 22: NATIONAL PARKS FOR THE NATION
1 C.Newbold, 'Environmental Effects of Aquatic Herbicides' and M.George, 'Mechanical Methods of Weed Control in Watercourses: An Ecologist's View', both in *Proceedings of a Symposium on Aquatic Herbicides*, T.O.Robson and J.H.Fearon (eds), British Crop Protection Monograph No.11, 1976.
2 Nature Conservancy Council East Anglia Region, 'Flood Control and Drainage in the Yare Basin: A Statement by the Nature Conservancy Council', 1978.

Index

Access, 62, 63, 78, 82, 217, 229-235
249, 252, 254
Access agreements, 231, 233-234
Advisory Committee for Agriculture
and Horticulture, 124
Afforestation, 45, 60, 82, 129
Agricultural revolutions: first, 11-12;
second,12, 13, 35, 66, 200; third, 13,
14, 200
Agriculture Act 1947, 21, 104
Alkham Valley, 71-75
Amberley Wildbrooks, 92-96, 254
Amphibia, 84, 183, 188-189, 193
Ancient Monuments and Archaeolog-
ical Areas Act 1979, 174, 206
Angling, 234, 254
Arable farming, 18, 19, 36, 37, 60, 89
Archaeology, 36, 53,65, 69, 76, 119-
120, 131, 173-182, 253
Art and the countryside, 191, 247
Association of Agriculture, 121
Avon, 38

Bedfordshire, 189, 230
Berkshire, 60, 67, 178
Birds, 19, 59, 68, 84, 86, 89-90, 93-94,
131, 183-185, 246
Blenheim Park, 232-233
Bristol, 227
British Field Sports Society, 231-232
British Trust for Conservation Volun-
teers, 211
Buckinghamshire, 187, 196, 230
Buildings, agricultural, 109-110, 173,
176-177, 206
Buses, 227-229, 249, 254
Butterflies, 56, 61-62, 65, 68, 72, 89,
93, 131, 183, 185, 187

Cambridgeshire, 37, 38, 41, 47, 59,
65, 223
Capital gains, 55, 214-215
Capital transfer tax, 30, 55, 214
Chalk downland turf, 59, 65-75, 141,
177, 206, 209-210, 222-223, 248
Cheshire, 35, 38, 230
Chichester District Council, 132-134,
245
Children, 121, 192-194, 235-236
Chilterns, 59, 65, 141, 211, 249-251
Chiltern Society, 211
Cliff roughland, 59, 140, 206, 209
Coastal marshes, 59-60, 115, 141, 206
Common Agricultural Policy, 14, 22-
25, 50, 85, 87, 95, 155, 201
Common land, 12, 249, 253, 256
Commons, Footpaths and Open Spaces
Preservation Society, 256

Compensation, payment of to farmers,
103, 108-113, 118
Coniferisation, 47, 50, 54-57, 205, 255
Conservation areas, 175
Conservation and the Countryside Heritage,
147-153
Conservation of Wild Creatures and
Wild Plants Act 1975, 73
Conservation Society, 256
Cornbury estate, 230
Cornwall, 34-36, 50, 58, 59, 77, 146,
168, 179-181, 230
Cotswolds, 37, 141, 144, 175, 176, 181
Council for British Archaeology, 70,
119, 209
Council for the Protection of Rural
England, 94, 95, 119, 120, 220, 237,
256
Country Code, 235-236
Country parks, 197, 249, 252
Countryside Act 1968, 111, 117, 125,
197, 206
Countryside action groups, 257-260
Countryside Commission, 119-122,
127, 140, 145, 198, 221, 230, 235,
236, 251
Countryside Review Committee, 123-
124, 127, 147-153
Cowslips, 72, 75, 131, 190, 247
Crafts, 38, see also Lake District

Dairy farming, 38, 44, 60, 78, 85, 93
Dartmoor, 50, 58-59, 62, 77, 80, 136,
149, 178, 181-182
Department of the Environment, 175,
218
Development control, 99-101, 137,
146-147, 174-175, 204-210, 215-216
Devon, 34, 35, 47, 49, 141, 146, 167-168
Dorset, 38, 55, 56, 59, 60, 65, 67,68,
69, 86-88, 136, 141, 144, 186, 208,
209, 215, 230
Dower, John, 141-142, 145
Dower, Michael, 196-197
Drainage, 34, 40, 83-97, 105, 127, 173,
180, 189, 205, 252, 255
Durham, 35

Economics, 155-169
Education, 119-128, 237
EEC, 21, 77, 155, 213
Employment, 166-167
Energy and agriculture, 20, 159-160
Essex, 35, 49, 144, 213
Exmoor, 34, 58, 59, 62, 77, 78, 79,
80, 111, 113, 136, 137, 140, 223,
244; National Park Committee, 112-
113, 134, 244; Society, 79

Farmers: attitudes to conservation, 14, 215; incomes, 213-215; in local government, 106
Farming and the Nation, 155-156
Farming and Wildlife Advisory Group, 121
Farm workers, 15-16
Felling Licences, 53, 117-118, 131-132
Fencing, 26, 38, 39, 62, 245
Fens, The,83, 85, 90-91
Fertilisers, 18-19, 58, 66, 69, 89, 92-93, 206, 255
Financial institutions, 51-53
Food: surpluses, 14, 23, 85, 87, 155; wastage, 162-164
Food from our own Resources, 155-156
France, 24, 34, 58, 136, 148, 150
Fritillaries, snake's-head, 189-190
Fungi, 56

Genetic variation, 63
George, Susan, 157, 162, 164
Germany, 24, 27, 94
Gloucestershire, 230, 232
Government policy on agriculture, 13-14, 21-22, 102, 104, 155-158
Graffham and Woolavington Down, 129-135, 195, 243-246, 254
Grants, farm improvement, 25-28, 73, 86, 105, 111-112, 201-202, 216-217
Green belts, 147, 226
Grouse shooting, 229, 231

Hampshire, 51-53, 59, 67, 181, 253-254
Hay meadows, 58-60, 140, 206, 209, 247
Heathland, 59, 141, 186, 206, 209, 210, 248
Hedgerows, 17, 35-42, 43-46, 52, 173, 177, 200, 205, 222, 229, 253, 255
Herefordshire, 37, 46, 59 136, 141, 215, 246
Hereford and Worcester County Council, 195
Hertfordshire, 38, 57
Highclere estate, 51-52
Hobhouse Committee, 26, 66-67, 143, 253
Hudson, W.H., 61, 66, 129, 190
Humberside, 38, 73-74, 83, 223
Huntingdonshire, 44, 185, 189

Industrial revolution, 11
Insects, 20, 41, 56
Internal drainage boards, 91, 248
Ireland, 77
Isle of Wight, 70, 114, 189

Kent, 35, 59-60, 71-73, 192-194, 227

Lake District, 37, 58-59, 136, 140, 151, 173, 176-177
Lancashire, 35, 60, 76, 115, 207
Land law, 100, 137, 205
Landownership, 51-55, 200, 246
Land prices, 53, 124-125
Lincolnshire, 29, 37-38, 47, 49, 59, 65, 116, 223
London, 227-228, 235, 237, 249
Luton, 189

Machinery, agricultural, 15-18, 36, 45, 61, 66, 69, 74, 87, 159
Maintenance of landscape features, 17, 46, 49, 64, 210-211, 248, 260
Malvern Hills, 12, 46, 141, 144
Mammals, 41-42, 84, 131, 183, 185
Manufacturing industry, 20, 31, 204
Maud Committee on Local Government Reform, 106, 220
Midlands, The, 34-35, 43, 58
Milk production, 23, 38, 85, see also dairy farming
Minster, 192-194
Ministry of Agriculture, 73, 77-79, 86-87, 91, 96-97, 105, 111-112, 117, 126, 128, 134-135, 163, 168, 187, 201, 218, 221, 245-246, 259
Ministry of Rural Affairs, 127-128
Moore, Henry, 80, 191

Nature Conservancy Council, 48, 62, 87, 90, 91, 96-97, 114-116, 206, 209, 221, 247
National Farmers' Union, 103-106, 120-121, 124, 127, 155, 187, 212-213, 258
National parks, 99, 136-153, 239-253; administration of, 137, 244, 245; Commission, 68, 145, 253; future of, 147-153; selection of, 136, 141-145, 239-243; spending on, 111, 140, 217, 244
National Trust, 150-151, 195, 250
National Union of Agricultural and Allied Workers, 105, 216
Norfolk, 37-38, 44, 60, 65, 116, 230; Broads, 59, 83, 126, 141, 143-144, 251-253
Northamptonshire, 223, 230
Northfield Committee, 30, 214
Northumberland, 29, 35, 37, 58-59, 76, 83, 136
North York Moors, 59, 62, 76-78, 111, 113, 136-137, 140
Nottinghamshire, 37-38, 230

Open-field system, 35
Orchids, 56, 60, 66, 74, 75, 84, 89, 131, 247

Otters, 84, 86, 185
Oxfordshire, 35, 59, 230-231

Paddock grazing, 38
Parkland, 43, 45, 196, 229-230, 232-233, 248-249, 253
Partridges, 19, 50
Peak District, 80, 116-117, 136-137, 251
Peak Park Joint Planning Board, 117, 140, 231
Pennines, 12, 59, 77, 80
Pesticides, 18-19, 61, 63, 69, 88-89, 93, 164, 185, 206, 248, 255
Pheasants, 50-52, 196, 223, 229-234, 246
Planning, 101-103, 204, 217; public participation in, 107, 132, 221-222
Price support, 21-26, 51, see also Common Agricultural Policy

Ramblers' Association, 209
Rates, 29, 216-217
Reconstitution, landscape, 223-224, 229
Recreation, 67, 70-71, 87, 131, 171, 179, 191-199, 222, 224, 229-238, 245, 247
Regional councils for sport and recreation, 218, 224
Regional countryside planning authorities, 202, 206, 217-225, 233, 238, 243, 259
Regional economic planning councils, 218-220
Reptiles, snakes, lizards, 185-186, 193
Ribble Marshes, 115-116
Roads, farm, 26, 173, 206
Royal Commissions: on Environmental Pollution, 164; on Local Government, 216
Royal Society for the Protection of Birds, 94, 116, 121, 184-185, 187
Rounds (Cornish), 180
Ryegrass, 26, 60-62, 66, 78, 168, 180

Sandford Committee on National Parks, 144, 148
Scotland, 77
Self-sufficiency, 155, 158
Selborne, 254
Select Committee of the House of Lords on Sport and Leisure, 199
Sheep farming, 77-78, 233, 246
Sherborne, 86
Shropshire, 35, 38, 83
Sites of Special Scientific Interest, 69, 71, 114-115
Snowdonia, 136-137, 141
Society of Sussex Downsmen, 245-246
Somerset, 38-39, 44, 46, 86, 227; Levels, 58-59, 83-92, 96-97, 141, 247-248

South Downs, 51, 59, 62, 65, 67, 93, 119-120, 129-135, 136, 141, 143-144, 253-254
Spiders, 41, 60, 89, 183, 193
Staffordshire, 38, 230
State support to agriculture, 21-31, 155-161, 213-214, 216-217
Structure planning, 107, 133, 195-196, 221, 244, 248
Stubble burning, 19-20, 164
Suffolk, 35, 37, 49, 59, 63, 110, 230; County Council, 106
Surrey, 59, 186
Surrey Rambler, 228-229, 238, 250
Sussex, 35, 59, 62, 67, 74, 83, 93-96, 102, 129-135, 185, 189, 253-254; Ornithological Society, 133, 185
Tax concessions, 17, 29-31, 54-55, 201, see also rates
Thing-mount, 176-177
Town and country planning acts, 100, 108, 177, 202, 256
Tourism, 165-168
Trees, 12, 43-46, 52, 63, 84, 86-88, 194, see also hedgerows, woodland
Tree preservation order, 108-109, 244

USA, 10, 34, 58, 70, 78, 98, 100, 137, 142, 148, 150, 152, 156-157

Voluntary work, 209, 211, 216, 259-260

Wales, 50, 59, 77, 136, 141
Walker, Peter, 25, 28, 160, 213
Warwickshire, 35, 38
Water authorities, 85-88, 90-91, 93-95, 125-126, 207-208, 248
Water meadows, 59, 189, see also Somerset Levels
Weald, The, 34, 37, 39-40, 141, 144, 223, 234
West Sussex: County Council, 94, 119, 133-134, 244-245, 254; Structure Plan, 133
Wibberley, Gerald, 103, 217
Wild animals, 56, 60, 84, 183-190
Wild flowers, 19, 36, 40, 56, 58-59, 65-66, 72, 74, 79, 84, 89, 93, 183-190, see also cowslips, fritillaries, orchids
Wildlife and Countryside Bill, 123
Wiltshire, 59, 62, 67, 70, 74, 230
Woodland, 47-57, 69, 71, 140, 173, 193, 205, 210, 229, 249, 255, see also coniferisation, trees
Worcestershire, 37, 223, 232
Wye Valley, 50, 144, 246-247

Yorkshire, 37, 44, 59, 65, 73-74, 189, 223; Dales, 44, 59, 136, 140, 141; see also North York Moors